Sharon Heidenreich

Englisch für Architekten und Bauingenieure –
English for Architects and Civil Engineers

Aus dem Programm   **Bauwesen**

Bauentwurfslehre
von E. Neufert

Haustechnik
von Th. Laasch und E. Laasch

Architektur der Bauschäden
von J. Schulz

Bausanierung
von M. Stahr (Hrsg.)

**Englisch für Architekten und Bauingenieure/
English for Architects and Civil Engineers**
von S. Heidenreich

Sichtbeton Planung
von J. Schulz

Auslandsbau
von R. Kulick

Hochbaukosten – Flächen – Rauminhalte
von P. Fröhlich

Sichtbeton Mängel
von J. Schulz

Energieausweis – das große Kompendium
von A. Weglage (Hrsg.)

Baukosten bei Neu- und Umbauten
von K. D. Siemon

www.viewegteubner.de

Sharon Heidenreich

Englisch für Architekten und Bauingenieure – English for Architects and Civil Engineers

Ein kompletter Projektablauf auf Englisch mit Vokabeln, Redewendungen, Übungen und Praxistipps –
All project phases in English with vocabulary, idiomatic expressions, exercises and practical advice

Mit 61 Abbildungen

VIEWEG+
TEUBNER

Bibliografische Information Der Deutschen Nationalbibliothek
Die Deutsche Nationalbibliothek verzeichnet diese Publikation in der
Deutschen Nationalbibliografie; detaillierte bibliografische Daten sind im Internet über
<http://dnb.d-nb.de> abrufbar.

1. Auflage 2008

Alle Rechte vorbehalten
© Vieweg+Teubner Verlag | GWV Fachverlage GmbH, Wiesbaden 2008

Lektorat: Karina Danulat | Annette Prenzer

Der Vieweg+Teubner Verlag ist ein Unternehmen von Springer Science+Business Media.
www.viewegteubner.de

Das Werk einschließlich aller seiner Teile ist urheberrechtlich geschützt. Jede Verwertung außerhalb der engen Grenzen des Urheberrechtsgesetzes ist ohne Zustimmung des Verlags unzulässig und strafbar. Das gilt insbesondere für Vervielfältigungen, Übersetzungen, Mikroverfilmungen und die Einspeicherung und Verarbeitung in elektronischen Systemen.

Die Wiedergabe von Gebrauchsnamen, Handelsnamen, Warenbezeichnungen usw. in diesem Werk berechtigt auch ohne besondere Kennzeichnung nicht zu der Annahme, dass solche Namen im Sinne der Warenzeichen- und Markenschutz-Gesetzgebung als frei zu betrachten wären und daher von jedermann benutzt werden dürften.

Technische Redaktion: Annette Prenzer
Umschlaggestaltung: KünkelLopka Medienentwicklung, Heidelberg
Druck und buchbinderische Verarbeitung: MercedesDruck, Berlin
Gedruckt auf säurefreiem und chlorfrei gebleichtem Papier.
Printed in Germany

ISBN 978-3-8348-0315-3

Preface

The mobility of architects and building engineers is increasing. This is not due merely to globalisation brought on by technology, but also the mutual recognition and international validation of degrees. Throughout Europe, the Bologna Process seeks to introduce common course modules leading to BA and MA degrees. As a result of the European Credit Transfer System (ECTS), students are encouraged to travel, and periods spent abroad are credited. This mobility and diversification has a significant common denominator and that is the English language. A good knowledge and understanding of English is essential for persons working or studying abroad.

This book may be used either in class or for self-study. The aim is to give German students, graduates and professionals an insight into the terminology common to the building industry and, at the same time, to provide opportunity to practise and consolidate vocabulary and grammar. The 12 chapters – in the book referred to as units – accompany the reader through all planning phases of a project, from the brief and feasibility study through to the completion and acceptance of a building. Business skills, such as telephoning, writing e-mails, letters, etc., are practised throughout the book. The development of a single-family home, which is planned and realized during the course of the book, provides a background for dialogues and letter writing. Some of the more important grammar elements have been included, offering readers the opportunity to refresh and practise functions appropriate to the phase of construction.

This book does not purport to be a dictionary or a set of rules. It points out major differences between the UK and Germany, but does not cover all the rules and regulations. The purpose is to support those wishing to enhance their architectural knowledge with the equivalent English expressions and vocabulary. All terminology is introduced in an appropriate context, giving readers a lexical phrase, a short expression in English, rather than single words lacking context.

Acknowledgements

I am very grateful to all those who have made this book possible. Comments, suggestions and criticism have provided valuable insights and contributed immensely towards what "English for Architects" is today.

This book would never have been possible without the patience and support of my husband, Nicholas Heidenreich, with looking after our three children. I would have been lost without his help at the computer. The many diagrams, which he produced, illustrating architectural situations and phases are an incredible asset to the book.

I would like to thank my father, James Hawken, for spending endless hours reading and checking texts and for the e-mails with suggestions from across the globe. Susanne Zech, who contributed towards the book with her drawings, has also been a great help and support.

Furthermore, I would like to thank my sisters, Janice Göhns and Lisa Billin, Ursula Barth, Ingrid Gürtler and Prof. Josef Reindl for their support in reading and checking single units or sometimes even the whole book.

Contents

Introduction 1

Overview 2

1 Project Basics 3
    1.1 Work stages 3
    1.2 People involved 4
    1.3 Project organisation 6
    1.4 Architect's appointment 8
    1.5 Architect's workplace 9
    1.6 Vocabulary 12

2 Preliminary Enquiries 15
    2.1 Feasibility 15
    2.2 Site visit 17
    2.3 Plots 19
    2.4 Survey 21
    2.5 Communicating with the client 22
    2.6 Vocabulary 24

3 Briefing 27
    3.1 Accepting the brief 27
    3.2 Consultants 28
    3.3 Building costs 31
    3.4 Vocabulary 34

4 Preliminary Design 37
    4.1 Presentation 37
    4.2 Proportions 38
    4.3 Comparisons 39
    4.4 Shapes 41
    4.5 Roofs 43
    4.6 Appearance 44
    4.7 Vocabulary 46

5 Final Design 49

5.1 Coordination 49
5.2 Structural frameworks 51
5.3 Structural analysis 53
5.4 Final design proposal 55
5.5 Vocabulary 60

6 Planning and Building Permission 63

6.1 Permission 63
6.2 Planning permission 64
6.3 Building regulations 66
6.4 Fire safety 67
6.5 Vocabulary 69

7 Tender Documentation 73

7.1 Procurement procedure 73
7.2 Production information 74
7.3 Tender documents 77
7.4 Language in tender documents 79
7.5 Selection of contractors 80
7.6 Vocabulary 83

8 Tender Action 87

8.1 Tendering 87
8.2 Estimating 88
8.3 Opening of tenders 89
8.4 Negotiations 91
8.5 Building contract 94
8.6 Vocabulary 97

9 Pre-Construction Phase 101

9.1 Background to building operations 101
9.2 Time management 104
9.3 Construction programme 106
9.4 Site set-up 108
9.5 Vocabulary 111

10 Construction 115
10.1 Work progress 115
10.2 Site meetings 119
10.3 Variations 120
10.4 Project diary 123
10.5 Ceremonies 123
10.6 Vocabulary 124

11 Completion 129
11.1 Completion stage 129
11.2 Delays 130
11.3 Acceptance 132
11.4 Remedial work 134
11.5 Payment procedures 135
11.6 Vocabulary 137

12 Education, registration and more 141
12.1 Education 141
12.2 Registration 143
12.3 Practicing architecture 144
12.4 Finding work 145
12.5 Curriculum Vitae 147
12.6 Job application and interview 148
12.7 Vocabulary 149

Answer Key 151

Bibliography 161

Vocabulary English–German 163

Vocabulary German–English 177

Abbreviations and acronyms

Abbreviation	English meaning	German meaning
adj	adjective	Adjektiv, Eigenschaftswort
v	verb	Verb
sb	somebody	jemand/en/em
sth	something	etwas
pl	plural	Mehrzahl
fig	figurative	im bildlichen Sinne
eg	for example (Latin: exempli gratia)	zum Beispiel
ie	in other words (Latin: id est)	das heißt
etc	and other similar things (Latin: et cetera)	und so weiter
BE	British English	
AE	American English	
sqm, m²	square metres	Quadratmeter
cbm, m³	cubic metres	Kubikmeter

Acronym	English meaning	German meaning
ARB	Architects Registration Board	Britische Kammer zur Registrierung von Architekten
BA	Bachelor of Arts	
BGB	Civil Code	Bürgerliches Gesetzbuch
BSc	Bachelor of Science	
CAD	Computer Aided Design	computergestütztes Zeichnen
CPD	Continuing Professional Development	weitere berufliche Entwicklung
CV	Curriculum Vitae	Lebenslauf
EEC	European Economic Community	Europäische Wirtschaftsgemeinschaft
EHEA	European Higher Education Area	Europäischer Hochschulraum
ETCS	European Credit Transfer System	Europäisches System zur Übertragung und Akkumulierung von Studienleistungen

Acronym	English meaning	German meaning
FIDIC	French: Fédération Internationale des Ingénieurs-Conseils	Internationale Vereinigung der Beratenden Ingenieure
FFL	Finished Floor Level	Fertigfußboden (FFB)
HOAI	Official Scale of Fees for Services by Architects and Engineers	Honorarordnung für Architekten und Ingenieure
JCT	Joint Contracts Tribunal	Arbeitsgruppe für Bauverträge
MA	Master of Arts	
MSc	Master of Science	
RIBA	Royal Institute of British Architects	Königlicher Britischer Architektenverband
UFL	Unfinished Floor Level	Rohfußboden (RFB)
UK	United Kingdom	Vereinigtes Königreich
VOB	construction contracts procedures	Verdingungsordnung für Bauwesen

Introduction

The contents of the book are arranged in the same way as a project. Units 1 and 2 start with the fundamentals, the feasibility studies and first meetings with clients. Units 10 and 11 describe the realization and completion phases of a project. The final unit takes a look at the diverse career opportunities in architecture.

It is possible to access the book at any stage; however, vocabulary explained in earlier units is not repeated and might have to be referred to in the alphabetic lists at the end of the book. The overview on the following page will help the reader to locate the appropriate construction phase, business skill or grammar item.

Each unit offers reading texts describing a process or situation arising during the course of a project. These texts introduce vocabulary in a context corresponding to the phase. By working through the units, the reader will become aware of collocating verbs, nouns and adjectives. The significance of collocations is explained in Unit 11. Word spiders have been added in Units 2 and 8 to point out the importance of lexical phrases. Readers may find this method of illustration useful in understanding word families. Exercises and tasks are included, which invite the reader to check and experiment with the terminology and phrases introduced. Some exercises are designed for practice, whereas others invite the reader to reflect on personal situations and consolidate the elements learned.

New words are written in italics and listed at the end of each unit according to the order in which they appear. Words appearing in diagrams and drawings have not been highlighted, but are included in the vocabulary lists. The words from the individual units can be found in alphabetical order at the end of the book, either English to German or German to English with a page reference. At the end of the book there is also a section containing the answers to the numerous exercises.

According to the Common European Framework of Reference for Languages, the level of this book is B2.

Overview

	Title	Grammar	Lexis	Business skill	Situation
1	Project Basics	Simple past, simple present	Project participants Appointment	Project organisation	
2	Preliminary Enquiries	Questions and short answers	Plot description; survey	E-mails	First site meeting
3	Briefing		Costs	Telephone calls	Client's brief, consultants
4	Preliminary Design	Comparison of adjectives, modifiers	Description of appearance		
5	Final Design	If-clauses	Structural engineering	Informing, presenting	Presentation of final design
6	Planning and Building Permission		Planning application/permission; fire safety		
7	Tender Documentation	Passive and active speech	Procurement	Business letters	Selection of contractors
8	Tender Action	Comparison of adjectives	Contracts	Negotiations	Price negotiation
9	Pre-Construction Phase	Present perfect; prepositions of time	Time	Time management	Construction programme
10	Construction	Cause and effect	Construction trades	Inspections	Requesting an alteration
11	Completion	Collocations	Payment	E-mail	Requesting extension of time
12	Education, Registration and more			CV, interview	

1 Project Basics

1.1 Work stages

Every construction project no matter how small or large is based on the *client*'s desire for change. Sometimes the client already owns a *property* and would merely like to make some *alterations*, in other cases, he/she owns a *plot of land*, which could be developed. In some cases, the architect supports the client in finding a suitable plot for a *development*.

There is some confusion regarding the *services* provided by the architect. On the one hand, it is often believed that the *architect's fee* for a *commission* covers anything and everything the client desires, provided that it has some relation to the project. On the other hand, and equally erroneously, it is sometimes believed that the architect will prepare a *set of plans*, but anything else will cost extra. There is some truth in each belief, which is why it is often difficult to explain the architect's services satisfactorily.

In most countries the work of an architect is divided into stages. The stages function as a basis for fees and as a means of separation if several architects are working on different phases of the same project. Whereas the HOAI, the Official Scale of Fees for Services by Architects and Engineers in Germany, divides the development process into 9 stages, the RIBA, the Royal Institute of British Architects, divides the building process into 11 stages. However, because the process is continuous and some activities can be accommodated in more than one stage, there is not always a clear separation of stages.

The following table shows the subdivision used by the RIBA in Great Britain and the HOAI for building works in Germany.

The RIBA Plan of Work		HOAI Service Phases	
A	Appraisal	1	Establishing the basis of the project
B	Strategic brief	2	Preliminary design
C	Outline proposals		
D	Detailed proposals	3	Final design
E	Final proposals	4	Building permission application
F	Production information	5	Execution drawings
G	Tender documentation	6	Preparation of contract award
H	Tender action		
J	Mobilisation	7	Assisting award process
K	Construction to practical completion	8	Project supervision
L	After practical completion	9	Project control and documentation

1.2 People involved

A construction project is not usually a one-person job, but a process taken care of by a project team, which comprises designers, *consultants* and constructors working on behalf of the client. A building project may begin relatively simply with a client and an architect, but over a few months, depending on the size of the project, many more people become involved. The client is the customer and therefore the most important member of the team. Because the development of a project includes a mix of materials, a team often involves many different *trades* offering a variety of *skills*. The following sections list the parties usually involved in an architectural development.

1.2.1 Client

The client is the person who commissions the design and the construction. He/she is the initiator of every project and the ultimate *owner* of the building. Under standard *building contracts*, the client is known as the e*mployer* and is the one who makes the investment and finances the project. A good relationship between the client and the architect is extremely important and should *be based on trust*.

1.2.2 Architect

It is the architect's task to translate the client's ideas into an acceptable design and produce a building that meets the client's needs. He/she must ensure that the result is properly related to the requirements of the owner and *occupier* and that the design is developed within the budget set by the client. In achieving the result, the architect has to relate to the surroundings, respect the natural and built environment and take account of social factors. The architect should always strive for an ecological, sustainable design. The architect requires creative skills and a professional understanding of materials, construction techniques and their application on site. Furthermore, the architect must be able to manage a project team and maintain a clear overview of operations and cost.

Across Europe, the relations between team members and the *responsibilities* of an architect differ slightly. Whereas in England the architect is the *mediator* between the client and other project parties, particularly between the client and the *contractor* during the second half of a project, the architect in Germany is quite clearly the *client's representative* and acts on his/her behalf.

1.2.3 Consultants

The design team may also include the following consultants:

A *structural* engineer offers advice on the structural design from the *foundations* to the roof. The structural stability of the building as well as the *thermal insulation calculation* are the responsibility of the structural engineer. The work includes *advice, specifications*, design and *supervision* of the works in progress.

A *building services engineer* is responsible for the mechanical and electrical aspects of a project. A building services engineer provides advice and drawings, and is sometimes involved in the tendering procedures with specialist firms.

A *landscape architect* is involved in the design and supervision of external works. Ground formation, planting and arboreal work provide the finishing touches to every project.

Most projects in the UK also include a *quantity surveyor*. Their work is often described as the financial management of a project. Traditionally quantity surveyors were employed to prepare *bills of quantities*. Nowadays they advise on, forecast and plan costs, take part in the *procurement procedure*, prepare *final accounts* and settle *contractual disputes*. The type and the size of the project determine the level of involvement. However, it is advantageous for the entire development process if the quantity surveyor is involved from the very beginning in order to become familiar with the special needs of the client and properly evaluate all options.

1.2.4 Contractor

The building contractor is the second major party in the project team. The contractor is usually selected by *competitive tender* and has a contract directly with the client. The contractor turns the architect's design into reality. Depending on the size of the contractor's company, a contract manager may be responsible for the management of the work. It is from the contract manager that the *site agent* receives instructions.

1.2.5 Site agent

The site agent has control of all construction processes on site. The site agent initiates each particular operation, coordinates it with other trades, ensures that it has a clear run and is supplied with appropriate plant, labour and materials.

1.2.6 Subcontractor

As the name suggests, work is sub-let to subcontractors by the (main) contractor. The contractor retains responsibility for all construction operations and remains *liable* to the client for any defects in sub-contracted work.

1.2.7 The clerk of works

Depending on the degree of the architect's involvement during the completion period, the British client may employ a clerk of works as a full-time inspector on the construction site. The clerk of works is responsible for checking that the materials and *workmanship* conform to the drawings and specifications set out in the contract documents. The clerk of works collaborates with the architect, who is kept informed about all activities on site.

1.2.8 Who is who?

Read the paragraphs above and decide which person fulfils the tasks described on the left.

1. They know all about foundations. ....
2. He/she pays the bills. ....
3. In the UK, they offer advice on cost matters. ....
4. They calculate structures. ....
5. The UK client's representative on site. ....
6. The contractor hires them for a specific task. ....
7. The architect needs one before he/she can practise. ....
8. In the UK, they help to evaluate tender documents. ....

1.3 Project organisation

Organigrams are diagrams displaying the organisation of people involved in a company or a project. Because there are so many different contract formats and structures and roles within a construction project, an organigram is a useful way to present the functions of individuals and the relationships between them.

1.3.1 Traditional contract

The organigram shown below is typical of one for a traditional contract for a medium-sized project. The client commissions the architect to lead a project from beginning to end. The architect advises the client to *appoint* consultants to deal with particular tasks, such as calculating structures, *cost estimating*, landscape design or technical matters.

Contractors are selected by the client and commissioned to execute the work according to the drawings and specifications produced by the design team. The contractor's site agent controls site operations and coordinates all trades. Contractors order material from *suppliers* and employ subcontractors to complete certain tasks within the project.

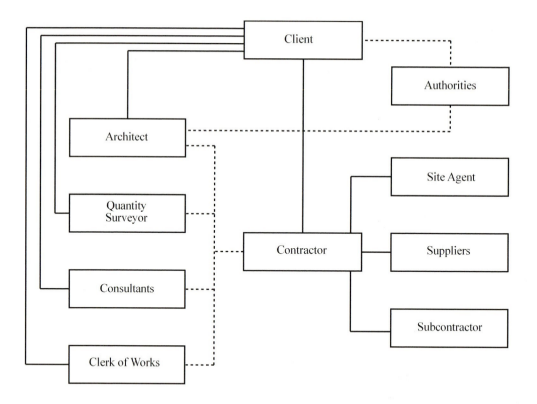

1.3 Project organisation

1.3.2 Design and build contract

The following organigram shows a contract form which has become very popular in recent years – especially in the UK. In this case, the contractor carries the responsibility for both design and construction. The concept is to offer the client a package or, what is known as, a *turnkey development*. The contractor is responsible for providing everything, sometimes even furniture and pictures on walls. As the name suggests the client simply turns the key and starts using the building.

It goes without saying that this system also involves architects. However, in this case, the architect's employer is not the client, but the contractor.

Insert the functions below into the organigram and describe the relationships. The lexical phrases used in 1.3.1, such as to appoint sb, to be responsible for, etc., should be helpful to create a similar description.

architect · authorities · supplier · subcontractor · client · quantity surveyor · consultants

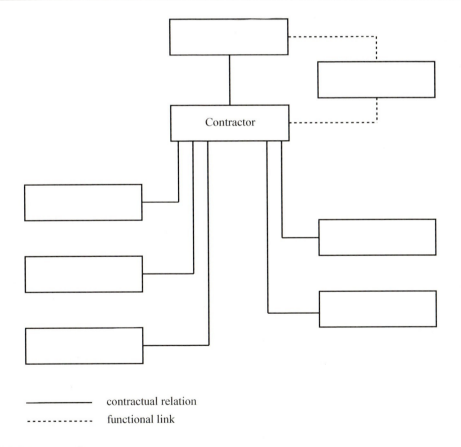

———————— contractual relation
- - - - - - - - functional link

1.3.3 Your project

Think about a project you are working on at the moment or have already completed. Which people or trades were represented in the project team?

1.4 Architect's appointment

The relationship between an architect and his or her client is contractual. A contract is a *binding agreement* between two or more parties. It sets down mutual rights and duties, which are enforceable at law.

A contract can exist by word of mouth. However, the dangers of an *oral contract* are often misunderstandings sometimes due to imperfect memory. A written contract has the advantage that it protects both parties' rights in the event of disputes, if necessary before a court of law.

Before signing a contract, the architect should pay careful attention to the *terms and conditions*. It is wise, wherever possible, to contract on the basis of standard terms. In contrast to Germany, the RIBA offers standard forms for the appointment of architects in the UK. There are several different forms depending on the size and the type of work. The form SFA/99 is intended for general use for the appointment of an architect. To find out more about different contract formats in Britain go to www.riba.org.

1.4.1 Code of conduct

All persons wishing to use the title architect for business purposes have to register with a *professional association*. In Germany, this is the Architectural Chamber of the Land in which the architect is practising; in the United Kingdom, the ARB (Architects Registration Board) holds and maintains the UK Register of Architects.

The *registration conditions* prescribed by most boards include adequate qualifications awarded by a school of architecture and usually at least two years of practical experience. Sometimes a written and/or oral examination is also required.

These professional associations, including the European Architect's Directive (85/384/EEC) and the UNESCO/UIA Charter for Architectural Education, on an international basis, issue guidelines regulating the actions of members between themselves, to their clients and the public. The codes published by the boards list guidelines regarding the professional conduct and the practice expected of architects, including *complaints handling* and client service. The principle of all codes is the requirement for architects to act with complete honesty and integrity at all times. Architects should carry out their professional work faithfully and conscientiously and with due regard to relevant technical and professional standards.

A failure to follow the guidance of a code may be taken into account should it be necessary to examine the conduct and competence of an architect. A shortcoming or failure to comply with the guidelines may give rise to *disciplinary proceedings*. The codes do not replace obligations placed upon architects by law.

1.4.2 Lexis: Architect's appointment

Match the expressions 1 – 9 with the correct definitions a – i on the right.

1.	sign a contract	a.	a building completed as a package requiring little more of the client than payment
2.	turnkey development	b.	agreement made in writing between two or more parties with their signatures expressing consent
3.	oral agreement	c.	the behaviour expected of a board member, usually described in detail in the association's code of conduct
4.	contract terms and conditions	d.	a specialist employed to provide the services of designing and realizing a building
5.	appoint a consultant	e.	the subject matter of a legal document
6.	written contract	f.	not a written, but a spoken arrangement with legally binding effect
7.	commission an architect	g.	possible result of not complying with the code of conduct
8.	professional conduct	h.	to write one's name on a document to show that one agrees with the contents
9.	disciplinary proceedings	i.	to select a specialist for expert advice in a specific trade, e.g. heating, ventilation, etc.

1.5 Architect's workplace

Architects who have been in practice for more than 15 years are fully aware of the changes, which have taken place due to information technology. Over the years, *drawing boards*, *tee squares*, *stencils* and *tracing paper* have been replaced by computer applications. There is no longer a need for large *filing cabinets* to store *dyelines*. Today the originals are nicely stored on disks and printed out on plotters when required. Changes are simply made by a mouse click without requiring *razor blades* to remove the *drawing ink* once used to make the drawings.

Nowadays, all office staff are computer trained and multi-skilled in that they not only prepare their own drawings, but also draw up diagrams and charts, as well as write a lot of their own letters and e-mails. The *cable clutter*, which once occupied much of the floor space behind and under tables and desks, has disappeared since introduction of *wireless* equipment. Wireless phones, printers, monitors and keyboards bring great flexibility to once very rigid office arrangements.

Despite all these changes, architecture is one profession which will never be able to cope as a *paperless office*. Paper and pencils will always remain the architect's first tool. A pencil is small, quick, totally independent of electricity and able to express such a lot in a small space of time.

1.5.1 Grammar: Simple present and simple past

If you take a look at the two pictures you will notice a lot of differences between the past and the present situation.

Simple Present is used to describe current facts and regular activities.

Signal words:	adverbs of frequency such as always, usually, normally, sometimes, never, hardly ever, every day, etc.
	adverbs contrasting the present and the past such as nowadays, today, currently, etc.
Form:	The simple present has the same form as the infinitive but adds an s in the third person singular (I work, you work, he/she/it works, etc.). The negative is formed with the negative of the verb to do + the infinitive of the full verb (I don't work, he doesn't work).
Example:	Today architects use computer programs.

Simple Past is used to describe completed activities or facts of the past.

Signal words:	yesterday, last week, last year, time + ago, on + date, in + year
Form:	In regular verbs, the simple past is formed by adding -ed to the infinitive (I worked). There are no inflexions, i.e. the same form is used for all persons. In irregular verbs, forms vary considerably and they simply have to be learnt. Most dictionaries include a list of irregular verbs. Like regular verbs, there are no inflexions.
	The negative of regular and irregular verbs is formed with did not + the infinitive (I did not work).
Example:	15 years ago, draughtsmen sat at drawing boards.

1.5 Architect's workplace   11

1.5.2 Exercise: Simple present versus simple past

Complete the text below by putting the verb in brackets into either the simple present or simple past tense.

Architecture has always been practised. Even in ancient times *master-builders* .... (design) buildings and .... (manage) their construction. Up until the late 80ies *draughtspersons* .... (sit) at drawing boards using tee squares, *compasses* and stencils. In 1938, Konrad Zuse .... (invent) the Z1 – the first digital computer. The first CAD programmes .... (appear) in the 70ies, however, they .... (not become) affordable for smaller offices until the early 90ies. Nowadays, most architects .... (sit) in front of flat screens and .... (give) instructions to the computer by clicking the mouse. Despite all the changes, architects .... (still use) paper and pencil to jot down first thoughts.

1.5.3 Office equipment

Architects, draughtspersons, civil engineers are dependant on a wide range of equipment to fulfil their daily tasks of designing. Can you find the following pieces of equipment in the two drawings.

scanner · plotter · T-square · tracing paper · monitor · mouse · mobile phone · printer · file *folding rule · power outlet strip* · pencil · keyboard · a pair of scissors · bin · calculator

1.6 Vocabulary

1.1	work stages		Leistungsphasen
	client		Auftraggeber, Bauherr
	property		Immobilie
	alterations		Umbauarbeiten
	plot of land		Baugrundstück, Parzelle, Flurstück
	development		Bebauung
	services		Leistungen
	architect's fee		Architektenhonorar
	commission		Beauftragung
	set of plans		Plansatz
	RIBA, Royal Institute of British Architects		königlicher Britischer Architektenverband
	appraisal		Bewertung, Evaluierung
	brief		Übermittlung der Planungsgrundlagen an den Planer durch den Bauherrn
	outline proposal		Vorentwurf
	final proposal		Entwurf
	production information		Ausführungsplanung
	tender documentation		Ausschreibungsunterlagen
	tender action		Angebotseinholung
	mobilisation		Mobilisierung, Bauvorbereitung
	construction to practical completion		Bauausführung bis zur Fertigstellung
	after practical completion		nach Fertigstellung
1.2	consultant		Fachplaner, Fachingenieur
	trade		Baugewerbe
	skill		Fertigkeit
1.2.1	owner		Eigentümer, Besitzer
	building contract		Bauvertrag
	employer		Auftraggeber
	to be based on trust		auf Vertrauen basieren
1.2.2	occupier		Bewohner
	responsibility		Verantwortung
	mediator		Vermittler
	building contractor		Auftragnehmer, Bauunternehmen
	client's representative		Bauherrenvertreter
1.2.3	structural engineer		Statiker, Tragwerksplaner
	foundations		Fundamente
	thermal insulation calculation		Wärmeschutznachweis
	advice		Beratung
	specifications		technische Daten

1.6 Vocabulary

	supervision	Bauüberwachung
	building services engineer	Haustechnik-Ingenieur
	landscape architect	Landschaftsarchitekt, -planer
	quantity surveyor	Kosten- u. Abrechnungsingenieur (Berufsstand mit eigenem Studiengang in GB u. anderen Ländern; berät auch bei Vertragsgestaltung u. Vergabe)
	bill of quantities	Leistungsverzeichnis
	procurement procedure	Vergabeverfahren
	final account	Schlussrechnung, Endabrechnung
	contractual disputes	Vertragsstreitigkeiten
1.2.4	competitive tender	Ausschreibung
	site agent	Bauleiter des Auftragnehmers
1.2.6	subcontractor	Subunternehmen
	liable adj	haftbar
1.2.7	clerk of works	Bauaufseher (meist des Auftraggebers)
	workmanship	Ausführungsqualität
1.3	organigram	Organisationsdiagramm
1.3.1	to appoint sb	beauftragen
	cost estimate	Kostenanschlag
	supplier	Lieferant
	contractual relation	Vertragsverhältnis
	functional link	funktionale Bindung
1.3.2	turnkey development	schlüsselfertige Bebauung
1.4	appointment	Beauftragung
	binding agreement	verbindliche Vereinbarung
	oral contract	mündlicher Vertrag
	terms and conditions	Konditionen
1.4.1	conduct	Verhalten, Betragen
	professional association	Berufsverband
	registration conditions	Eintragungsbedingungen
	complaints handling	Beschwerdebearbeitung
	disciplinary proceedings	Disziplinärverfahren
1.5	drawing board	Reißbrett, Zeichenbrett
	tee-square	Reißschiene
	stencil	Schriftschablone
	tracing paper	Transparentpapier
	filing cabinet	Aktenschrank
	dyeline (copy)	Lichtpause
	razor blade	Rasierklinge
	drawing ink	Tusche

	cable clutter	Kabelsalat
	paperless office	papierloses Büro
1.5.2	master-builder	Baumeister
	Draughtsperson/-people draughtsman/-men pl draughtswoman/-women pl	Bauzeichner/in
	compass	Zirkel
1.5.3	folding rule	Zollstock
	power outlet strip	Mehrfachsteckdose
	(rubbish) bin BE, trashcan AE	Mülleimer, -kübel
	to bin sth (e.g. old things, an idea/concept)	etw. wegschmeißen

2 Preliminary Enquiries

2.1 Feasibility

Before the architect gets too involved in the project, a decision has to be made as to whether it is at all feasible to build. Feasible means possible as well as practicable and is influenced by a number of factors. For example, the decision may depend on the *access* to the site, *building lines* and specific requirements regarding the *number of storeys*, *parking provisions* and, of course, *geological conditions*. The decision to proceed or to stop lies with the client; however, it is the architect's task to present the information in a structured way so that it is possible for the client to come to a decision.

2.1.1 Planning authorities

In order to judge the feasibility of a project, the architect or civil engineer should consult the *local planning authority*. Planning authorities have a wealth of information and will be able to advise on *development plans*, *conservation areas*, *listed buildings* and trees with *preservation orders*. Local planning authorities will also have a view on the *acceptability* of the proposed development. It is possible to submit an *outline application* to determine the likelihood of a *proposal* being accepted; this is especially useful for more daring designs and costly projects.

Frequently state or local authorities draw up development plans for specific areas. The intention of development plans is to balance business, *residential and community needs* and, at the same time, protect areas from the adverse effects of development. Development plans influence the *scale*, location and timing of land development and redevelopment. Therefore the starting point for the local planning authority in considering any *planning application* will be the development plan. Any provisions in it relating to the specific site, area or type of proposed development will affect the *scheme*.

The local planning authority will also be able to provide a *water table*, information on the *liability to flooding* and information on the *nature of the subsoil*. Furthermore, they will be able to indicate the position and depths of all main *services*.

2.1.2 Feasibility study

In order to prepare a *feasibility study* the architect needs to check various aspects of the site. Some questions will be quite straightforward, however, others may require input from a consultant or might have to be based on assumptions, at least before making a detailed *survey*. In the following, there are some typical considerations that an architect will make before putting together a feasibility study.

- Is the site appropriate for the client's proposed scheme?
- How does the topography suit the scheme?
- Does the size of the plot seem reasonable for the scale of the project?
- What is the nature of the soil?

- Will it be necessary to make a *soils report*?
- Can the project be realised for the money the client wishes to spend?
- Does the project involve any existing buildings?

2.1.3 Grammar: Questions

Take a look at the questions above. There are two different types of questions:
- those which can be answered with yes or no (Yes/No questions) and
- the others which require a more detailed answer (Wh-questions).

Yes/No questions using a form of **do** (do, does, did) at the beginning:
Question: Form of do + subject + full verb
Example: Does the project involve any existing buildings?

Yes/No questions using a form of **be** at the beginning:
Question: Form of be + subject
Example: Is the site appropriate for the client's proposed scheme?

Yes/No questions using a helping verb (have, be, will, might, etc.) at the beginning:
Question: Helping verb + subject + full verb
Example: Will it be necessary to make a soils report?

The short answers should always repeat the helping verb used in the question.
Is there access to the plot? – Yes, there is. / No, there isn't.
Will it be necessary to make a soils report? – Yes, it will. / No, it won't.

Wh-questions are formed with **do** unless the question word itself is the subject or the full verb is a form of be.
Question: Question word + form of do + subject + full verb
Example: How does the topography suit the scheme?

2.1.4 Exercise: Questions and answers

Match the questions on the left with the appropriate short answers on the right.

1. Will it be fairly easy to obtain *planning permission*?		a.	No, they aren't.
2. Does the client's time schedule seem reasonable?		b.	Yes, it will.
3. Is the client aware of the infrastructure offered?		c.	Yes, it might.
4. Are the existing buildings protected?		d.	No, it hasn't.
5. Might it be possible to fell some of the trees?		e.	Yes, there are.
6. Are there any requirements regarding the number of storeys?		f.	No, he isn't.
7. Has a water table been provided by the local planning authority?		g.	Yes, it does.

2.2 Site visit

A site visit at the beginning of each project is absolutely essential to understand the full scope of the job. It is a fundamental part of a feasibility study and should be performed by all persons involved.

In the case of this project, which will accompany the reader through the book, the client owns a plot he would like to develop. He was *recommended* to an architect, whom he has contacted and with whom he has arranged a meeting on site. We will simply assume that the client and the architect get on well, that the architect is competent and his current *commitments* allow him to take on another job. The *terms of appointment*, the *programme of work and costs* will be discussed in a later meeting.

Conversation: A first meeting

George Brown: Hello, you must be Tim Smith, the architect.
Tim Smith: Yes, that's right.
George Brown: I'm George and this is my wife, Helen.
Tim Smith: Hello, pleased to meet you.
George Brown: So this is the piece of land we *inherited* last year. We've spent quite a long time thinking about it, but we've decided we'd like to build a house and move to this part of the town.
Tim Smith: Well, it's a wonderful location, isn't it. And the plot is an adequate size, too.
George Brown: Yes, we think it should be big enough for a small house leaving a bit of garden.
Tim Smith: I presume there won't be a problem obtaining planning permission.
George Brown: No, I don't think so. We're not sure how far back we can build or how close to the neighbours, but surely that isn't a problem to find out.
Tim Smith: No, not at all. The local authority will be able to provide all the necessary information. So, what is it you actually have in mind?
Helen Brown: Well, we're thinking of something quite normal really. Living, dining, kitchen on the ground floor; the bedrooms, we'll be needing two for the children and one for us, maybe an extra guest bedroom, upstairs. I'd love either a cellar or a utility area to take care of all the technical equipment and offering *storage facilities*; oh, and of course, we'll need a garage.
Tim Smith: Okay, I've made a note of all of that. Have you got an idea how many square meters you're looking at.
Helen Brown: The house we're living in at the moment is a 4-bedroom *semi*. It would be great to have a bit more space.
George Brown: I suppose we're thinking of something between 150 and 200 sqm. But of course a lot depends on the costs.
Tim Smith: Yes, I can understand that. I'll tell you what. Let me speak to the local authority, take some measurements of the site and I'll get back to you in a week or two with some first ideas and thoughts.
George Brown: That sounds wonderful. I'll give you my card so that you know where we are and I look forward to hearing from you soon.

2.2.1 Comprehension

Are the following statements concerning the dialogue true or false.

		true	false
1.	Tim Smith and Helen Brown had never met before.	☐	☐
2.	The Browns' *purchased* the site.	☐	☐
3.	The plot of land is extremely large.	☐	☐
4.	There are several neighbours.	☐	☐
5.	The Browns' would like at least 3 bedrooms.	☐	☐
6.	There has to be cellar for technical equipment and storage.	☐	☐
7.	They are currently living in a *flat*.	☐	☐
8.	The architect is going to contact the local authorities.	☐	☐

2.2.2 Scales

In the UK and other English-speaking countries, people – especially those not involved in jobs requiring measurements – still tend to use inches and feet instead of centimetres and metres. For an easier understanding, we have used the metric system throughout this book as it is intended mainly for German readers.

Imperial system		Metric system
1 inch (in) = 1"		25.4 millimetres (mm)
1 foot (ft) = 1' 0"	= 12 inches	30.48 centimetres (cm)
1 yard (yd)	= 3 feet	0.914 metres (m)
1 mile	= 1760 yards	1.609 kilometres
1 acre	= 4840 square (sq) yards	0.405 hectare

2.2.3 Building types

A building's function strongly influences its design and construction. Domestic, public and commercial buildings have different requirements. Their form, scale and appearance is dependant on the use and the persons using it. There are many different types of buildings with differing characteristics. As a general rule, we separate them into *residential* and *non-residential buildings*.

- Non-residential buildings are quite simply all buildings which are not used for living purposes. These include public buildings (schools, hospitals, libraries and museums), buildings for sport (stadiums and swimming pools), commercial buildings (shops, factories, warehouses and offices) and buildings for transport (stations, airports and bus terminals).

- Residential buildings are all buildings required for living purposes and include:

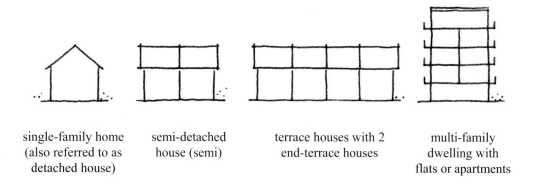

| single-family home (also referred to as detached house) | semi-detached house (semi) | terrace houses with 2 end-terrace houses | multi-family dwelling with flats or apartments |

2.3 Plots

A plot is an undeveloped piece of land. A developed piece of land is referred to as a *property*; a piece of land under construction is a building or construction site. All have boundaries encompassing the *curtilage* and separating it from *adjacent properties*.

When submitting a planning application, a *site location plan* has to be included indicating the *site boundary*. In the UK, the site boundary is indicated in red; in Germany, red is used to highlight the new construction whereas the site boundary is indicated in green. A site location plan is a copy from an official map supplied by a *cadastral office*.

Ordnance Survey is the national mapping agency of Great Britain. They produce digital and paper maps, which can be ordered online at www.ordnancesurvey.co.uk or may be obtained from local authorities for a certain fee.

2.3.1 Considerations

When making plans for a plot of land the architect should consider the following aspects:
- Is there access to the plot?
- What are the approximate dimensions of the plot?
- If there are existing buildings, where are they positioned?
- What about the *orientation* of the site?
- What are the general characteristics of the landscape, planting and trees?
- Are there any buildings *adjoining* or *overlooking* the site?
- What about services such as *sewers*, water, electricity, gas and communications?
- Does the neighbourhood have special features or characteristics which might affect the scheme?

2.3.2 Situations

The two plots presented below are very different. Assign the vocabulary to the appropriate situations. For a clear, unambiguous description, it might be necessary to add a noun, e.g. a narrow road.

A

B

in town
on a slope
constricted
spacious
small
rural
commercial
wide
busy
narrow
in the countryside
close
urban
friendly
dense
large
distant

2.3.3 Descriptions

Read the following passages describing two very different plots. Try to imagine what they look like.

The plot is a narrow *gap* between houses in an urban, very dense, environment. It is rectangular measuring about 6 by 20 meters. It is totally flat. To the north and south, tall 5-storey buildings, with *gable roofs,* border the site. To the west there is a busy road with a mixture of shops and offices. At the rear, facing east, the plot has a typical courtyard atmosphere. Tall buildings surround a large inner courtyard with a variety of tall trees.

The plot is rectangular measuring about 20 by 80 meters. It is on a slope and slightly wider at the top than at the bottom. In total the difference in height is about 5 meters. There is a small area of woodland beyond a small path at the top of the site, which faces north. To the east and south there is a quiet road. There are 3 plots with detached two-storey houses to the west, however, none of the houses border the plot directly. There is a view from the top of the plot; the town centre with about 500,000 inhabitants is 10 minutes walking distance away.

2.3.4 Your plot

Think about a plot for which you are planning or have planned a structure. It could also be the piece of land you are living on. Extract the lexical phrases from the sections above and write an appropriate description highlighting the main characteristics.

2.4 Survey

The term survey has several different meanings. Here, the term refers to the activity of taking *measurements* and performing *levelling* operations to ascertain the various levels of the ground. Finally all data collected is translated into drawings.

If the site or buildings are fairly simple, the architect will probably perform the surveying work without difficulty. In more complex situations, a survey should be produced either by a land *surveyor* for undeveloped plots or a building surveyor for already developed property.

However, a detailed survey prepared by a qualified surveyor should not prevent the architect from visiting the site. A *site investigation* also includes reference to the nature of the ground under the site. Depending on the site and the proposed building, a special consultant engineer should be employed to investigate ground conditions. Usually the work of a specialist *ground consultant* includes *sinking boreholes* and *examining soil samples*.

2.4.1 Lexis: Survey

The term survey is a very complex term with several different meanings. It is both a verb and a noun. Take a look at the term survey and some collocations.

to survey: to study, inspect or examine sth, to describe the general condition of sth; in architecture this is often a plot of land or a building examined by taking measurements and preparing plans

a survey: the result of surveying, either a map, plan or report

surveying: the process of a person preparing a map, plan or report

Noun + noun collocations:
building surveyor
land surveyor
quantity surveyor
surveying authority
surveying vehicle

Verb + noun collocations:
to make/perform/prepare a survey
to commission/employ a surveyor
to recommend a surveyor to sb
to brief a surveyor about sth
to instruct a surveyor to do sth

2.4.2 The Browns' plot

Tim Smith, the architect, makes a trip to the local authority's planning office the next morning. He obtains a copy of the Ordnance Survey map showing all boundaries of the site and the surrounding properties. He also receives information regarding the building lines and services.

He then returns to the site. He is equipped with a digital camera, a *levelling instrument* and a *staff*, pencil and paper. As it is a lot easier to perform site measurements in a team, a member of staff accompanies him. The architect and his assistant spend a few hours on site taking measurements and photos, making a note of trees and other important features.

Since the plot is on a slope and the neighbouring building to the east is very close, the architect decides to make a rough model of the plot.

The architect decided to perform the site analysis himself, as the plot is undeveloped and very straightforward. In many cases, a surveyor would have been commissioned to perform this work. However, the architect does come to the conclusion that a soils report is necessary. He has worked with a good consultant before and recommends him to the client. The consultant is briefed by the architect and, after the client obtains an estimate of cost and time, is instructed to proceed with the work.

2.5 Communicating with the client

Architects are expected to report to their clients at various stages throughout the project. It is often difficult to decide when to contact the client in advance. Usually some kind of communication takes place whenever the architect needs the client to make a decision. Naturally there will be situations when no decision is required, but it is simply good for relations to report on progress. Take a look at the following methods used for reporting:

Formal letter: A formal letter sent by post may seem inappropriate if the matter is fairly trivial and the aim is simply to keep the client informed.

Telephone call: A telephone call is appropriate for immediate decisions.

Facsimile (fax): A fax is employed for urgent matters, which need to be transmitted and received the same day. Faxes are still ideal for sending sketches directly to the building site. In comparison to an e-mail, a fax is immediately visible.

E-mail: More recently e-mail has replaced faxing. E-mail is valuable for transmitting large quantities of text and diagrams from one place to another. The system is especially useful because the recipient can make alterations. However, the ease with which an e-mail can be sent encourages the sending of messages even about the most trivial matters.

Here are a few aspects, which should be considered when writing e-mails:

- Even though e-mails are different to formal letters, they should still be clear, use concise language, correct grammar and appropriate vocabulary.
- The structure of an e-mail is similar to that of a formal letter in that it consists of a salutation, the body with an introduction and an appropriate ending and a close. For more information regarding the structure of letters see 7.5.2.
- The *subject line* is not only useful for telling the recipient what the e-mail is about before it is read, but it is also helpful for finding the e-mail later when it is filed away in the sender's inbox or the recipient's outbox.

2.5 Communicating with the client

2.5.1 E-mail

The architect sends the client an e-mail informing him about the outcome of his visit to the local authority and some thoughts concerning the next steps.

Insert the correct words from this chapter.

> photographs · site location plan · boundaries · *constraints* · planning permission · services
> soils report · measurements · site · restrictions · properties · water level · ground consultant

Hello George,

I would just like to let you know that I was able to get the .... from the local authority. It clearly shows the .... and beyond these the .... of your future neighbours. It shouldn't be a problem to obtain .... for the site and there are luckily no major .... or .... Due to the proximity to the river and the ...., it is necessary to have a .... made. I have worked together with John Taylor, a very good ...., who I could recommend. If you would like me to give him a ring, please let me know.

All ...., except for gas, are available. I have been back to the .... to take some .... and a few .... Naturally a lot of questions have cropped up. I would therefore like to suggest arranging a meeting for next week. Wednesday or Thursday would suit me best.

I look forward to hearing from you.

Best regards
Tim

2.5.2 Register

The register of an e-mail (how formal or informal it is) depends on the type of message you are writing and who you are writing to. An e-mail about rescheduling a meeting might be less formal than a first enquiry or an apology. Similarly, an e-mail to a new client would probably be more formal than an e-mail to an old client or friend.

As you will have noticed this e-mail, as are most e-mails, is fairly informal. Read it again and decide which words you would replace by this more formal vocabulary.

> to inform · to receive · to present · to contact · to return · to arise

2.6 Vocabulary

	preliminary enquiries	Voruntersuchungen
2.1	feasibility	Durchführbarkeit, Machbarkeit
	access	Zufahrt, Zugang
	building lines	Baulinien
	number of storeys	Geschosszahl
	parking provisions	Stellplatzrichtlinien
	geological conditions	geologische Bedingungen
2.1.1	local planning authority	kommunale Projektierungsbehörde
	development plan	Bebauungsplan
	conservation area	Denkmalerhaltungsgebiet
	listed building	denkmalgeschütztes Gebäude
	preservation order	Denkmalschutzauflage
	acceptability	Genehmigungsfähigkeit
	outline application	Bauvoranfrage
	proposal	Vorschlag
	residential and community needs	Bedürfnisse der Anwohner u. Gemeinde
	scale	Größenordnung
	planning application	Bauantrag, Baugesuch
	scheme	Plan, Projekt
	water table	Grundwasserspiegel
	liability to flooding	Überschwemmungsgefahr
	nature of the subsoil	Bodenbeschaffenheit
	services	Hausanschlüsse, Versorgungsleitungen
2.1.2	feasibility study	Durchführbarkeitsstudie
	survey	Aufnahme, Untersuchung
	soils report	Bodengutachten
2.1.4	planning permission	Baugenehmigung
2.2	site visit	Ortsbegehung
	to recommend sb/sth to sb	empfehlen
	commitments	Verpflichtungen
	terms of appointment	Bedingungen der Beauftragung
	programme of work	Arbeitsaufwand
	programme of cost	Kostenrahmen
	to inherit sth	erben
	storage facility	Abstellraum, Lagermöglichkeit
	semi, semi-detached house	Doppelhaushälfte
2.2.1	to purchase	erwerben
	flat	Etagenwohnung
2.2.2	scale	Maßstab

2.6 Vocabulary

2.2.3	residential building	Wohnungsbau
	non-residential building	Nichtwohnbau
	single-family home, detached house	Einfamilienhaus
	terrace house	Reihenhaus
	end-terrace house	Reiheneckhaus
	multi-family dwelling	Mehrfamilienhaus
2.3	plot	Parzelle, Flurstück, Baugrundstück
	property	Immobilie
	curtilage	Hausgrundstück
	adjacent property	Nachbarbebauung
	site location plan	Lageplan
	site boundary	Grundstücksgrenzen
	cadastral office	Katasteramt
	Ordnance Survey	engl. Landvermessungsagentur
2.3.1	orientation	Ausrichtung, Himmelsrichtung
	adjoining adj	angrenzend
	overlooking adj	einsehend, mit Blick auf
	sewer	Abwasserleitung
2.3.2	rural adj	ländlich
	urban adj	städtisch
	dense adj	dicht besiedelt
2.3.3	gap	Baulücke
	gable roof	Satteldach
2.4	survey	Aufnahme, Vermessung, Baugutachten, Bestandsaufnahme eines Gebäudes
	measurement	Aufmaß
	levelling	Höhenmessung, Nivellieren
	surveyor	Vermessungsingenieur
	site investigation	Baugrunderkundung
	ground consultant	Bodengutachter
	to sink a borehole	Bohrloch ausheben
	to examine a soil sample	Bodenprobe untersuchen
2.4.1	surveying	Vermessungsarbeit
	surveying authority	Vermessungsbehörde
	surveying vehicle	Vermessungsfahrzeug
2.4.2	levelling instrument	Nivelliergerät
	staff	Messlatte
2.5	subject line	Betreffzeile
2.5.1	constraints	Beschränkung
	proximity to sth	Nähe zu etwas

3 Briefing

3.1 Accepting the brief

The brief is a set of instructions given to the architect by the client. In this sometimes very delicate and lengthy process, it is the architect's task to understand, interpret and finally produce possible solutions. It is not always clear whether what the client says he wants or requests is also what he/she actually needs. For the architect or engineer this phase is quite clearly about listening and interpreting.

The architect has to analyse the client's needs in terms of activities and identify, in respect of each activity, a number of key criteria including *areas*, *volumes*, requirements for *finishes* and *orientation*, interaction with other activities, number of persons involved, social and psychological needs. Usually the result of taking a brief is the preparation of a *space-utilisation schedule*, a *user requirement programme* or at least something in writing or in graphical form. The brief should always be *confirmed* by the client before the next stage is commenced.

Here is a sketch showing the outcome of an architect's meeting with a client.

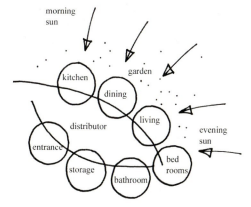

3.1.1 Client's needs

During a meeting with the architect, the client, George Brown, says the following:

We are thinking of a light and *spacious* house. We would like to enter the house through a large *entrance area*, which offers enough space to store all the jackets and shoes. Also on the ground floor, we could imagine having a fairly open-plan arrangement with the kitchen, dining and living areas interlinked. We would definitely like a *larder* close to the kitchen. The garden should be *accessible*, too, with a terrace for eating outside in the summer.

Then, above the ground floor, we visualise having two further *storeys* one for the adults and one for the children, each with their separate bathrooms. A *walk-in wardrobe* connected to the *master bedroom* would be great. We'll also need a *study* somewhere. We'd like a *utility room* and a *workshop* in the *cellar*. Of course we'll also need a garage and lots of storage space throughout the house.

As you can see here, the client already has quite clear ideas, at least concerning the scale and *arrangement of rooms*. He has not said anything about the *technical installations* or their location. It is the architect's job to point out these technical details and clarify any other uncertainties.

3.1.2 Needs and worries

As you can see from the following questions and answers, the client's needs do not always correspond with the architect's thoughts. The whole process may require numerous meetings before the complete information, especially for a large job, is obtained.

Match the client's needs with the architect's worries.

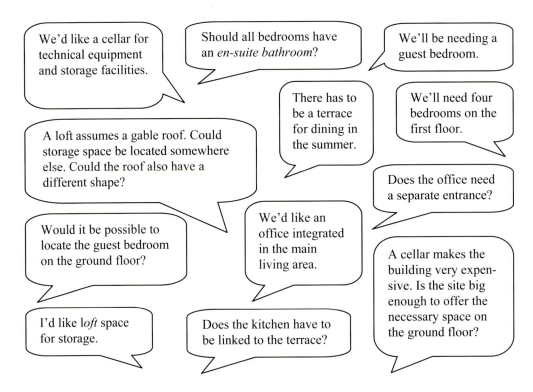

3.2 Consultants

During early design stages, it is the architect's task to decide whether any support regarding a particular part or function of the development is required. Consultants are qualified in a particular field and are able to give expert advice or assistance. Common types of consultants in connection with construction work are:

- Structural engineers
- Electrical engineers
- Mechanical services engineers
- Quantity surveyors or cost managers
- Interior designers
- Landscape architects

3.2 Consultants

On smaller projects, the architect may feel capable of carrying out the entire design work alone, except for the structural engineering. If the project is large or has special features, the architect may nominate several consultants to deal with the areas of work which are outside the architect's competence.

Consultants should be appointed as soon as their need is identified. Usually this is shortly after the architect has clarified the brief with the client. Because of the client's natural desire to limit fees, it is sometimes difficult to convince him/her that additional consultants are necessary.

A first design team meeting should clarify the *scope of* each consultant's *work*. Consultants are generally employed directly by the client. A *contractual link* between the consultant and the client is clearly useful in the event of problems with regard to *liability* or fees.

On some projects, the architect has the role of consultant when another construction professional has been appointed as the *lead consultant*.

3.2.1 Appointing a consultant

Read this telephone conversation with a structural engineer. You will notice that the conversation is taking place at a fairly early stage in the design, since the architect has only just received the brief. However, it is good to refresh contacts and *forewarn* possible contractors sooner rather than later.

Secretary:	Good morning, White Engineers. Can I help you?
Tim Smith:	Er, yes, it's Tim Smith. Could I speak to Joe White, please?
Secretary:	Yes, of course. I'll put you through.
Joe White:	Hello, Tim. Nice to hear from you. What can I do for you?
Tim Smith:	Hello, Joe. Well actually, I'm phoning about a new project I'm working on.
Joe White:	Is it a big one?
Tim Smith:	No, not really. It's a single-family home, but the clients are interested in timber construction and would like everything spacious and open plan.
Joe White:	I understand. Could be difficult, but not impossible.
Tim Smith:	I've really only just started with some sketches, but wanted to let you know that I'll be needing some support regarding the structure. Are you available for some additional work over the next few weeks?
Joe White:	Well, we're fairly busy at the moment, but I'm sure we'll be able to help you out. It would be nice to work on something other than steel and concrete.
Tim Smith:	That would be great. I'll let the client know you're interested and get back to you in a couple of weeks, if that's okay.
Joe White:	Yes, certainly. Well, thanks for phoning Tim and I look forward to hearing from you. Bye.
Tim Smith:	Bye, bye, Joe.

3.2.2 Standard telephone phrases

As you can see from this simple phone call, there are many standard phrases used on the telephone. The phrases at the beginning and the end of the call tend to be rather repetitive.

Function	Standard Phrases
Introduction	This is … This is …. speaking. Good morning/Hello …, …. here.
Request	Could I speak to … I'd like to speak to …
Replies to requests	Yes, certainly. I'll put you through. Hold the line, please. I'll see if I can find …. I'm afraid the line's busy. Would you like to wait? I'm afraid he/she is in a meeting. Would you like to leave a message? I'm sorry he/she is out of the office. Can I take a message?
Communication difficulties	I'm sorry, I can't hear you very well. Could you speak up a bit? The line's not very clear. Could you repeat that, please? Could you spell that, please?
Reason for calling	I'm phoning to inquire/ask … The reason I'm phoning is … I'm calling about …
Ending	I'll be in touch as soon as possible. Thank you for your call. I look forward to seeing you on …/hearing from you next … Thank you very much. Goodbye.

3.2.3 Exercise: Telephoning

Put the sentences of this telephone conversation between the architect and the client into the correct order. Number the boxes.

☐ That sounds good. So how about our meeting then? How does Thursday late afternoon suit you?

☐ Yes that suits me fine. I'll be round at 5.

☐ I'm just phoning to let you know that I've spoken to Joe White and he'd be interested to do the structural planning for your house.

☐ George Brown.

☐ Oh, that's good news. Should I arrange a meeting with him?

☐ Goodbye.

☐ Yes, definitely, but there's no rush at the moment. I'd like you to take a look at some sketches first and confirm the brief. And once I have got some preliminary drawings prepared, we could all sit down together.

☐ Excellent, I look forward to seeing you. Goodbye George.

☐ Hello, George. It's Tim.

☐ Thursday would be fine. Shall we say 5 o'clock? Would you like to come round to the office?

☐ Hello, Tim. Nice to hear from you. What can I do for you?

3.3 Building costs

The building costs include all the *expenses* for goods, services and charges necessary to carry out a development. Before planning and constructing a property, the client needs to be aware of all the expenses associated with the development. Architects and engineers have a detailed knowledge of the costs involved and are able to support the client by preparing a realistic *cost estimate*. The client will then be able to determine the *feasibility* and *affordability* of the project. The design team may need to recommend adjustments in order *to bring the scope of the project into line* with the *client's means*. The final step in this process is the agreement of the *budget* for the project.

The total *expense budget*, at the start, is the sum of a large number of individual items. As work progresses, the expense budget is replaced by *actual costs* until, on completion, the *final statement* is drawn up with the total cost of the project. Throughout the period of development, as actual costs are *invoiced*, it is essential to monitor progress against the original budget or revised budget if alterations have been agreed along the way. Since there is a tendency for all parties *to pitch* estimates *on the low side*, it is always prudent to allow for a *contingency sum*.

The different *cost categories* for an average sized building are shown in the diagram below.

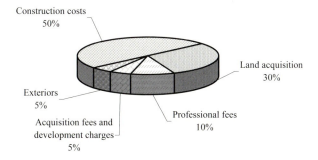

3.3.1 Cost categories

As mentioned above, the subdivision of the total costs enables the client to understand the different cost categories. In Germany, the DIN 276 is concerned with the *determination of cost* and the structure of cost categories.

Land acquisition: In most cases, clients already own a plot when they approach an architect for the first time. It follows that the costs involved in purchasing a plot seldom really affect the architect. In addition to the acquisition price, the client may need to pay for a survey before the architect can proceed with design work. Giving advice on the acquisition of a site or building is regarded as an *additional service*.

Development charges: This cost category includes the connections to all services, the *public sewer*, the *water mains*, *gas supply mains*, *power connection* and *cable connection*. The costs deriving from these connections are payable to the appropriate supplier.

Construction costs: These costs cover the entire construction of the building, from the foundations to the paintwork including all materials and the labour costs to perform the work. The client's budget can easily be translated into areas (cost per square metre) or volumes (cost per cubic metre) based on different constructional systems and finishes, e.g. expensive or basic. This calculation gives the client and the architect a rough guide as to the feasibility.

No project is ever designed perfectly – there will always be unforeseen items, situations or misjudgements. A contingency sum allows for these unknown factors. Depending on whether it is a new construction, an extension or a renovation, between 10 and 15 % is usually included as a *provision*.

Incidental building costs: The incidental building costs, also called on-costs, include the costs of professional services before construction begins as well as those incurred during the course of development. In other words, all fees, costs for the *planning permission application*, which is usually a percentage of the total building costs, *legal charges*, *insurance* and *finance costs* arising during the total planning and construction period.

Architects and other consultants charge either a percentage of the building construction cost, a *time charge* or a *lump sum*. Higher rates apply for work involving existing buildings.

- Percentage Charge:

  In most countries there is an *official scale of fees*, which applies to services offered by architects, engineers and other building professions. In Germany, architects and engineers consult the HOAI (Honorarordnung für Architekten und Ingenieure – Official Scale of Fees for Services by Architects and Engineers). For architects practising in Great Britain, the RIBA has published a chart, "A Client's Guide to Engaging an Architect", which indicates percentages for each class, simple, average and complex, over a range of construction costs. Usually these fees are paid in *instalments* based on the *estimated final cost*. The final instalment fee is adjusted to match the total fees to the actual cost of the building.

- Time charge:

  Time charges are based on an *hourly rate*. In comparison to the rates stated by the HOAI, there are no recommendations given by the RIBA and the actual amount charged per hour varies from practice to practice. An hourly rate is appropriate for *partial or additional services*.

- Lump sum:

  A lump sum fee is often *quoted* if the extent of the work required is absolutely clear and the time scale of the service is known. Therefore when architects offer clients a lump sum, the services included should be specified precisely.

Others: Clients should also be aware of the costs for *removal*, furnishings, such as kitchen and lighting, telephone and computer cabling, since it is not usual for these to be included in the construction costs.

3.3.2 Loans

A client usually requires additional capital to purchase land or develop a property. This is normally achieved by *borrowing* from a bank or *building society*. The client takes out a *mortgage,* which grants the *lender* a charge on the property as security for the loan.

There are numerous types of mortgage offered today, but most involve regular payment of *interest* and capital to the lender to ultimately repay the *loan*. When a property is being developed, the lender may agree to make capital available in stages as the construction proceeds, and the architect or other professionals may be asked to supply certificates confirming stage completion.

3.3.3 Cost management

A major difference between practising architecture in the UK and Germany is the availability of quantity surveyors in Great Britain. Even though all architects are able to, or should be able to, look after the financial aspects of construction work and determine the *probable cost of a building* from a set of drawings, architects in the UK are often relieved from this work and may concentrate on design and realisation.

Quantity surveyors are qualified to prepare *cost plans* of building costs from a brief at a very early design stage. Quantity surveyors then work hand in hand with architects and engineers and manage cost matters throughout a project. Depending on the stage at which the determination of cost is prepared, the *margin of error* should be reduced towards the completion of the scheme.

No matter who is responsible, it is necessary to develop a cost plan at an early design stage *allocating a sum of money* to each element. The cost plan, which reflects the client's estimated expenditure, needs to cover everything forming part of the project i.e. all aspects of construction, fixtures and fittings, furniture (if included) and professional fees. The person involved in setting up the cost plan has to take account of all outstanding and potential risks with potential cost implications.

3.3.4 Lexis: Building costs

Match the term on the left with the correct definition on the right.

1.	contingency	a.	a loan to buy, build or refurbish a property
2.	lump sum	b.	a sum of money withheld in case of unforeseen events
3.	hourly rate	c.	charges for services offered by architects, engineers and other consultants
4.	professional fees	d.	amongst other things, the costs for the planning application and insurance
5.	to purchase	e.	a guarantee issued by a company for compensation in case of damage in return for a payment
6.	on-costs	f.	a fixed charge for a clear task
7.	mortgage	g.	to buy
8.	insurance costs	h.	a time charge

3.4 Vocabulary

	briefing	Vorbesprechung, Bedarfsermittlung
3.1	brief	Übermittlung der Planungsgrundlagen an den Planer durch den Bauherrn
	to brief sb	jmdn. unterrichten, informieren
	area	Fläche
	volume	Rauminhalt, Kubatur
	finishes	Ausbau
	orientation	Ausrichtung
	space-utilisation schedule	Raumprogramm
	user requirement programme	Bedarfsanalyse
	to confirm sth	bestätigen
3.1.1	spacious adj	geräumig
	entrance area (hall)	Eingangsbereich
	larder	Speisekammer
	accessible adj	zugänglich
	storey/s (AE story/ies)	Geschoss, Stockwerk, Etage
	walk-in wardrobe	begehbarer Kleiderschrank
	master bedroom	Elternschlafzimmer
	study	Arbeitszimmer (im Wohnhaus)
	utility room	Wirtschaftsraum
	workshop	Werkstatt
	storage space	Lagerfläche, Stauraum
	arrangement of rooms	Raumanordnung
	technical installations	betriebstechnische Anlagen
3.1.2	en-suite bathroom	an ein Schlafzimmer direkt anschließendes Badezimmer
	loft	Dachboden
3.2	consultant	Fachplaner, Fachingenieur
	structural engineer	Statiker, Tragwerksplaner
	electrical engineer	Elektroingenieur
	mechanical services engineer	Haustechniker
	quantity surveyor or cost manager	Kosten- u. Abrechnungsingenieur
	interior designer	Innenarchitekt
	landscape architect	Landschaftsarchitekt
	scope of work	Leistungsumfang
	contractual link	Vertragsverhältnis
	liability	Haftung
	lead consultant	leitender Fachplaner
3.2.1	to forewarn sb	jmdn. vorwarnen

3.3	building costs	Baukosten
	expenses	Aufwendungen
	cost estimate	Kostenschätzung, Voranschlag
	feasibility	Durchführbarkeit, Machbarkeit
	affordability	Erschwinglichkeit
	project scope	Leistungsbedarf
	to bring sth into line with sth	in Einklang bringen
	client's means	Bauherrenmittel
	budget	Haushalt
	expense budget	Kostenplan
	actual costs	tatsächliche Kosten
	final statement	Schluss(ab)rechnung
	to invoice	in Rechnung stellen
	to pitch sth on the low side	unterschätzen
	contingency sum	Summe für Unvorhergesehenes
	cost categories	Kostengruppen
	construction costs	Baukosten
	development charges	Erschließungskosten
	exteriors	Außenanlagen
	land acquisition	Grundstückserwerbskosten
3.3.1	professional fees	Honorare für Freiberufler
	determination of cost	Kostenermittlung
	additional (planning) service	besondere Leistung
	public sewer connection	Kanalisationsanschluss
	water mains	Wasseranschluss
	gas supply mains	Gasanschluss
	power connection	Stromanschluss
	cable connection	Kabelanschluss
	provision	Vorkehrung, Vorsorge
	incidental building costs	Baunebenkosten
	planning permission application	Antrag auf Baugenehmigung
	legal charges	gesetzliche Gebühren
	insurance	Versicherungen
	finance costs	Finanzierungskosten
	time charge	Vergütung auf Stundenbasis
	lump sum	Pauschale
	official scale of fees	Honorarordnung
	instalment	Abschlagszahlung
	estimated final cost	geschätzte Endkosten, Kostenanschlag
	hourly rate	Stundensatz
	partial or additional services	Teilleistungen oder bes. Leistungen

	to quote sth	anbieten, Preis angeben
	removal costs	Umzugskosten
3.3.2	to borrow sth	sich etwas leihen
	building society	Bausparkasse
	mortgage	Hypothek
	lender	Kreditgeber
	interest	Zins(en)
	loan	Kredit, Darlehen
3.3.3	probable cost of a building	voraussichtliche Baukosten
	cost plan	Kostenaufstellung
	margin of error	Abweichung
	to allocate a sum of money to sth	eine Geldsumme für etw. zur Verfügung stellen

4 Preliminary Design

4.1 Presentation

Taking into account the client's brief and the additional information obtained, the architect will commence to prepare drawings illustrating a possible solution. The first drawings may not be very detailed, but will show what the architect has in mind. They should illustrate and make it possible to appreciate the general *massing*, the *external appearance* of the building, its position on the site and the *arrangement of the interior*.

Usually several meetings take place with the client during this phase. The architect takes along drawings, sketches etc. to these meetings. While these should, of course, be *self-explanatory*, it is absolutely necessary for the architect to guide the client through the presentation.

Presentation form

There are numerous terms used to describe the various forms of presentation. Match the terms with the correct explanation.

1.	a sketch	a.	a drawing made with paint
2.	a diagram	b.	often used to express the preparation of a technical drawing and still found in many collocations such as draughtsperson (AE draftsperson) or draughting machine (AE drafting machine)
3.	a plan	c.	a free-hand drawing made very quickly and not including a lot of detail
4.	a painting	d.	a computer-aided presentation offers the viewer a realistic understanding of the building by for example *taking a virtual walk through the various rooms*
5.	a drawing	e.	*compilation of* drawings showing all views
6.	to draft	f.	often used to sketch out the functional arrangement of rooms or routes within a building
7.	computer simulation	g.	a usually *to-scale illustration* in pencil or ink often made by using rulers, stencils or CAD

Adding an appropriate adjective can help to qualify these expressions. A *rough sketch* might be a sketch made with a thick pen with only a few lines, whereas a detailed drawing offers a clearer insight. The scale of a drawing also gives some indication of the amount of detail. Naturally a 1:50 drawing is more detailed than a 1:200 drawing. 1:50 is read as one to fifty.

Other forms of presentation are possible; for example, a model showing part or all of the development, a collection of *material samples*, illustrations or simply a *concise report*.

4.2 Proportions

The *cubage* of a building gives us an indication of the size, whether it is a small or a large building. However, it tells us nothing about the proportions, the relation between *width*, *depth* and *height*. The cubage is measured in cubic metres (cub m; m³). Similarly the *gross floor area* only indicates the size of the *covered area*, not the *relation* between width and depth. In some areas, especially in non-residential ones, the proportion of a site, which may be covered, is determined by the *plot ratio*.

Cubage and areas are particularly relevant when it comes to costs and calculations. Architects apply the *volume method* when preparing a preliminary cost estimate. In order to determine the construction costs, the cubage is multiplied by an average cubic metre price, which includes everything from the structure to the finishes. The client is especially interested in the *net floor area* as it indicates the number of square metres *excluding* the *external walls*, which may be sold or *let*. Architects and designers are interested in the individual *dimensions*, the proportions, as these characterize the appearance of a building, a room or even a piece of furniture.

4.2.1 Dimensions

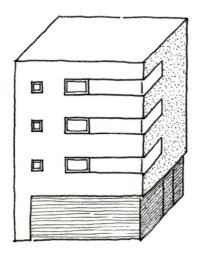

high/height
The structure is 12 m high.
The height of the structure is 12 m.

deep/depth
The structure is 8 m deep.
The depth of the structure is 8 m.

long/length
The ribbon window is 5 m long.
The length of the structure is 5 m.

wide/width
The structure is 9 m wide.
The width of the structure is 9 m.

4.2.2 Modifiers

It is possible to add modifiers to the adjectives in order to intensify their meaning.

Example: The building is very wide.

Here is a list of modifiers. The degree of intensification varies. Sort them according to their meaning from the least extreme to the most extreme intensification.

| really · not very · rather · extremely · very · -ish (e.g. tallish) · not at all · fairly |

4.3 Comparisons

Usually a design does not consist of just one element, but of several. Pointing out the relationships between the various elements helps the listener to gain a better understanding of the overall appearance. Making a comparison is an easy method to *emphasize* a difference.

4.3.1 Adjectives

Adjectives have three forms of comparison: positive, comparative and superlative.

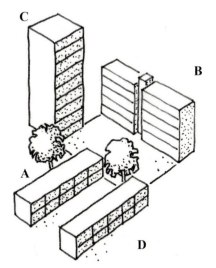

Building A is tall.   (positive adjective)

Building B is taller.   (comparative adjective)

Building C is the tallest. (superlative adjective)

If we compare two elements, we use **than** in the comparison:
Building B is taller than building A.
If we compare more than two elements, we use **the** in the superlative:
Building C is the tallest of the three.
If we compare two elements that are the same, we use **as** ...... **as**:
Building A is as tall as building D.

There are various groups of adjectives. Depending on the positive form, the comparative and superlative change according to the following table.

Form	Positive	Comparative	Superlative	Note
one syllable	tall	taller	tallest	add -er/-est
two syllables, ends in -y	busy	busier	busiest	change -y to -i and add -er/-est
one syllable, ends in -e	wide	wider	widest	add -r/-st
one syllable, ends in t or g	big	bigger	biggest	consonant is doubled
two or more syllables	interesting	more interesting	most interesting	add more and most
exception	good	better	best	
exception	bad	worse	worst	
exception	little	less	least	
exception	far	further	furthest	

4.3.2 Exercise: Comparisons

Use the information below to complete the following exercise.

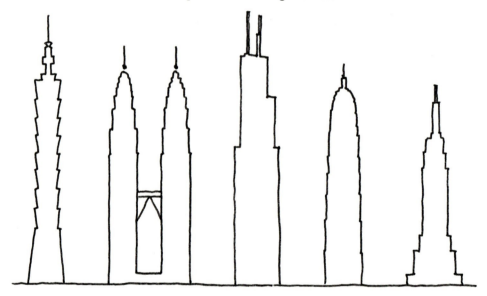

Taipei 101
in Taipei, Taiwan

Completed in 2004
Height: 509 m

Petronas Towers
in Kuala Lumpur, Malaysia
Completed in 1998
Height: 452 m

Sears Tower
in Chicago, USA

Completed in 1974
Height: 442 m

Jin Mao Building
in Shanghai, China

Completed in 1999
Height: 421 m

Empire State Building
in New York, USA
Completed in 1931
Height: 381 m

Taipei 101 in Taiwan is ………………….. (tall) building in the world. It is also ………………..………….. (recent) construction. It is ………………….. (high) than both the Petronas Towers and the Sears Tower in Chicago. The Petronas Towers are only slightly ………………….. (tall) than the Sears Tower. The Commerzbank Zentrale in Frankfurt measuring 259m is ………………….. (high) building in Germany. However, it is ………………….. (low) than all the buildings mentioned above. The Empire State building in New York is by far ………….……………. (ancient) skyscraper. It is not ………………….. (tall) the Jin Mao Building in Shanghai, but it is a lot ………………….. (old).

4.4 Shapes

The appearance of a building is not only characterised by its dimensions and proportions but also by its shape. Some shapes are very straightforward like a cube or a rectangle. Others are slightly more difficult and require language skills to be described. We often use letters or appearances in nature – like L-shaped or *egg-shaped* – to describe a design to a client. The following vocabulary and expressions should help you to prepare a precise presentation.

4.4.1 Standard shapes

Match the terms from below with the correct shape.

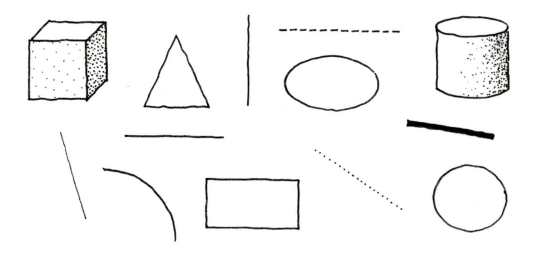

rectangle · ellipse · horizontal line · *broken line* · cube · *curved line* · *triangle* · circle
cylinder · vertical line · *dotted line* · *thin line* · *thick line*

Instead of using a noun to describe the shape of a building - the building is a rectangle – an adjective is often more elegant – it's a rectangular building. Note that not all adjectives are formed in the same way.

The panel is a rectangle.	– a rectangular panel
The pool is an ellipse.	– an elliptical pool
The house is a cube.	– a cubic house
The window is a circle.	– a circular window
The rooms are arranged in a line	– a linear arrangement

4.4.2 Expressions

Sometimes the shape of a structure is so obvious, that we use a letter, a shape or an element from nature to describe it. Some descriptions, such as shaped like a *horseshoe*, *U-shaped* or looks like a ship, are used quite frequently. There is no limit to the number of possibilities. Some appearances have even given the building a *nickname*. To name just a few, the Congress Hall in Berlin, the American contribution to the International Building Exhibition in 1957 designed by Hugh A. Stubbins, which is nicknamed "pregnant oyster" or 30 St. Mary Axe in London, designed by Norman Foster, which is now known as "The Gherkin".

Here are some useful expressions to describe the appearance of a structure:

It resembles …	It is shaped like a …	It has *similarities* with …
It looks like …	It appears as ….	It is similar to a …
It is …-shaped.	It is comparable with …	It is arranged as a …

4.4.3 Exercise: Description

Read this text and underline all the descriptive terms. Try to imagine what the building looks like and make a sketch.

The main building is a rectangular, *two-storey* structure with a *mono-pitched roof*. A smaller rectangular one-storey structure *protrudes* at a *right angle approximately* a third of the way along the longer and taller side of the larger element. From a *bird's eye view* it looks like a T with differing lengths. The smaller element is a single-storey structure with a flat roof. There are no organic shapes or circles; the right angle *prevails*.

4.4.4 Further practice

You can practise this activity of characterising shapes at any time. Look at things when you are out and about and try to find the right words to describe them.

4.5 Roofs

The roof, the top covering of a building, is a universal element found in all structures. Its purpose is to protect the building from the effects of the weather. Primarily this means to shed water off the building and to prevent it from accumulating on top. Depending on the location of the building it may also be required to prevent *heat loss*. Nowadays, *roof areas* are also used to install solar panels, which provide electricity for the inhabitants of the building.

The roof areas with the *roof covering* can be detailed in many different ways. There is a major distinction between *roof sealing* for flat or *low-pitched roofs* and *roofing* for *pitched roofs*. *Bituminous materials* are used to seal flat or low-pitched areas most commonly found on industrial and commercial type structures. Materials for pitched roofs range from *roofing tiles*, *corrugated roof panels*, *zinc sheet* to *thatching*.

4.5.1 Roof shapes

Roof shapes not only have a significant effect on the appearance of a building, they also determine how well the structure can withstand certain elements. The slope of the roof and its *overhang* system are often dictated by the climate. This phenomenon leads to specific styles becoming dominant and characteristic for certain regions.

Connect the roof descriptions with the appropriate drawings.

flat roof with one horizontal surface

single-pitched roof with one inclined surface

tent roof with 4 identical surfaces forming a point at the top

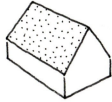
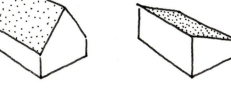
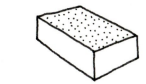

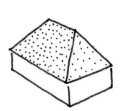
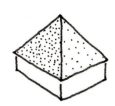
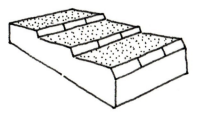

gable roof with two usually identical surfaces

the profile of the sawtooth roof looks like the teeth of a saw

a hip roof is similar to a gable roof, except that the gables are also inclined

4.5.2 Roof parts

The shape, *pitch*, covering and overhang with the *verge* and the *eaves* have a significant effect on the external appearance of the building. The roof elements can also tell you something about the use and the character of the interior space.

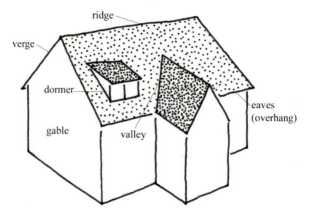

4.6 Appearance

In most projects we are not simply dealing with a single cube, but with a complex arrangement of elements. The organisation of horizontal and vertical members creates a form meeting the demands of the functions within. The relations between the elements are fundamental factors, which play a vital role in characterising the design.

Two elements of a scheme may be totally independent, separated by a path, passage or even a road. Elements may be linked by a bridge, a further structure, perhaps emphasized by a different *skin* or a different size or shape. A further possibility may be to overlap elements creating *intersections*.

In every building, there is a relationship between the exterior and the interior. Depending on the type of building, the climate, the surroundings and its purpose, the *shell* separating interior and exterior fulfils different functions. Glass enables the architect to create a *visual link*, a view from the interior to the exterior and visa versa. Solid materials, such as brick or concrete, create a visual barrier between inside and out. Some surfaces can have a *repellent* character, are intended to emphasize a certain feature or add contrast to a complex arrangement of structures. Others are more inviting and *blend in* with the surroundings. Some buildings appear to be *embedded* in their environment and harmonise, while others are made to *stand out*. The wide spectrum of materials available gives the architect the opportunity to define the relationships between the various elements.

4.6.1 Material functions

Exterior walls have to fulfil several functions simultaneously. They protect the interior space from the effects of the weather as well as from intruders. Depending on the size of the element, exterior walls can emphasize a significant border and become a very distinct and dominant feature. Despite the weight of the materials, elements can be made to look *light* and sometimes appear to *float*.

4.7 Vocabulary

The surface treatment characterises the appearance of both the exterior and the interior. It may be the architect's intention to have the brickwork of a solid brick wall visible (*fair-faced brickwork*). Brickwork can also be *rendered* or plastered to create a smooth or textured appearance on exterior and interior surfaces respectively. Very often exterior walls are made up of several layers enclosing a *core of insulation*. The load-bearing component made of either timber, steel, concrete or brick supports a second skin. All sorts of materials can be fixed to the substructure; these range from concrete panels or blockwork, timber lining, corrugated sheet metal or *ashlar stone facing*.

Glass enables light to penetrate and to flow into the rooms beyond. There is a connection, a link, despite the barrier of *single, double or even triple glazing*. Depending on the size of the elements, a fully glazed wall enhances the transmission of light; punctuated or pierced walls allow only a reduced amount to enter or offer a very specific view to the outside. Larger buildings are often provided with *curtain walls*. These large glass surfaces are interrupted merely by narrow *posts and mullions*. The load-bearing structure supports the façade. If the skin of a building is a curtain wall, different materials can be substituted for the glass elements to create closed areas in the façade.

4.6.2 Exercise: Building materials

Match the terms from below with the materials in the pictures.

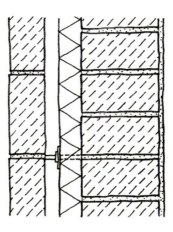

40 mm cavity
200 mm concrete blockwork
60 mm insulation
stainless-steel cavity tie
13 mm gypsum plaster
100 mm fair-faced concrete blocks

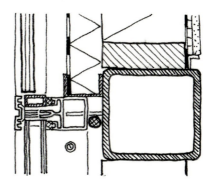

18 mm boarding
double glazing
waterproof membrane
vapour barrier
8 mm plywood
mineral-wool insulation
12 mm plasterboard
aluminium clamping strip
steel tube shore

4.7 Vocabulary

4.1		massing	Massenverteilung, Ausmaße
		external appearance	äußere Erscheinung
		arrangement of the interior	Anordnung im Innenbereich
		self-explanatory adj	selbsterklärend
4.1.1		painting, to paint	Gemälde
		drawing, to draw	Zeichnung
		to draft	Zeichnen, entwerfen
		to take a virtual walk	einen virtuellen Spaziergang machen
		compilation of sth	Zusammenstellung von etw.
		to-scale illustration	maßstabsgetreue Darstellung
		rough sketch	grobe Skizze
		material samples	Bemusterung
		concise report	kurzer und prägnanter Bericht
4.2		proportions	Verhältnisse
		cubage	Kubatur, umbauter Raum
		width n; wide adj	Breite, breit
		depth n; deep adj	Tiefe, tief
		height n; high adj	Höhe, hoch
		length n; long adj	Länge, lang
		gross floor area	Bruttogeschossfläche
		covered area	überbaute Fläche
		relation	Verhältnis
		plot ratio	Grundflächenzahl
		volume method (of construction cost estimate)	Kostenschätzung nach umbautem Raum
		net floor area	Nettogeschossfläche
		excluding external walls	Außenwände ausgenommen
		to let	vermieten
		dimensions	Abmessungen, Dimensionen
4.3		to emphasize	betonen
4.4		egg-shaped	eierförmig
4.4.1		broken line	gestrichelte Linie
		curved line	gebogene Linie
		triangle	Dreieck
		dotted line	gepunktete Linie
		thin line	dünne Linie
		thick line	dicke Linie
4.4.2		horseshoe	Hufeisen
		U-shaped	U-förmig

4.7 Vocabulary

	nickname	Spitzname
	to resemble	ähneln, gleichen
	similarity/ies	Ähnlichkeit/en
4.4.3	two-storey adj	zweigeschossig
	mono-pitched roof (single-pitched roof)	Pultdach
	to protrude	herausragen, vorstehen
	right angle	rechter Winkel
	approximately	ungefähr
	bird's eye view	Vogelperspektive
	to prevail	überwiegen, vorherrschen
4.5	heat loss	Wärmeverlust
	roof areas	Dachflächen
	roof covering	Dacheindeckung
	roof sealing	Dachabdichtung
	low-pitched roof	Dach mit leichtem Gefälle
	roofing	Dachdeckung
	pitched roof	geneigtes Dach
	bituminous materials	bituminöse Materialien
	roofing tile	Dachziegel
	corrugated roof panel	Welldachplatte
	zinc sheet	Zinkblech
	thatching	Strohbedachung
4.5.1	overhang	Ausladung, Überhang
	hip roof	Walmdach
	tent roof	Zeltdach
	sawtooth roof	Sheddach
4.5.2	pitch	(Dach-)Neigung
	verge	Ortgang
	eaves	Traufe
	ridge	First
	dormer	Gaube
	gable	Giebel
	valley	Kehle
4.6	skin	Außenoberfläche
	intersection	Überschneidung, Durchdringung
	shell	(Außen-)Hülle
	visual link	Sichtbezug
	repellent adj	abstoßend
	to blend in	sich harmonisch einfügen
	to embed sth in	eingliedern
	to stand out	auffallen

4.6.1	light adj		leicht
	to float		schweben
	fair-faced brickwork		Sichtmauerwerk
	to render		Außenwände verputzen
	core insulation		Kerndämmung
	ashlar stone facing		Natursteinverkleidung
	single/double/triple glazing		Einfach-/Doppel-/Dreifachverglasung
	curtain wall		Vorhangfassade
	posts and mullions		Pfosten und Riegel
4.6.2	cavity		Hohlraum
	stainless-steel cavity tie		Edelstahlanker
	gypsum plaster		Gipsputz
	waterproof membrane		Dichtungshaut, Abdichtungsfolie
	vapour barrier		Dampfsperre
	plywood		Sperrholz
	plasterboard		Gipskartonplatte
	clamping strip		Klemmprofil
	steel tube shore		Stahlrohrstütze

5 Final Design

5.1 Coordination

The diagram below gives an indication of the development and the coordination during the final design planning stages.

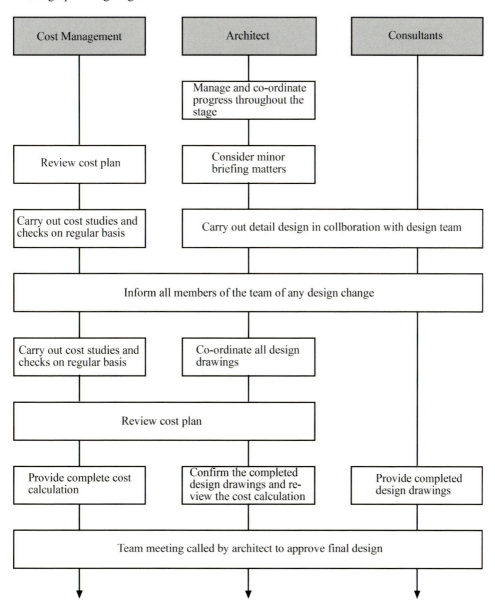

5.1.1 Flow of information

This stage of the architect's work is the completion of the design stage. Ideally, there should be no major changes to the design after this point. If the project is sufficiently large to support a design team, there has to be a constant flow of information between the architect and the consultants. It is the architect's task, or, if commissioned, the project manager's task, to coordinate the work of the design team and *iron out* all conflicts arising between team members.

Similar to the drawings becoming more precise and detailed during the course of a project, the method used for the *cost determination* should also become more refined. What was once a *cost estimate* should during the final design stage become a *cost calculation* allowing a smaller margin for variations. The margin is reduced further towards the realisation and completion of each project. At tendering stage, *quotations* offer fairly realistic outlooks; the *cost finding* prepared at completion lists the actual costs.

It is important to keep the client informed during this phase and regular meetings should take place. It may be necessary to report to the client on changes due to *incorporating* services or structural measures. The client has to approve all changes and make decisions on any *outstanding* items.

5.1.2 Informing the design team

E-mails are useful for ensuring that all people involved receive the same information at the same time. Here is an e-mail that the architect, Tim Smith, sends to the design team informing them about a decision the client has made. Find an appropriate subject line for the e-mail.

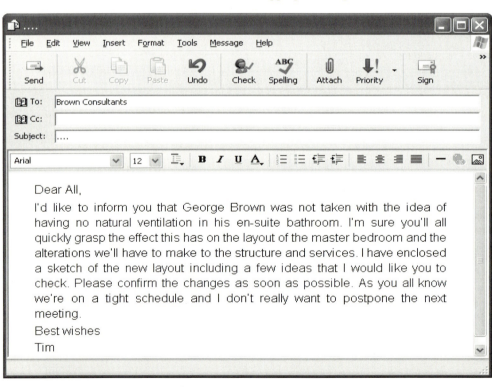

5.1.3 Exercise: Register

The language used in the e-mail is fairly formal. Match the vocabulary used in the e-mail with the less formal vocabulary below.

1. to let you know   ……………………   5. to attach   …………………
2. to put off   ……………………   6. no time to spare …………………
3. asap   ……………………   7. the changes   …………………
4. to agree   ……………………   8. does not like   …………………

5.2 Structural frameworks

All structural elements and their interaction form the structural framework of a building. No single element alone is responsible for the supporting structure, but the combination of members together with the *configuration of joints*.

Elements can either be distinguished according to their *alignment*, vertical or horizontal members, according to their configuration, *bar or panel system*, or according to their *effectiveness*, *slab* or *diaphragm*. Whereas slabs merely bear the strain of *deflection*, diaphragms have a *stiffening effect* bearing vertical forces.

The correct choice and dimensioning of elements prevent *deformation* and ensure the stability of the structure.

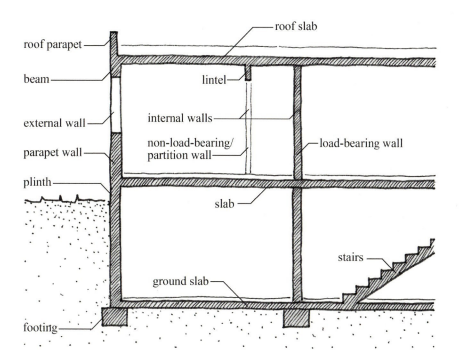

5.2.1 Structural elements

Vertical members

wall	a vertical panel
pillar	another word for column; usually applied for square or rectangular columns, which are integrated in walls
column	vertical member supporting a roof or beam; in Greek temples, there is a differentiation between e.g. Doric and Corinthian ones
post	a slender light column, sometimes a member in framing
stanchion	a vertical supporting member made of steel

Horizontal members

slab	a horizontal panel
beam	a horizontal bar
truss	a structure comprising several members in triangular units to span great distances; top and bottom boom are not parallel
girder	a structure comprising several members in triangular units to span great distances; top and bottom boom are parallel
joist	a horizontal supporting member that runs from wall to wall, or beam to beam; typically it is smaller than a beam and usually made of steel
lintel	a horizontal beam usually supporting the masonry above a window or door
cantilever	a beam only supported on one end; it allows for overhanging structures without external bracing

5.2.2 Connections

All structural members forming a *rigid* construction have to be connected in one way or another. Depending on the method used, it is either referred to as a *bond* for *glued connections*, a junction or joint for either metal or timber or sometimes even a link.

In steel construction, there are 3 main connection methods, namely *riveting*, *bolting* and *welding*. For riveting, which is the least common nowadays, a rivet is hammered into aligned holes. When bolting two members, a *bolt* is pushed through the aligned holes and a *nut* is threaded on and tightened with a spanner.

Many joints, especially those made *in shop*, are welded. Welding joins metals by melting and fusing. There are two basic types, the *butt weld*, which is employed to join parallel members, such as pipes, and the *fillet weld*, which is used to connect a vertical to a horizontal member.

Splice and *gusset plates* are used to connect timber as well as steel. More traditionally *carpentry connections* are applied in timber construction. The most frequently used are the *tongue and groove* connection for fitting boards in one plane, especially in flooring and panelling. *Mortise and tenon* is a method used to connect two timber members at an angle close to 90°. The mortise is the cavity cut into a timber to receive the tenon.

5.2.3 Exercise: Connectors

Label the following diagrams depicting methods for connecting structural elements.

> nut and bolt · gusset plate · fillet weld · screw · tongue and groove · splice
> mortise and tenon · butt weld

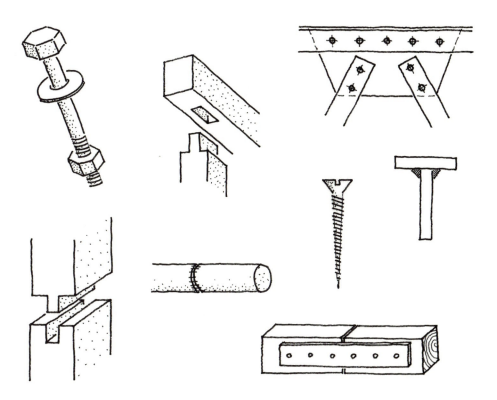

5.3 Structural analysis

The structural analysis usually begins with the determination of the *forces acting* on the *static system*. The analysis helps to find the most suitable, as well as economical form of construction, which will provide *adequate support* and *resist* all forces.

The forces acting on the system are *dead loads* or *live loads*. The dead load is the *weight* of the structure itself. The live load is a collection of changeable forces acting on the structure, such as the *imposed load*, which is machinery, furniture, vehicles, people, etc., wind and snow load. The live load can also be differentiated according to *concentrated*, linear or *area load*. The task of the structural engineer is to *prevent* these forces from moving the structure. This is achieved when all the active external forces and moments are *counterbalanced* with the inner forces and moments of the structure itself. Once these conditions are satisfied, the structure remains in *equilibrium*, or in other words at rest.

5.3.1 Calculations

Below is an example of a structural system. It is a simple *supported beam* with a *uniformly distributed load* and a cantilever with a concentrated load imposed on the end. A structural engineer will calculate the *shearing force* and the *bending moment* to determine the size of the beam.

The *span* of the beam is 4 m; the imposed load is a uniformly distributed load of 0.5 t/m; the length of the cantilever is 1 m; there is a concentrated load of 10 kN imposed on the end of the cantilever.

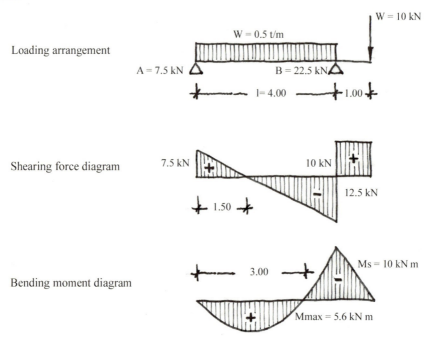

5.3.2 Structural design

Having completed the structural analysis, good design must follow. Members with sufficient strength have to be selected to resist the attacking forces, stresses and strains. The strength of the material and the moment of resistance have to be considered. In timber for example, the permissible shearing stress is only about one tenth of its permissible stress for compression or tension. Similarly the resistance strength against pulling in plain concrete is minimal. *Reinforcing steel* is embedded in concrete to resist these *tensile forces*. The *compressive force* is borne by the concrete itself.

When selecting a suitable member for a *suspended construction*, the permissible deflection also has to be considered. Normally the highest deflection for steel or timber beams is between $1/200^{th}$ and $1/500^{th}$ of the span (read $1/200^{th}$ as one two-hundredth).

In the calculation and design of a column, the tendency for the member to *buckle* sideways must be taken into account.

Foundation design is comparatively simple, if only vertical forces are present. The base area of the construction must be large enough to spread the load and thus avoid excess *settlement*. The determination of the vertical loads, resulting from the construction and from live loads is usually straightforward, but care must be taken in assessing the *bearing capacity* of the ground. In some cases it is necessary to have a soils report prepared by a specialist.

5.3.3 Lexis: Structural engineering

Combine a word in A with a word in B to form 10 terms used in structural engineering. Finally, choose the best definition for the term in C.

A	B	C
in	and strains	A force acting parallel to a plane
live	capacity	related terms defining the intensity of internal reactive forces caused by external forces
dead	equilibrium	the active external forces are balanced with the internal forces
stresses	force	bending of a vertical member due to a compressive load
bending	buckling	load imparted by the external environment and intended occupancy or use
shearing	concrete	the load-bearing properties of the ground
uniformly	moment	load generated by the weight of the structural member being considered
bearing	distributed load	concrete with steel mesh or bars embedded in order to increase the tensile strength
column	load	A load imposed evenly on a load-bearing member
reinforced	load	the result of internal forces in a member caused by external loads

5.4 Final design proposal

Before preparing documents and plans for the *planning application*, the client should *accept* the final design proposal and give instructions to proceed. Any second thoughts on the scheme after this point can cause serious *disruptions* and add cost. The architect should prepare a detailed presentation including a report, a *determination of cost* and a *time schedule*. The information from the consultants should be carefully *cross-referenced* to the design drawings.

5.4.1 Plan

Usually the architect will take along a plan to the presentation showing the building from all *angles*. Take a look at the following plan and add the correct vocabulary to the individual drawings.

east elevation · ground floor plan · longitudinal section · underground floor · south elevation
cross section · west elevation · drawing title · north elevation · first floor plan · north indicator

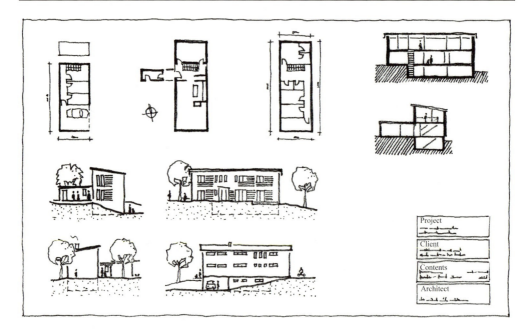

5.4.2 Presentation language

Architectural drawings should be self-explanatory. However, when *submitting* the proposal to the client, the architect should present the scheme orally. In some cases, the architect may present the project to a single client, in other cases, especially when dealing with larger schemes, the presentation may be made to a group, such as a company board or a committee. In either case, good presentation skills, including a good *command of* the presentation language, are extremely important.

What makes a presentation successful? Complete the following list of features using the words from the box.

humour · voice · structure · appearance · preparation · language · contact · *attitude*

To be a good presenter you need …

1. a simple and clear ……………
2. a smart and professional ……………
3. a good sense of ……………
4. good eye ……………
5. an enthusiastic ……………
6. a strong ……………
7. expressive body ……………
8. careful ……………

5.4.3 Presentation structure

A presentation usually consists of at least three parts. Typically there will be an introduction outlining the scope of the presentation and providing an overview of the project. The central part, or body, goes into greater detail and might be structured according to building sections or phases. The conclusion should sum up the scheme emphasising the key points and invite the audience to ask questions or take part in a discussion.

The introduction is perhaps the most important part of a presentation – it is the *first impression* the audience has of the presenter. The introduction should be used to:

- welcome the audience
- introduce the project
- outline the structure of the presentation.

The table below lists useful expressions that you can use to introduce the various parts of your presentation.

Function	Language	
Introducing the project	• I'd like to start by … • Let's begin by … • First of all, I'll …	• Starting with … • I'll begin by …
Moving on to next phase	• We'll now move on to … • Let's now look at … • Next … • I'd like to continue with …	• Another important aspect is … • I'd like to expand on … • I'd like to emphasize the importance of …
Sequence of events	• Firstly … secondly … thirdly … lastly … • First of all … then … next … after that … finally … • To start with … later … to finish up …	
Reference to visuals	• Let's take a look at … • As you can see … • I'd like to point out … • If you take a look at …, you will see …	• Here you can see … • This diagram points out … • This drawing shows …
Conclusion	• In conclusion … • Let's summarize briefly what we've looked at … • Finally, I'd like to point out … • If I can just sum up the main points …	
Dealing with questions	• I'll come back to this question later … • We'll be examining this question in more detail later on … • Are there any questions? • Would anybody like to comment on … ?	

5.4.4 Presentation

Tim Smith presents the final design to the client, George Brown. A few changes have been made since the last meeting, and it is the first time the client receives a presentation of the project as a whole. Put the parts of the architect's presentation into the right order.

- ☐ If you take a look at the cross section, you'll see that the single pitched roof rises towards the garden, which emphasizes the open character of the façade. The *overhang* of the roof is approximately 1m offering some structural shading to the sunny side of the house. As you can see here, the overhang is less on the north façade allowing as much light as possible to penetrate through the small windows.

- ☐ Well, I hope the proposal meets your expectations. Have you got any questions regarding any aspects of the house?

- ☐ It's nice to be here with you again today. I think we're nearly there, and if there are no major alterations to be made, we'll be able to submit the planning application next week.
  But before we start talking about business matters, let me talk you through the design. First of all I'm going to take you through the various floors, beginning on the ground floor, and then we'll look at the sections and the elevations.

- ☐ So, I've completed the little tour of the house. I think you can see that it is a very clear design. I know you envisioned a private adult area on a separate storey, however the extra height would be very difficult to manage on this site. Nevertheless, I think we have succeeded in offering clearly separated parent and children zones by adding the spacious hall on the first floor.

- ☐ Let's begin at the main entrance. You enter the building here and step into a large hall. Here you can see that the hall functions as both a *distributor* and as a separator. On the ground floor it separates the kitchen, dining and living area from the office, and on the first floor it separates the adult area from the children's area.
  Now let's take a look at the stairs. This set takes you up to the first floor. The stairs to the cellar are behind this door.
  Finally, the bedrooms on the first floor. The master bedroom with an en-suite bathroom and a walk-in wardrobe is situated above the office. The children's bedrooms are arranged in a row above the living and dining area.

- ☐ Good morning everybody,

- ☐ We'll now move onto the elevations. All bedrooms and living areas face southwest. Large windows with *movable shutters* look out onto the garden. All other facades, especially the north and east facing, are closed except for a few small windows.

5.4.5 Alternatives

Depending on the kind of presentation, discussions either take place during the presentation or immediately afterwards. During these discussions, the client or a person from the audience might propose an alternative or make a suggestion. A conjunction at the beginning of a conditional phrase is an indirect way of introducing a possibility and a careful way of making a suggestion.

Example:

If we increased the depth by half a metre, we'd *gain* a lot of extra *space* on the first floor.

5.5 Vocabulary

The if-clause, which is the first part of the sentence above, states the possibility; the main clause shows what the speaker thinks the result of that possibility might be. The if-clause can be positioned at the beginning or at the end of a sentence. When it comes at the end, there is no comma after the main clause.

Depending on the level of possibility, we either use conditional I, II or III.

Conditional I for real possibilities (simple present/future with will)	If the client chooses a photovoltaic system, we'll have to change the angle of the roof.
Conditional II for *remote possibilities* (past simple/conditional with would)	If the site were slightly wider, we'd locate the garage next to the entrance.
Conditional III for impossibilities (past perfect/past conditional with would have)	If we hadn't submitted the planning application, we would have encountered many more changes.

It is also possible to use other conjunctions to connect two related ideas in a conditional sentence. "*Provided/providing that*" and "so long as" have a similar meaning to if. "In case" and "in the event of" indicate that a future event may or may not happen. "Unless" can be used for real possibilities with the same meaning as "on the condition that".

5.4.6 Exercise: Conditional sentences

Match a part from the left with a part from the right to form conditional sentences.

1. Supposing you raised the ceiling height,
2. We'll cope with not having a larder
3. So long as there is sufficient space for my car,
4. The architect would have had to prepare the cost estimate
5. If you add another window to the room,
6. We'll go ahead with this scheme,
7. If you increased the distance between the posts,
8. Supposing the office has a separate entrance,

a. there'll be sufficient light to work.
b. unless you come up with a suitable alternative.
c. if the client hadn't appointed a quantity surveyor.
d. will the access from the hall still be necessary?
e. would the beam still be sufficiently dimensioned.
f. would the stairs still work in this way?
g. providing the kitchen is no narrower than three metres.
h. you may use the garage for technical equipment, too.

5.5 Vocabulary

5	final design		Entwurfsplanung
5.1	coordination		Abstimmung, Koordination
	in collaboration with		in Zusammenarbeit mit
5.1.1	flow of information		Informationsfluss
	to iron out		beseitigen, aus dem Weg räumen
	cost determination		Kostenermittlung
	cost estimate		Kostenschätzung
	cost calculation		Kostenberechnung
	quotation		Kostenanschlag
	cost finding		Kostenfeststellung
	to incorporate		aufnehmen, einbeziehen
	outstanding adj		ausstehend, ungelöst
5.1.2	to be taken with sth		angetan sein
	alteration		Änderung
	asap, as soon as possible		so bald wie möglich
	tight schedule		enger Terminplan
	to postpone		verschieben
5.2	structural framework		Tragwerk
	joint configuration		Gelenkausbildung
	alignment		Ausrichtung
	bar system		Stabbauweise
	panel system		Plattenbauweise
	effectiveness		Wirksamkeit
	slab action		Plattenwirkung
	diaphragm action		Scheibenwirkung
	deflection		Verformung infolge von Biegung
	stiffening effect		aussteifende Wirkung
	deformation		Verformung
	roof parapet		Attika
	parapet wall		Brüstung
	plinth		Sockel
	lintel		Sturz
5.2.1	pillar		Pfeiler
	post		(Stahl-)Pfosten
	stanchion		Stahlstütze
	beam		Balken
	truss		Binder
	girder		Träger
	joist		Stahlbalken

5.5 Vocabulary

	cantilever	Auskragung
5.2.2	rigid adj	biegesteif
	bond	Verbund
	glued connection	Klebeverbindung
	riveting	Nieten
	bolting	Verschrauben
	welding	Verschweißen
	nut and bolt	Schraube und Mutter
	in shop	in der Werkstatt
	butt weld	Stumpfnaht
	fillet weld	Kehlnaht
	splice plate	Stoßblech
	gusset plate	Knotenblech
	carpentry connection	Zimmermannsverbindung
	tongue and groove	Nut und Feder
	mortise and tenon	Zapfen und Zapfenloch
5.3	structural analysis	statische Berechnung
	forces	Kräfte
	to act on sth	auf etwas wirken, einwirken
	static system	statisches System
	adequate support	ausreichende Stützung
	to resist	sich widersetzen
	dead load	unveränderliche Last, Eigenlast
	live load	Verkehrslast
	weight	Gewicht
	imposed loads	veränderliche Last, Nutzlast
	concentrated load	Einzellast, Punktlast
	area load	Flächenlast
	to prevent	verhindern
	to counterbalance	ausgleichen
	equilibrium	Gleichgewicht
5.3.1	supported beam	Balken auf zwei Stützen
	uniformly distributed load	gleichmäßig verteilte Last, Gleichlast
	shearing force	Scherkraft
	bending moment	Biegemoment
	span	Spannweite, Stützweite
	loading arrangement	Lastbild
5.3.2	reinforcing steel	Bewehrungsstahl
	tensile force	Zugkraft
	compressive force	Druckkraft
	suspended construction	Hängekonstruktion

	to buckle	knicken
	settlement	Setzung
	bearing capacity	Tragfähigkeit
5.4	proposal	Vorschlag
	planning application	Bauantrag
	to accept	abnehmen
	disruption	Störung, Unterbrechung
	determination of cost	Kostenermittlung
	time schedule	Zeitplan, Terminplan
	to cross-reference	querverweisen
5.4.1	angle	Blickwinkel
	elevation	Ansicht
	longitudinal section	Längsschnitt
	cross section	Querschnitt
	drawing title	Plankopf
	north indicator	Nordpfeil
5.4.2	to submit	unterbreiten, vorlegen
	to have a good command of sth	gute Beherrschung von etw. haben
	attitude	Haltung, Einstellung
5.4.3	first impression	erste Eindruck
5.4.4	roof overhang	Dachüberstand
	distributor	Verteiler
	movable shutters	Schiebeläden
5.4.5	to gain space	Platz gewinnen
	remote possibility	geringe Wahrscheinlichkeit
	provided/providing that	angenommen dass

6 Planning and Building Permission

6.1 Permission

A form of permission is required for most new constructions or alterations to existing properties. In many countries, this process involves an application to the local authority. The aim of the authority is to check whether the building *blends in* with its environment, is in line with the *development plan* and *complies with* general rules of construction.

Despite international differences, the procedures for obtaining permission are very similar, and every application passes through a fairly well defined sequence of stages. Take a look at the process illustrated in the flowchart below.

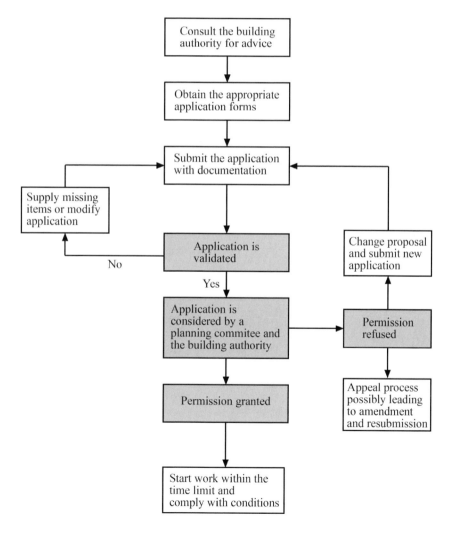

In Great Britain the application process is divided into two phases: Planning permission and *building regulations* approval. They are separate pieces of *legislation* dealt with by separate departments within the local authority. Basically planning permission is permission to erect, enlarge or make alterations to a building as presented in the application, whereas building regulations define how the new building must be constructed. Usually *applicants*, who have applied for planning permission, also have to obtain building regulations approval. Both applications involve a fee, which is normally related to the value of the development. In Germany, planning and building permission are combined in one single application.

If work is carried out without the necessary *approvals*, the local authority can issue an *enforcement notice* requiring at best *retrospective approval* or at worst *demolition* of the work already completed.

6.2 Planning permission

Planning authorities seek to guide the way towns, cities and countryside develop. This includes the use of land and buildings, the appearance of buildings, landscaping considerations, highway access and, increasingly, the impact the development will have on the general environment. Planning applications have to be put to the authority responsible for the place of construction. Sometimes notice of the application is published in the local press and at the property. Neighbours and anybody with an opinion are able to view the plans and make comments, which the local planning authority must take into account when making a decision on the application.

Whether an application is approved or refused largely depends on the development plan and the written guidelines. Planning permission is officially granted by a planning committee made up of elected members of the *council*. The meeting is normally open to public. However, a planning officer, not elected, but a paid employee of the council, will make *recommendations* to the committee. It is always worth *consulting* the official before an application is made and again before the application goes to the committee.

Certain minor works are granted automatic planning permission by the state. These developments are known as *permitted developments*. So long as the buildings are not *listed* or in a *conservation area*, for which separate pieces of legislation apply, permitted developments both in Germany and the UK include:

- Fences and walls along the plot boundary no taller than 2 m.
- The demolition of buildings.
- All changes concerning the exterior appearance such as paintwork, panelling, roof coverings and the replacement of windows and doors.
- *Loft conversions*; in Germany without dormer windows, in the UK subject to the additional volume not exceeding 10 per cent of the original building's volume.
- *Non-habitable rooms* such as *conservatories*, *sheds*, garages and carports.

  In Germany, these should not exceed 50 m³ if they are extensions and 10 m³ for sheds; garages should not exceed an average height of 3 m and a length of 9 m on the boundary.

  In the UK the floor area should not exceed 30 m², it should be no higher than 4 m and at least 2 m (garages and sheds 1 m) away from the boundary.

6.2 Planning permission

□   In the UK it is permitted to build *habitable* extensions so long as these do not exceed the limits related to the original building's volume and are no higher than 4 m. The limit is 10 per cent for a terraced house and 15 per cent for semi-detached or detached house. All extensions, including *porches*, must be at least 2 m from the site boundary.

If in doubt about the scale of planned work, local planning authorities are always able to provide the necessary information. If planning permission is required for a new building or alteration, building regulation approval is normally also necessary. Usually architects wait until planning permission has been granted before proceeding with the building regulations application.

The website www.planningportal.gov.uk provides useful information and links with regard to the planning regime in the United Kingdom.

6.2.1 Planning application

A planning application should be made on a form issued by the local planning authority. It must be submitted properly completed together with the relevant plans, documents and the fee. The application must at least provide details of the proposed design, external appearance, access, parking and landscaping. The application *curtilage* has to be defined on the *site location plan*.

The assessment of planning applications usually takes about 4 weeks, but depends upon the scale of the development. The authority may grant permission, grant it *subject to conditions* or refuse it, giving reasons for the conditions or refusal. Permission is given to the land not the applicant. It follows that when the land is sold, the permission is unaffected. In Germany, planning permission is valid for 4 years; in the UK, for 3 years. If permission is refused, the applicant has a right of appeal.

6.2.2 Exercise: Permitted development?

Not all developments require planning permission. Unfortunately it is not easy to assess whether or not permission is required, as many factors are involved. General rules such as "small house extensions are *exempt*" are misleading as they apply to some situations but not to others. It is always advisable to speak to a planning officer and allow him or her to make an assessment.

Nevertheless, take a look at this variety of projects and decide for which four developments planning permission has to be obtained in the UK. Do the same rules apply to Germany?

1. A porch with a total area of 4 m², approximately 1m away from the road.
2. A *greenhouse* with a floor area of 6 m².
3. A loft conversion for a terraced house to include new dormer windows, but adding less than 4 m³ volume.
4. A 2 m² extension to a dwelling in a conservation area.
5. A 1.80 m tall wall on the site boundary.
6. A garage with a total floor area of 24 m² set on the site *boundary*.
7. Insulation and wood panelling to be added to exterior walls.
8. A two-storey extension adding 90 m³ to the existing 550 m³ of a semi-detached house.

6.3 Building regulations

Rules for permitted buildings in Germany are stricter than those in the UK, the reason being that in Germany only one application is required. In England, more development is possible without planning permission, however, most permitted developments are subject to building regulations. The application for building regulations is fairly straightforward and often taken care of by the contractor; it is not always necessary to involve an architect for a building regulations application. In Germany, aspects considered in British building regulations form part of the general planning application. The building description demands information regarding the materials and their *combustibility* as well as a description of building services. A separate form has to be submitted for the *firing system*.

In the UK planning permission relates to the aesthetic and environmental aspects of construction work, whereas building regulations are concerned with *health and safety matters*. Generally building regulations are designed to:

- set standards for the design and construction of buildings; to secure the health and safety, *welfare* and *convenience* of people, including those with disabilities, in or about buildings and others affected by the buildings or matters connected with the buildings.
- further the *conservation of resources*
- *prevent waste, undue consumption, misuse or contamination of water*.

Based on the first building construction legislation drawn up after the Great Fire of London in 1666, which saw a need for buildings to have some form of *fire resistance*, the regulations are constantly reviewed to meet the growing demand for better, safer and more accessible buildings.

The most recent *amendments* have been to increase *thermal insulation* in order to conserve energy and reduce global warming, providing access and facilities for *disabled people* and more comprehensive *fire protection requirements*.

An application for building regulations approval is not advertised and only the person applying and the local authority are involved. Building regulations approval may be required even if planning permission is not. There are very few structures and alterations which require neither planning permission nor building regulations.

Exercise: Planning application and planning permission

There are some strong and likely verb/noun combinations for the words planning application and planning permission. Match the verbs below with the correct noun. Then insert the appropriate words into the exercise below. Make sure to use the correct grammatical form.

to assess · to require · to apply for · to handle · to refuse · to deposit · to submit · to grant

.... ⎫
.... ⎬ a planning application
.... ⎭

.... ⎫
.... ⎬ planning permission
.... ⎭

The architect, Tim Smith, is not only responsible for planning the dwelling for his client, but also for obtaining planning permission. First of all Tim Smith has to .... whether planning permission is necessary or not. Some simple features, such as the size of the house, the distance to the street, clearly indicate the necessity. The architect .... the plans together with the required documents. He is almost certain that the local planning authority .... planning permission. However, just in case they ...., he will wait and .... building regulations at a later date. The local planning authority .... the plans and the documents. In order to .... the scheme, they also .... a certificate of ownership.

6.4 Fire safety

For centuries, fire has proved to be a major *hazard* in buildings. Local building authorities enforce regulations dealing with fire safety matters and seek to ensure that adequate levels of safety are provided for people in and around buildings. All building codes include rules and regulations concerning *fire precaution* in buildings. Even though the contents of the building codes vary, there are common principles designed to ensure a means of warning and escape, limit the *spread* of fire, both internally and externally, as well as provide access and facilities for the *fire service*. The primary concern is *life safety* rather than the preservation of the structure or the protection of contents.

Fire regulations are enforced by the *fire protection authorities*, which issue a fire certificate once satisfied with the precautions taken. A *fire protection plan* containing a complete inventory and maintenance details of all *fire protection components* forms the legal basis for compliance with laws and regulations.

6.4.1 Fire protection

The fire protection system in a building has several equally important components. These include:

- Planned measures: Sufficiently dimensioned *escape routes* as well as access for fire brigades and firefighters; *compartmentalisation* of horizontal and vertical *fire sections*, including the necessary *firewalls* to prevent *flashovers*.
- Constructional measures: The selection of suitable materials, protective measures for *hazardous materials*, e.g. *encasings*. Steel is *incombustible* but deforms at high temperatures and therefore loses its *load-bearing capacity*. An encasing made either of concrete or fibreboard increases the *fire resistance* of structural elements.
- Technical measures: The installation of *fire-alarm and fire-detecting devices*, *fire-extinguishing systems*, such as hydrants, *fire extinguishers* and sprinkler systems, and the installation of *smoke exhausting equipment*.

Fire drills and training on what to do in an emergency are a further important aspect of fire protection. The purpose is to ensure that occupants and operators know how to handle and maintain systems. They should know how to evacuate, or where *to seek refuge*. Furthermore, they should have sufficient understanding not to disable any of the active or passive fire protection systems.

6.4.2 Fire resistance rating

The fire resistance rating indicates the duration of a passive fire protection system withstanding a standard *fire endurance test*. This is usually quantified as a measure of time. A fire door with a T90 designation is able to withstand fire and prevent fire from spreading for a duration of 90 minutes. A *certification mark* is displayed on the product to show that *product certification* was obtained in an appropriate fire endurance test. In most industrialised nations, product certification is *mandatory*.

The combustibility of materials selected depends on the *class of inflammability* required for the part of building under consideration, e.g. the walls of a staircase enclosure. The usual ratings for elements and structures range from 30 to 120 minutes. The fire rating describes the period for which the material has to maintain its load-bearing capacity and prevent fire from spreading. The minimum periods are reduced for buildings with sprinklers.

6.4.3 Escape routes

In an ideal situation, occupants of a building should be able to turn their backs on any fire and walk to a place of safety. Clearly, single staircase buildings, *rooms within rooms* and *dead-end corridors* have difficulties satisfying this demand. A measure often required is that staircase enclosures, especially in single staircase buildings, should have a high fire rating and should not be used for the storage of combustible materials. The same applies to dead-end corridors.

Alternative escape routes, which are exits from the building not usually used for access, must be fitted with special locks. These include break-the-glass bolts or locks, *panic bolts* or electric locks, which release on the operation of the fire alarm. All alternative exit routes have to be clearly indicated by "Fire Exit" signs.

An *escape and rescue plan* is drawn up and displayed to inform all occupants of appropriate escape routes. These plans also mark the locations of fire extinguishers, *hoses* and all other fire prevention and extinguishing equipment.

6.4.4 Lexis: Fire safety

Match the term on the left with the correct definition on the right.

1.	fire rating	a.	an exit from a building which is only used in emergencies
2.	combustible	b.	a value describing the combustibility of a product
3.	smoke exhausting system	c.	an activity which divides a building into zones in order to limit the spread of fire
4.	hazardous material	d.	fire spreading into an adjacent fire section

6.5 Vocabulary

5.	compartmentalisation	e.	a phase during which materials should maintain their load-bearing capacity and prevent fire from spreading
6.	escape route	f.	dangerous or risky product
7.	flashover	g.	something that catches fire and burns
8.	fire-resistance period	h.	a technical device to draw smoke from an area

6.5 Vocabulary

	planning permission	Baugenehmigung
6.1	to blend in	sich vermischen, einfügen
	development plan	Bebauungsplan
	to comply with sth	erfüllen, nachkommen
	building authority	Baubehörde
	application form	Antrag
	to submit	vorlegen
	fee	Gebühr
	planning committee	Planungsausschuss
	to refuse	ablehnen, verweigern
	to grant	bewilligen, gewähren
	appeal	Berufung, Einspruch
	building regulations	Baubestimmungen, -vorschriften
	legislation	Gesetzgebung
	applicant	Antragsteller
	approval	Genehmigung, Zustimmung
	enforcement notice	Vollstreckungsankündigung
	retrospective approval	rückwirkende Genehmigung
	demolition	Abbruch, Abriss
6.2	local planning authority	kommunale Projektierungsbehörde
	council	Gemeinderat, Stadtrat
	recommendation	Empfehlung
	to consult sb/sth	jmdn./etw. zu Rate ziehen
	permitted development	nicht genehmigungspflichtiges Bauvorhaben
	listed building	denkmalgeschütztes Gebäude
	conservation area	Denkmalerhaltungsgebiet
	loft conversion	Dachausbau
	non-habitable room	Raum ohne Aufenthalt

	conservatory	Wintergarten
	shed	Schuppen
	habitable room	Aufenthaltsraum (gemäß Bauordnung)
	porch	überdachter Eingangsbereich, Vorbau
6.2.1	curtilage	Hausgrundstück
	site location plan	Lageplan
	subject to conditions	unter bestimmten Bedingungen
6.2.2	to be exempt	(genehmigungs-) frei sein
	greenhouse	Treibhaus, Gewächshaus
	boundary wall	Grenzmauer
6.3	combustibility	Verbrennbarkeit
	firing system	Feuerungsanlage
	health and safety matters	Gesundheits- und Sicherheitsangelegenheiten
	welfare	Wohlergehen
	convenience of the public	Wohl der Öffentlichkeit
	conservation of resources	Ressourcenerhaltung, -schonung
	waste prevention	Abfallvermeidung
	undue consumption	unangemessener Verbrauch
	misuse	Missbrauch
	water contamination	Wasserverschmutzung
	fire resistance	Feuerwiderstand
	amendment	Berichtigung, Nachtrag
	thermal insulation	Wärmedämmung
	disabled people	Körperbehinderte
	fire protection requirement	Brandschutzanforderung
6.4	fire safety	Feuersicherheit
	hazard	Gefahr
	fire precaution	vorbeugender Brandschutz
	to spread	ausbreiten
	fire service	Feuerwehr
	life safety	Lebensrettung
	fire regulations	Brandschutzrichtlinien
	fire protection authority	Brandschutzbehörde
	fire protection plan	Brandschutzkonzept
	fire protection components	Bandschutzmaßnahmen
6.4.1	escape route	Fluchtweg
	compartmentalisation	Einteilung in Brandabschnitte
	fire section	Brandabschnitt
	firewall	Brandwand
	flashover	Brandüberschlag

6.5 Vocabulary

	hazardous material	Gefahrenstoff
	encasing	Ummantelung
	incombustible	nicht brennbar
	load-bearing capacity	Tragfähigkeit
	fire resistance	Feuerwiderstand
	fire-alarm and fire-detecting device	Feuermeldeeinrichtung
	fire-extinguishing system	Feuerlöschsystem
	fire extinguisher	Feuerlöscher
	smoke exhausting equipment	Rauchabzugsvorrichtung
	to seek refuge	Schutz suchen
6.4.2	fire resistance rating	Feuerwiderstandsklasse
	fire endurance test	Feuerwiderstandsprüfung
	certification mark	Zertifizierungszeichen
	product certification	Produktzertifizierung
	mandatory	obligatorisch, verbindlich
	class of inflammability	Brandschutzklasse
6.4.3	room within a room	gefangener Raum
	dead-end corridor	Sackflur
	panic bolt	Notausgangsverriegelung
	escape and rescue plan	Flucht- u. Rettungsplan
	fire hose	Feuerlöschschlauch

7 Tender Documentation

7.1 Procurement procedure

The procurement procedure is the process of selecting firms to perform the work described in the tender documents. Usually the size and/or the officialdom of the project determine which procurement path is to be taken. A common feature of procurement procedures is that all require the preparation of tender documents.

The tender documents enable the tendering contractors to price the work and *submit a tender* to complete the specified work. Whilst the composition of the documents varies, it is essential that it is in a form which enables the *tenderer* to fully understand the scope of the work. For major projects, it is common to prepare *bills of quantities*. In the absence of bills of quantities, the tender documents include *specifications* and drawings.

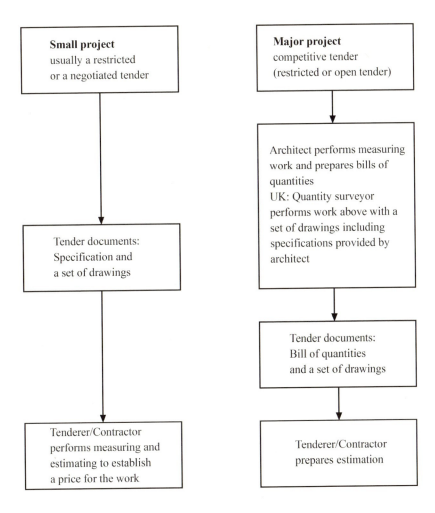

A competitive tender can either be an open tender, which is advertised and does not limit the number of contractors participating, or a restricted tender, which limits the number of tenderers to those selected by the client and the architect. If the client wishes to have the work executed by a particular contractor, a contract sum is negotiated.

Depending on the anticipated form of contract, traditional or design and build, as described at the beginning of the book, or others, the client will either have procurement documents prepared for *partial tenders* or a single *global tender*. In traditional contracts, each trade is *tendered for individually*. Architects or quantity surveyors perform the measuring work according to trades and compile a single bill of quantities for each trade. When dealing with a design and build contract and a *general contractor* is to be commissioned with the work, a clear definition of trades is not necessary and a global tender is issued.

7.2 Production information

The production information includes all instructions necessary to realise the project. Preparation of the production information usually takes place in stages as the project progresses. At the procurement stage, sufficient information has to be prepared to invite tenders. At this point, the architect should have confirmed all construction details and *compiled* the information in drawings and notes.

For the construction phase, contractors require further, more detailed information to *amplify* the contract drawings. The information received from the architect, enables the contractor to carry out and complete the work by the completion date stipulated in the contract.

Under most standard forms of building contract, the responsibility for supplying the contractor with correct information lies with the architect. It is therefore the architect's task to carefully check drawings prepared by consultants. In the event of *discrepancies, amendments* need to be made either by the architect or the appropriate member of the design team. A drawing, which has been amended and then *reissued*, should clearly state the amendment and be renumbered in order to avoid misunderstandings concerning the *up-to-dateness* of a drawing.

If drawings are not included in the tender documents, which is often the case if a bill of quantities has been prepared, a full set of drawings has to be made available in either the architect's or possibly the quantity surveyor's office.

7.2.1 Working drawings

Working drawings are the drawings prepared by the architect to realise the construction work on site. They contain a wealth of information. Depending on the size of the building, all necessary information might be contained in one set of plans. This system is fairly accurate and has its advantages; the bricklayer can see what the electrician has to do and can readily appreciate the reason for any fine tolerances. However, the complexity of these drawings makes them less suitable for large buildings.

The *elemental drawing* is part of a system which gives each trade a drawing or a set of drawings. Ideally there is a set of drawings to a scale of at least 1:50 for each trade involved in the realisation. Reinforced concrete drawings, for example, show every detail of the concrete including dimensions, but nothing else. Further drawings, *location drawings*, to a small scale of 1:100, or 1:200 for very large buildings, are provided to show the way in which the

7.2 Production information

elements fit together. Their intention is to show the location of the building enabling the site agent to set it out properly. Location drawings serve as an index offering reference numbers for further, more specific, drawings.

Neither system relieves the architect or the consultants from the task of preparing detail drawings. Large-scale drawings include details of specific items of construction not shown sufficiently clearly elsewhere. Details of *damp-proof courses* and *weatherings* need to be shown at a scale of 1:5, 1:10 or 1:20 to give those executing the work a full understanding of the construction.

This example of a traditional working drawing shows, in a single plan, the construction details for all trades involved in the project.

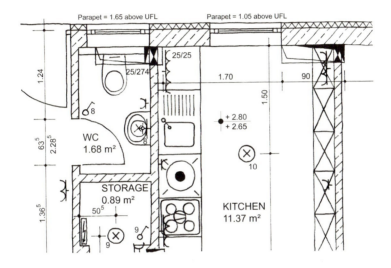

7.2.2 Dimensions

Dimensions are measurements of structural elements indicated on *dimension lines* in and around drawings. The dimensions can be indicated in metres, centimetres or millimetres depending on the level of detail. Some practices in the UK still work in feet and inches (see comment in section 2.2.2). It may be the client's request to use the imperial system.

Architects, engineers, quantity surveyors and contractors require *overall dimensions*, measurements of total lengths, to calculate the *girths* of walls. Excavations, foundations, damp-proof courses, copings, etc. are all dependant on the girths. *Internal dimensions* determine the lengths and widths of the interior layout. These measurements are necessary to calculate the internal girths, e.g. for *plastering, skirting*, etc. as well as positioning interior walls correctly. Dimensions relating to structural elements, such as posts, doors, windows, etc., are not of interest to the person preparing the tender documents or the person estimating costs. Merely the quantity and the dimension of the structural element itself is of importance. However, these dimensions are absolutely essential for site staff positioning structural elements on site.

All the dimensions on plans refer to the *shell of the building*; this means the lengths between wall faces before plastering. The architect should make quite clear whether the heights indicated in sections are finished levels (FFL = *finished floor level*) or unfinished levels (UFL

= *unfinished floor level*). *Allowances* have to be made for the thickness of *finishes*, especially concerning minimum heights and widths. Architects and engineers should ensure that the dimensions on drawings are comprehensive and correct.

7.2.3 Exercise: Dimensions

There are three categories of dimensions:

- Overall dimensions, the total lengths of building elements
- *Structural* dimensions, a subdivision of overall dimensions indicating structural elements, such as doors, windows
- Internal dimensions indicating lengths and positions of internal walls

Identify these three types of dimensions in the drawing and fill the gaps in the text below.

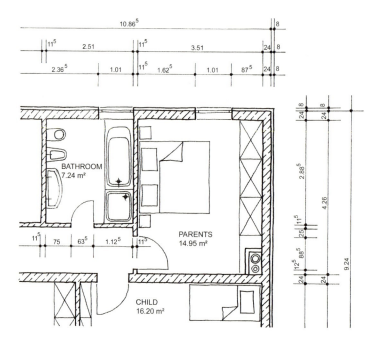

The width of the bathroom is ....; the depth is .... leading to a total floor area of .... A window, ... wide, is positioned above the bath. The master bedroom is located at the end of the hall, which is .... wide. Wardrobes are located against the longer exterior wall measuring .... The bed could be placed against the bathroom wall. .... should be sufficient for a king-size bed and two bedside cabinets. The total floor area of the master bedroom is .... Whereas the door to the master bedroom is .... cm wide, the door to the bathroom only measures .... cm. The external walls are made of .... mm brickwork and a further .... mm of insulation material. It goes without saying that all dimensions refer to the *carcass*.

7.3 Tender documents

Tender documents include all the information necessary for tenderers, a company wishing to or requested to submit a tender for construction work, to estimate the costs of building work. The composition of such documentation differs. However, it is essential that it is in a form adequate for the tenderer to fully understand the scope of the work. As already mentioned, it is often the size of the project which determines the contents of the documents. A *form of tender*, which is returned to the architect with the *tender price*, is always included.

During the preparation work for tendering, the quantities have to be determined. The person responsible for this task varies. It may be performed by a member of the planning team or, when merely supplying plans and specifications, by the tendering contractors themselves.

In the UK, the architect is often relieved of this task through the appointment of a quantity surveyor. The quantity surveyor prepares bills of quantities based on the information provided by the architect. This happens even when the project is relatively small. The quantity surveyor is commissioned by the client or, on some occasions, by the architect. The information required by the quantity surveyor to complete this task includes a full set of drawings and specifications. Since the specifications are not part of the tender documents, they may be in the form of notes. The bills of quantities itemise all the work necessary to complete the project. They are usually prepared in accordance with s*tandard methods of measurement*.

7.3.1 Specifications

Specifications contain descriptive information, which together with the drawings, form the basis for all construction work. In small contracts, the contractors prepare their tender from drawings and specifications only. The contractor's estimator takes measurements from the drawings and relies on the specifications for a full description of quality, materials and *workmanship*. Whereas quantities and materials are fairly easy to define, workmanship is not. If something is not mentioned in the specifications, but is required during construction, the contractor is entitled to additional payment. In this case the specifications are a contract document, which precisely convey what the client wants.

If a bill of quantities is prepared by a quantity surveyor, the specifications are not a contract document. The architect's descriptions can be less formal and could appear in the form of notes on the drawings. Whereas in the previous case the contractor's *estimator* was responsible for the measuring work, it is now the quantity surveyor's task to take the measurements and prepare the bills of quantities.

When construction work commences, the *site agent* and *forepeople* require instructions in greater detail than available in the contract documents. The architect therefore produces working drawings and forwards them to the contractor in good time. Despite the supply of these detailed drawings, the specifications remain a fundamental document incorporating the architect's instructions and are frequently referred to on site.

7.3.2 Bill of quantities

A bill of quantities is a set of descriptions defining the quantity and quality of construction work. It is required to provide sufficient information for the contractor to tender efficiently and accurately. Once the contract has been entered into, it functions as a *priced bill*, which is used for the *periodic valuation* of completed work.

All items are listed with an indication of the quantity. The measure can either be a dimension (metre, square metre, cubic metre), a time (hour, day, week) or a weight. The work is itemised in sufficient detail to distinguish between the different classes of work or between work of the same nature carried out in different locations or in other circumstances. Differing conditions may give rise to different considerations in terms of cost. The layout and content of a bill of quantities should be as simple and brief as possible.

Bills of quantities are prepared by taking measurements from architect's drawings and translating the instructions in the specifications. This is performed by dividing the building into sections according to trades and construction sequences. Nowadays, there are standard methods of measurement, which divide the work into categories. The most commonly used in the UK is called CAWS (Common Arrangement of Work Sections for Building Works). CAWS includes more than 300 work sections, which describe an extensive range of products and materials. Sections that are not required can be deleted; new work sections can be inserted.

A bill of quantities often includes *prime cost sums* for work or services to be executed by a *nominated subcontractor* or for materials to be obtained from a *nominated supplier*. A separate procurement procedure is normally carried out by the employer to select such specialized contractors. These sums are followed by an item inviting the tenderer *to quote* a *price* for any facilities, *amenities*, attendance, etc. required. *Provisional sums* are provided for work lacking sufficient information for proper measurement and/or pricing at tender stage. A bill of quantities may also include *contingency items* and *alternate specification items*. The inclusion of such items, provisional sums and prime cost sums facilitates *budgetary approval* and avoids the need to obtain prices for alterations and modifications during the realisation.

Bills of quantities like specifications incorporate contract particulars, employer's requirements and contractor's liabilities as well as a full specification of materials and workmanship. Unlike bills of quantities, specifications never contain quantities.

7.3.3 Lexis: Procurement

Match the terms 1 – 10 with the correct descriptions a – j.

1. tender
2. tenderer
3. bill of quantities
4. competitive tender
5. open tender
6. negotiated tender
7. procurement
8. to estimate
9. quantity surveyor
10. specifications

a. somebody who prepares bills of quantities instead of the architect
b. the scheme is advertised publicly and any contractor may tender
c. the process of selecting a contractor through tender action
d. descriptions of quality, material and workmanship; they do not contain any quantities
e. procedure involving the pricing of quantities
f. document containing the price offered by a contractor for the work specified in a bill of quantities
g. the contractor with the lowest offer is *awarded the contract*
h. an itemised list of all construction work including quantities
i. a specific contractor is selected and a price for the construction work is agreed upon between the client and contractor
j. a person, usually a contractor, making an offer to perform the work

7.4 Language in tender documents

The language used in tender documents, *site diaries*, *minutes*, etc. describing activities of construction work is very specific. If you take a close look, you will realise that the person performing the action is not mentioned. Most activities are described either by using passive voice or the imperative. Take a look at the following example.

L 05 Suspended ceilings

False dry-construction ceilings comprising a membrane of tiles are supported by concealed suspended metal grids. The membrane is *demountable*, in part or in whole, to give access to the ceiling space. Lighting, ventilation and other services are integrated in the suspended ceiling.

Compare the following sentences:

Passive voice: Ventilation ducts are to be integrated in the suspended ceiling.

Imperative: Integrate ventilation ducts into suspended ceiling.

Active voice: The contractor is to integrate ventilation ducts in the suspended ceiling.

Whereas the person performing the action is not mentioned in the first two sentences, the third sentence names the obvious person, the contractor, as the person performing the work. This information is unnecessary and inappropriate in specifications and bills of quantities.

7.4.1 Grammar: Active versus passive

Passive voice is formed by using the verb be in its correct form plus the past participle. Passive voice can be used in all tenses. The use of modal verbs in passive sentences is very useful for descriptions and instructions.

Tense	Active	Passive
Present Simple	Contractor removes existing structures.	Existing structures are removed.
Present Continuous	Contractor is performing excavation work.	Excavation work is being performed.
Past Simple	Contractor laid foundations.	Foundations were laid.
Past Continuous	Contractor was pouring concrete for slab.	Concrete was being poured for slab.
Present Perfect	Contractor has prepared *formwork* for ceiling.	Formwork for ceiling has been prepared.
Going to future	Contractor is going to start brickwork.	Brickwork is going to be started.
Future Simple	Contractor will finish ground floor walls tomorrow.	Ground floor walls will be finished tomorrow.
Modal verbs (shall, must, may, , etc.)	Contractor must complete the construction work by 31 April.	Construction work must be completed by 31 April.

7.4.2 Exercise: Active versus passive

Insert the correct verb form into the description of a cavity wall.

The external walls .... (to make up) of several layers. The load-bearing wall, on the inside, ... (to make) of 240 mm *vertically perforated brickwork*. It .... (to *plaster*) creating a smooth surface in the interior. The exterior surface of the load-bearing wall .... (to not *render*), but a second *fair-faced brick wall* .... (to placed) at a distance in front of it. The two *leaves* .... (to enclose) a partially filled *cavity*. The cavity .... (to consist) of a rear ventilation and insulation, which is fixed to the inner leaf. *Wall ties* .... (to require) to provide structural stability. They .... (to embed) in the brickwork at regular intervals. *Perpends* in the exterior leaf .... (to leave open) in order to secure ventilation and control moisture.

7.5 Selection of contractors

The selection of contractors should be made in consideration of the nature and the size of the project. In order to obtain comparable offers with realistic prices, the contractors invited should be of similar standing. Contractors suitable to build a complex shopping centre may not be suitable to build a small house. It is therefore necessary to consider the contractors' experience and reputation, as well as their workforce and financial capacity.

The result of open tenders, which are advertised publicly, is often a very mixed list of firms, many of which might be unknown to the client. It is therefore not uncommon for the client to request that the successful contractor provides a *guarantee bond*. If the contractor fails to fulfil obligations, the bond would become available to the client to cover any additional expenses. Guarantee bonds are usually 10% of the contract value; they can be obtained from banks or insurance companies.

Public sector construction contracts within the European Union exceeding 6 million euros have to be advertised. The procurement process has to be performed according to the procedures laid down in the EEC Directives 89/440 (EEC – European Economic Community). According to the directive, contractors have to apply to advertisements in the official journal of the European Union if they wish to be on the list of tenderers. The firms selected during this process are then officially invited to tender.

7.5.1 Advising the client

During the preliminary design phases of the project, used as an example in this book, the architect advised the client not to appoint a general contractor for all the work, but to commission a main contractor for the *carcass work* and several smaller companies for the *interior construction work*. The architect, Tim Smith, is in the process of preparing the tender documents.

7.5 Selection of contractors

Before sending the documents out to a selection of contractors, the client should confirm the list of possible tenderers. Read the following letter addressed to the client requesting the confirmation of the list of contractors.

Tim Smith & Partners

Mr George Brown
Pepper Road
Great Missenden
Bucks HP6 2BP

2 April 2007

Re: Confirmation of list of contractors

Dear George,

As you are aware, I am currently preparing the tender documents and would like you to confirm the list of companies to be approached.

As discussed in previous meetings, the idea is not to appoint a general contractor to undertake all aspects of the work, but to have a main contractor for the carcass work and a selection of contractors for the interior construction work, sanitary installations, electrics and finishes.

The quantity surveyor is going to prepare bills of quantities for the carcass work and the sanitary fittings, and I hope to meet him on 4 April to hand over the drawings and specifications. With regard to the other trades, we will prepare some detailed specifications and send these to the firms together with drawings for them to make estimates.

I have enclosed a list of contractors with some comments. As you will see, I have worked with some of the companies before, others have been recommended. All in all, I feel it is a good selection, which will hopefully get us the price we are looking for. If you would like to make any changes or add some further contractors, please feel free to do so. I would like to contact the selected companies next week. I am hoping that most of them will be prepared to submit a tender.

I would be very grateful if you could confirm the list by next Tuesday.

Yours sincerely

Tim Smith

Encl.: List of contractors

Tim Smith & Partners   6 Willow Road   Chorleywood   Herts WD4 3RS
Tel 01494 37894 Fax 01494 37895   e-mail timsmith@btconnect.com

7.5.2 Business letters

A business letter is more formal than an e-mail or a phone call. It is used to highlight the official character and importance of a certain topic. A letter enables the sender to enclose further documents, which are immediately available to the recipient. Even though the contents of a letter differentiate, the structure of a letter remains the same.

The sender's and recipient's address as well as a date and a reference should be positioned at the top of the letter. The salutation follows. In English, "Dear" is suitable for everybody. Whether you use Mr or Ms (only use Mrs if you know the person would like to be addressed in this way) or first names, depends on how well you know each other.

The actual contents of the letter are made up of an introduction, the body and an ending. The introduction should accomplish three aims: It should attract the readers' interest, explain the purpose for writing and provide a preview of the document. Unlike in German the letter begins with a capital letter.

- Purpose of letter: With reference to your phone call/your letter of 20 March, I would like to ….

  I am writing to enquire about/inform you/apologize for/confirm/ remind you that …
- Adding enclosures: Please find enclosed …/I have enclosed …

The ending should state your conclusions or recommendations. It is also typical to close a letter with an action step or a feedback mechanism.

- Action step: I'll call you next Thursday to discuss this matter.

  Once I have your approval, I will proceed with the plan to …
- Feedback mechanism: I would be grateful, if you could…

  Please let me know if I can be of any further assistance.

  I look forward to hearing from you.

  I look forward to meeting you on …/at …

To ensure that your document flows use appropriate transitions like:

- First … second … third …
- First of all … then … finally …
- Furthermore, …
- On the one hand … on the other hand …

There are numerous possibilities to end a letter in English. The close "Yours faithfully" is very formal and slightly old fashioned. "Yours sincerely" is still formal, but works for people you know as well as people you have never met. "Best regards" and "Best wishes" are less formal and should only be used in business letters if you are using first names.

Even if you have referred to enclosures in the letter, it is wise to add a list of enclosures after the close.

Remember to use the spell-check before printing the document. A spell-check is not *foolproof*; misspelled words could be correctly spelt, but have a different meaning, e.g. form and from. In order to ensure correct spelling and overall accuracy, it might be necessary for somebody to *proofread* the document. Active speech, rather than passive speech, makes your letter more interesting and livelier. Passive speech in a letter addressed to somebody personally is impersonal and makes it sound quite clumsy.

Don't forget to sign your letter.

7.5.3 Exercise: Business letter

The letter below contains numerous mistakes regarding the style. Correct the letter from the client addressed to the architect.

>
> Tim Smith & Partners   Pepper Road
> 6 Willow Road   Great Missenden
> Chorleywood   Bucks HP6 2BP
> Herts WD4 3RS
>
>
> 5th April 2007
>
> Hi Tim!
>
> I received your letter with the list of contractors. Your selection looks fine to me. Some of the names ring a bell, but most companies are unknown to me. A friend of mine has used Company X on your list and had great difficulties with the quality of workmanship and meeting deadlines; therefore I would like to take them off the list. I have added two further companies: Company Y, for whom my brother-in-law works and Company Z, who built our current neighbour's house. If you have no objections to these changes, I suggest you go ahead and we get this tendering business sorted out as soon as possible. Please don't ask any more questions.
>
> Cheers, George
>
>
> List of contractors

7.6 Vocabulary

	tender documentation	Ausschreibungsunterlagen
7.1	procurement procedure	Vergabeverfahren
	to submit a tender	ein Angebot abgeben
	tenderer	Anbieter, Bieter
	bill of quantities	Leistungsverzeichnis
	specifications (of works)	Baubeschreibung
	restricted tender	beschränkte Vergabe
	negotiated tender	freihändige Vergabe

	competitive tender	Ausschreibung
	open tender	öffentliche Ausschreibung
	estimation	Schätzung
	partial tender	Einzelvergabe
	global tender	Gesamtvergabe
	to tender for a trade individually	gewerkeweise Vergabe
	general contractor	Generalübernehmer
7.2	production information	Ausführungsplanung
	to compile sth	etw. zusammenstellen
	to amplify sth	etw. ergänzen, ausführlicher erläutern
	discrepancy	Unstimmigkeit
	amendment	Berichtigung
	to reissue	neu herausbringen, -geben
	up-to-dateness	Aktualität
7.2.1	working drawing	Werkplan
	elemental drawing	Teilzeichnung
	location drawing	Übersichtsplan
	damp-proof course	Feuchtigkeitssperre
	weathering	Wetterschutzabdeckung
7.2.2	dimension line	Maßkette
	overall dimension	Außenmaß
	girth	Abwicklung, Umfang
	internal dimension	lichtes Maß
	plastering	Putzarbeiten, innen
	skirting	Sockelleiste
	shell of the building	Gebäudehülle
	FFL finished floor level	FFB Fertigfußboden
	UFL unfinished floor level	RFB Rohfußboden
	allowance	Spielraum, Toleranz
	finishes	Oberflächenbehandlung
7.2.3	structural dimension	Rohbaumaß
	carcass	Rohbau
7.3	form of tender	Angebotsformular
	tender price or amount	Angebotssumme
	standard method of measurement	Aufmassnorm
7.3.1	workmanship	Ausführungsqualität, Bearbeitungsgüte
	estimator	Kalkulator, Baukalkulator
	site agent	Bauleiter (der ausführenden Firma)
	foreperson, pl forepeople foreman, pl foremen forewoman, pl forewomen	Polier/in

7.6 Vocabulary

7.3.2	priced bill	ausgefülltes Leistungsverzeichnis
	periodic valuation	fortlaufende Kostenkontrolle
	prime cost sum	Selbstkostenbetrag
	nominated subcontractor	benannter Subunternehmer
	nominated supplier	benannter Lieferant
	to quote a price	anbieten, einen Preis angeben
	amenities	nützliche Anlagen
	provisional sum	vorläufiger Betrag
	contingency item	Eventualposition
	alternate specification item	Alternativposition
	budgetary approval	Kostengenehmigung
7.3.3	to award a contract	einen Auftrag vergeben
7.4	site diary	Baustellentagebuch
	minutes	Protokoll
	suspended ceiling	abgehängte Decke
	demountable adj	demontierbar, abnehmbar
7.4.1	formwork	Schalung
7.4.2	vertically perforated brick	Hochlochziegel
	to plaster	Innenwände verputzen
	to render	Außenwände verputzen
	fair-faced brickwork	Sichtmauerwerk
	leaf, pl leaves	Mauerwerksschale (einer zweischaligen Wand)
	cavity	Hohlraum
	wall tie	Maueranker
	perpend	Stoßfuge
7.5	guarantee bond	Bürgschaft
	public sector construction contract	öffentlicher Bauvertrag
7.5.1	carcass work	Rohbauarbeiten
	interior construction work	Ausbau
7.5.2	foolproof	absolut sicher, narrensicher
	to proofread	Korrektur lesen

8 Tender Action

8.1 Tendering

Tendering is the activity which eventually determines the three factors of principal interest to the client: Cost, quality and time. The contractor is the party offering the services to meet the demands of the client, who ultimately pays the bills. The contractor needs to be able to source *labour*, materials, capital and *plant* before he is able *to bid* for work.

The process of tendering involves a complex arrangement of stages. In the case of public authorities, which have to advertise their contracts publicly, these stages are very formal and have to be strictly observed. However, even when dealing with small projects, tendering contractors should be treated in the same way, receiving the same information at the same time.

Tendering action:

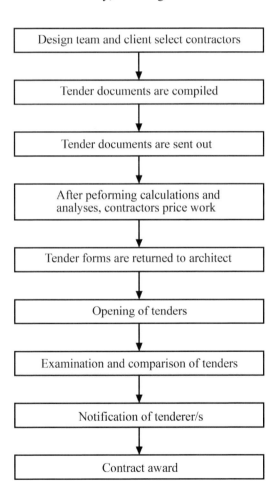

Invitation to tender

Once all the documents have been completed, they are sent out to the firms wishing to tender. The invitation to tender is the title page of this sometimes very extensive conglomeration of information. It should clearly state the project name and the work, which is to be completed. In the invitation to tender, the tendering firms are frequently requested to return a *letter of acknowledgement*, a document attached to the invitation. The acknowledgement enables the tendering firm to confirm the receipt of all enclosed documents and state whether they will be submitting a tender or not.

The invitation to tender should always include the date and place for delivery of the completed tender. If plans are not included in the documents, it may be necessary to specify a time and place for their inspection. Furthermore, if the site is not accessible – this especially applies to extensions and refurbishments – information has to be added concerning necessary arrangements to view the site. Every invitation to tender contains a statement regarding the *confidentiality* of information.

8.2 Estimating

The estimator of a construction company is responsible for pricing work and securing contracts *in competition with* others. The *tender sum* is usually the result of careful analysis.

A lot of factors influence the price, and before estimators actually set to work, they usually investigate the likely competition from other interested contractors. Depending on the *current workload*, the tendering contractor might try to keep the price as low as possible in order to secure work or hold on to its close association with a particular client or architect. On the other hand, if the competition is not likely to be fierce, the estimator might choose to price the job deliberately high. Should the contractor be awarded the contract at a high price, the *margins* allowed could well compensate for the problems of taking on unattractive work.

The preliminary research prior to compiling the tender figure involves enquiries to various suppliers for the current prices of materials and decisions on which sections of work should be *sublet* to sub-contractors.

8.2.1 Pricing

Whatever the basis is for pricing, the fundamental principles of estimating generally remain the same. First of all *lump sum prices* are determined for the items listed in the opening bill or the early section of the specification headed *"Preliminaries"*. These items do not describe the actual work, but *associated works* including insurances, site offices, storage sheds, *temporary water and electricity supply*, *scaffolding* etc.

The next stage is to *breakdown* the work and price individual items. *Unit rates*, which are the prices for either a cubic metre, square metre or linear metre or single unit, are inserted against each item description. The *extended price* for each item is arrived at by multiplying the quantity by its unit rate.

As mentioned in 7.3.2, the contractor is also requested to quote prices for alternate specification and contingency items. Alternate specification items provide a second price for a single item, enabling the person performing the *comparative analysis of tender items* to select the most reasonable one. A priced bill, which already lists prices for possible contingency items, enables the architect to *authorise variations* without having to obtain client approval.

8.2.2 Unit rates

Unit rates are a combination of costs for labour, material, plant, *overheads* with an additional profit margin.

The labour constant is the anticipated length of time that a craftsman or labourer will require to complete a unit of a particular item, for example laying a square metre of 240 mm brickwork in cement mortar.

The material content is straightforward and simply consists of the basic material cost including delivery to site.

The plant content includes all the equipment required to fulfil the item described. Very often the overall cost of plant is covered by a lump sum in the prelims. If additional equipment is required to perform a particular task, it should be included in the unit rate.

The contractor's overheads include the cost of running the head office, staffing the site, paying directors' fees and expenses, taking out certain *blanket insurances*, financing, *back-up services*, like a *joinery shop*. It is important not to allow overheads to become disproportionate to the company's workload. If the organisation is *top-heavy*, the contractor cannot expect to be competitive enough in his pricing for work, because overheads have to be borne by the contracts.

The *profit margin* is sometimes the deciding factor in the winning or losing of a contract. In difficult economic times, the profit margin may have to be reduced.

8.3 Opening of tenders

Tenders must be opened at the time appointed in the tender form; those arriving late must be excluded. The architect, or when commissioned the quantity surveyor, checks the tenders making sure that the contractors arithmetic is correct, that the rates for labour and materials are reasonable and that they compare favourably with the *target costs*. An architect may go back to ask a contractor to correct errors before compiling a report on tenders for the client. If all the tenders are higher than anticipated, the design team might approach the contractor who submitted the most favourable price and *negotiate*. In order to meet the target, it may be necessary to remove certain items from the bill or *downgrade* the specifications. It should be noted that there is seldom an obligation to select the cheapest offer; value for money is the overriding criteria.

If the priced bill has not already been submitted with the tender, the tenderer whose offer is under consideration is asked to supply a copy of the bill of quantities. The architect checks the items in the bill of quantity, and, if there are no serious errors, recommends it for acceptance.

All the tendering contractors should be notified as soon as a tender has been accepted. For future pricing and policy purposes, all tendering contractors like to know what margin there was between their bid an the next lowest. It is common practice to publish a list of the prices received. However, for reasons of confidentiality, the amounts should be published without the firms' names. Tendering contractors will recognise their price and will be able to judge their position in relation to the accepted tender price.

8.3.1 Comparative analysis of tender items

When evaluating tenders, architects and quantity surveyors will usually draw up a chart enabling them to compare unit, item and total prices. The procedure selected should also include aspects such as the bidder's financial, economic, technical and professional capacity. The persons making the evaluation should also list their estimated price in order to see whether they are in line with the offers or whether any measures need to be taken to obtain lower prices.

The following chart is a comparison of three tenders for carpentry work. It compares the unit and extended prices as well as the overall price offered by companies A, B and C.

Trade: 05 Carpentry work								
Bidder:			Company A		Company B		Company C	
Item	Text	Quantity	Unit price £	Total price £	Unit price £	Total price £	Unit price £	Total price £
5.1	Structural solid timber	0.50 m³	670.00	335.00	745.00	372.50	930.00	465.00
5.2	Roof sheathing	15.00 m²	16.95	254.25	19.10	286.50	25.20	378.00
5.3	Parapet of main roof	60 m	14.60	876.00	16.60	996.00	18.50	1,110.00
5.4	Extra for corners	8	5.40	43.20	4.30	34.40	6.00	48.00
5.5	Parapet of roof overhang	15 m	11.30	169.50	8.00	120.00	14.10	211.50
5.6	Extra for corners	2	4.00	8.00	2.70	5.40	4.70	9.40
5.7	Underside sheathing	15.00 m²	16.95	254.25	23.50	352.50	27.90	418.50
Total				1,940.20		2,167.30		2,640.40
			1ˢᵗ	100%	2ⁿᵈ	112%	3ʳᵈ	137%

8.3.2 Exercise: Comparison of tendered prices

No two prices are the same and careful comparison is important. Add the correct adjectives to the text below to describe the information from the comparative analysis in 8.3.1. You may like to consult section 4.3.1 for the comparative and superlative forms of adjectives.

Company A has submitted …………..……….. (favourable) tender with ……………….. (low) total amount. It is in line with the offer made by Company B. Company C's tender is by far ……………….. (high). The unit prices submitted by Company C are all ……………….. (high) than those of Company A and B – they are obviously not interested in submitting a competitive tender. Company A's unit prices are all ……………….. (low) than those of Company B except for the items 5.4, 5.5 and 5.6. In the tender of Company A, the unit price for roof sheathing is ……………….. (high) than the unit price for the sheathing of the roof overhang's underside. Company B, on the other hand, regards the sheathing of the underside as being ………….……….. (labour-intensive) and therefore …………..……….. (expensive) than the sheathing of the roof. Since Company A has submitted ……………….. (reasonable) offer, they will most probably be commissioned with the carpentry work.

8.4 Negotiations

A negotiation is a discussion aimed at meeting an agreement. This form of communication is used to resolve disputes between parties or to *bargain for an advantage* over an individual or a group. Negotiations involve two basic elements, process and substance. The process refers to how the parties negotiate, whereas the substance refers to what the parties negotiate over.

Negotiations can take place at any time during the lifetime of a construction project. However, they frequently take place when finalising business matters prior to the signing of contracts. The content and objectives of negotiations vary, but will often be concerned with price, length of construction period or simply better contract terms and conditions.

In the 1960s and 1970s, practitioners and researchers started to develop *win-win approaches* to negotiation. In contrast to the *winner-takes-it-all approach*, the philosophy of the win-win approach assures that all parties should *benefit* from the negotiation process. Win-win negotiations are aimed at finding solutions which are acceptable to both parties and leave them both feeling that they have a benefit.

More than any other form of communication, negotiation is very much dependant on tactics. The choice of tactic, is not only a matter of personal preference, but also cultural background. On which side of the line below would you place people from your own culture? What about you personally, how direct is your approach to negotiation?

Negotiator prefers diplomatic approach ← | → Negotiator prefers *straight-talking*

It is important that the person *conducting the negotiation* is aware of any cultural differences, particularly when dealing with companies from abroad. If the aim is to build a long-term business relationship, it may be necessary to adopt a negotiation approach suited to the *counterparty*'s character or his/her country of origin. Only consider a *win-lose negotiation* if there is no intention of an ongoing relationship with the other party.

8.4.1 Preparation

Depending on the nature of a difference or the scale of the *disagreement*, good preparation may be key to a successful outcome. The negotiators need to define their own objectives and be aware of the aims of the other parties. Negotiations will lead to one of the parties making a *proposal* with an *initial offer*. The other side may then react with a *counter proposal*. During the bargaining phase, which hopefully leads up to an agreement, each party needs to be aware of its *walk-away position*, which is the point at which a negotiation would break down, the *fall-back position* and the *best alternative to a negotiated agreement (BATNA)*.

The choice of words and the grammar used can have a powerful effect on the outcome of a negotiation. Compare the following sentences:
- We *reject your offer*.
- Unfortunately we are unable to accept your offer.

The first sentence is direct, leaving no *margin for negotiation*. The second sentence uses the softener "unfortunately" and the rephrased negative "unable to accept". Both features make the statement sound more diplomatic and less final.

Function	Expression	Example
Softener	unfortunately; I'm afraid; to be honest	I'm afraid your offer doesn't meet our expectations.
Modal verbs	Modal verbs make the negotiator sound less direct. would, could, may, might	We might have to look for an alternative.
Qualifiers	Qualifiers soften the impact of an argument, but don't actually change the content. slight, a bit, rather, quite, fairly, etc.	We're fairly close to reaching a *breakthrough*.
Restrictive phrases	A restrictive phrase does not exclude the possibility of future movement. at the moment, at this stage, so far, etc.	That's our position at the moment.
Rephrased negatives (adjective)	Even when used with a negative, positive adjectives sound more diplomatic. unhappy – not very happy; unconvinced – not totally convinced, etc.	We're not entirely happy with the proposal you made, but …
Rephrased negatives (verb)	Avoid direct negatives; rephrased negatives sound less final. can't accept – unable to accept; can't agree – not in a position to agree, etc.	We're not in a position to meet your expectations.
Question forms	Questions can be used to make suggestions and warn the opponent. They are more powerful and persuasive than statements. shouldn't we …; wouldn't it …;	Wouldn't it be better to resume negotiations tomorrow?

8.4.2 Price negotiation

The architect, Tim Smith, meets the company which submitted the lowest bid for carcass work. The contractor, John White, offered to perform the job for £124,000.00. The architect had estimated £110,000.00. They meet to discuss the tender.

John White:	Hello Tim, nice to see you again. When did we complete the office in Aylesbury? It must be 18 months ago.
Tim Smith:	Yes, you're right. It was in February last year. Anyway, thank you for submitting a tender. Unfortunately, it's not quite as straightforward this time, and there are a few aspects I would like to take a look at with you.
John White:	Yes, certainly.

Tim Smith:	Well, you'll be pleased to hear that you are amongst the lowest tenders, but the price you quoted is unfortunately still quite a bit higher than our estimate. To be precise, you're still £14,000.00 above our target price.
John White:	As much as that? Are you sure the bill is in line with your estimation?
Tim Smith:	We're quite sure. The quantity surveyor has checked; £110,000.00 is the price we're looking at. Is your quoted price your final offer?
John White:	Well, to be honest, I'm very interested in the work, and considering it's so close to our shop, I suppose we could offer 120.
Tim Smith:	That's better, but still gives us a problem. Do you see any possibility to get the price down a bit further?
John White:	You requested *sandlime* be used for the brickwork. A thought that did cross my mind during the estimation work was that we could save a few thousand by using *vertically perforated brick* instead of the sandlime. I'd have to check this exactly, but it would make a difference of, let me think, at least two thousand. But really that's as far as we can go without making any major changes.
Tim Smith:	So that puts you at £118,000.00. We had hoped for rather more. Might there be a *discount for early payment*?
John White:	Yes, I'll offer you a 3 % discount for payment within 10 days. And you know you can *rely on us* to meet your deadlines.
Tim Smith:	Yes. That sounds quite good. I'll be speaking to the client this afternoon, and I'll let you know the outcome once we have reached a conclusion. Hopefully, I can get back to you tomorrow morning.

8.4.3 Comprehension

Are the following statements concerning the dialogue above true or false.

		true	false
1.	John White and Tim Smith have never worked together before.	☐	☐
2.	John White submitted the lowest tender.	☐	☐
3.	The contractor is prepared to negotiate.	☐	☐
4.	John White immediately gives in to the architect's pressure.	☐	☐
5.	The architect accepts the contractor's first proposal.	☐	☐
6.	The contractor makes a suggestion to reduce the price.	☐	☐
7.	A 3 % discount is agreed for early payment.	☐	☐
8.	The final offer is approximately halfway between the architect's target price and the contractor's originally quoted price.	☐	☐

8.5 Building contract

A building contract is an agreement between two parties, a client or an employer and an individual or an organisation, to *undertake* an agreed amount of work, to an agreed standard and for an agreed sum of money. The size and nature of contracts varies widely, but there are common elements, which every contract should include.

- Provisions for every party to deal fairly with each other and to co-operate mutually
- A fair *distribution of risk*
- A clear separation of the roles and responsibilities of all persons involved
- Established methods of payment
- Clear description of the work involved
- An agreed timescale for *commencement* and *completion*
- An *adjudication system* acceptable to all parties

Standard forms contain a wide range of clauses designed to ensure protection to both the client and the contractor, which can be modified or deleted as necessary. The most widely used forms of contract for building in the UK are the JCT contracts. They are drawn up by the Joint Contracts Tribunal and their contents correspond with the rules and regulations contained in the VOB (Verdingungsordnung für Bauleistungen) in Germany.

8.5.1 FIDIC

In order to create common international contract terms for engineering work, FIDIC, the International Federation of Consulting Engineers (Fédération Internationale des Ingénieurs-Conseils), was founded in 1913. The aim of the cooperation is to eliminate the national differences and create standard contract forms and conditions to be used in *cross-border operations*. Peter L Booen has been actively involved in the preparation of standard terms since 1993. He is the principal drafter of these four major books:

- CONS: Conditions of Contract for Construction, which was commonly referred to as Red Book. These conditions are recommended for building works designed by the Employer or by his representative, the Engineer.
- P&DB: Conditions of Contract for Plant and Design-Build, which was commonly referred to as Yellow Book. These are recommended for the *provision* of electrical and/or mechanical plant, and for the design and execution of building or engineering works. Usually the contractor designs and provides in accordance with the Employer's requirements.
- EPCT: Conditions of Contract for EPC/*Turnkey Projects*, which was commonly referred to as Orange Book. These are recommended when one institution takes total responsibility for the design and execution of an engineering project.
- Short Form of Contract: This is recommended for building or engineering works with relatively small capital value.

FIDIC contracts and conditions are becoming more widely known. Especially since the opening of the East European markets, there is a growing need for contracts and conditions independent of *national jurisdiction*. The contract language is generally English. If you would like to find out more about FIDIC, take a look at the website www.fidic.org.

8.5.2 Contract award

The contract documents are prepared as soon as the client has approved the *tender report*. It is usually the architect's task to prepare the contract documents by completing the various blanks in the *articles of agreement*. It may be necessary to *add* special *clauses* to the conditions of contract, to *delete* or *amend* them. All documents contained in the contract (drawings, bills of quantities, specifications) should be marked as contract documents and signed by the contract parties. It is important that all the contract documents are consistent with each other.

Take a look at the term contract with some collocations and useful expressions.

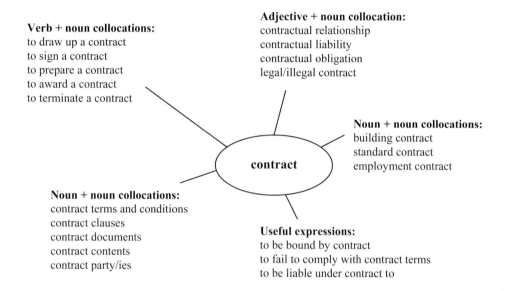

8.5.3 Contract termination

Most contracts are concluded when both parties have completely fulfilled their obligations. The contract simply *ceases* to have a purpose and comes to an end. However, there are events which require the contractor's employment be brought to an end prior to completion. Most building contracts include provisions for terminating the contract. Other than the natural ending according to performance, termination can be effected by *agreement, frustration* or *breach*. In all cases the parties to the contract are released from their *contractual obligations*.

Agreement: The parties of a contract may agree at any time to end the contract. It is wise to record the agreement in writing.

Frustration: If a contract becomes fundamentally different due to events completely outside the control of the parties, the contract is said to have been frustrated. A good example of frustration would be if the contractor were unable to perform a refurbishment because the building was destroyed by fire, earthquake, etc. Death of either party is also a reason for frustration.

Breach: A breach of contract takes place when a party fails to perform their contractual obligations. Breach entitles the *innocent party* to either treat their obligations as ended or *sue* *for damages*. The party wishing to terminate must comply with the contractual terms governing termination. For a termination to be valid, the contract usually requires a *notice period* and that the notice is in writing. Typical reasons for the employer to terminate the contract are:

- in the event that the contractor does not perform or fails to perform according to the programme
- in the case of defective work due to poor workmanship and failure to rectify appropriately
- if the contractor fails to comply with regulations
- in the event of the contractor's insolvency

The situation is more serious when the contractor terminates the contract. In this case the contractor may *claim for the loss of profit*, which would have been made had the contract continued. It is the architect's responsibility to prevent such an occurrence. Possible trigger points are:

- If the employer fails to pay certified sums within the period stated.
- *Suspension* of the work due to actions, inactions or *defaults* by the employer or architect
- In the event of the employer's insolvency

8.5.4 Lexis: Contracts

Combine a word in A with a word in B to form 10 terms dealing with contracts. Finally, choose the best definition for the term in C.

A	B	C
contract	report	a document put together by the architect enabling the client to award a company with a contract
risk	analysis	companies or individuals signing an agreement
terms and	method	responsibility for dangers is shared between contract partners
breach	project	agreement concerning the details of *remuneration*
tender	of contract	all agreements making up the contents of a contract
contract	distribution	a service including everything, from the design to the pictures on the wall
payment	award	overview of prices offered by tenderers as a basis for comparison
turnkey	parties	contract termination due to failure of performing contractual obligations
comparative	conditions	decision on which company will be performing the work

8.6 Vocabulary

8.1	tendering	Angebotseinholung
	labour	Arbeitskraft, -kräfte
	plant	maschinelle Einrichtung, technische Ausstattung
	to bid for sth	ein Angebot machen
	opening of tenders	Angebotseröffnung
	contract award	Auftragsvergabe, - erteilung
	invitation to tender	Angebotsaufforderung
	letter of acknowledgement	Empfangsbestätigung
	confidentiality	Vertraulichkeit
8.2	estimating	Preisermittlung, (Baukosten-) Kalkulation
	to be in competition with sb	mit jmdm. konkurrieren/im Wettbewerb stehen
	tender sum	Angebotssumme
	current workload	momentane, aktuelle Arbeitsbelastung
	margin	Spanne
	to sublet	untervergeben
8.2.1	lump sum price	Pauschalbetrag
	Preliminaries, short form: prelims	Vorbemerkungen
	associated works	Nebenleistungen
	temporary water and electricity supply	Baustrom u. -wasser
	scaffolding	Gerüst
	to breakdown sth	etw. aufschlüsseln, -gliedern
	unit rate	Stückpreis
	extended price	Gesamtpreis einer Position
	comparative analysis of tender items	Preisspiegel
	to authorise a variation	eine Änderung genehmigen, billigen
8.2.2	overheads	Gemeinkosten, indirekte Kosten
	blanket insurance	allgemeine Versicherung
	back-up services	Hilfsbetriebe
	joinery shop	Tischlerwerkstatt
	top-heavy, adj	kopflastig
	profit margin	Gewinnspanne
8.3	target costs	Zielkosten
	to negotiate	verhandeln
	to downgrade	niedriger einstufen, niederstufen
8.3.1	sheathing	Holzverkleidung, -verschalung
8.4	to bargain for an advantage over sb	sich einen Vorteil über jmdn. erschaffen

	win-win approach	Doppelsieg Strategie
	winner-takes-it-all approach	Einzelsieger Strategie
	to benefit from sth	von etw. profitieren
	negotiator	Verhandlungsführer/in
	to do some straight-talking	Klartext reden
	to conduct a negotiation	eine Verhandlung führen
	counterparty	(Verhandlungs-) Gegner
	win-lose negotiation	Gewinner-Verlierer Verhandlung
8.4.1	disagreement	Meinungsverschiedenheit, Uneinigkeit
	proposal	Vorschlag
	initial offer	erstes Angebot
	counter proposal	Gegenvorschlag
	walk-away position	Verhandlungsabbruch
	fall-back position	Kompromiss
	best alternative to a negotiated agreement (BATNA)	Nichteinigungsalternative
	to reject an offer	ein Angebot ablehnen
	margin of negotiation	Verhandlungsspielraum
	breakthrough	Durchbruch
8.4.2	sandlime	Kalksandstein
	vertically perforated brick	Hochlochziegel
	discount for early payment	Skonto
	to rely on sb	sich auf jmdn. verlassen
8.5	building contract	Bauvertrag
	to undertake an obligation	Verpflichtung übernehmen, sich verpflichten
	distribution of risk	Risikoverteilung
	commencement	Baubeginn
	completion	Fertigstellung
	adjudication system	Rechtssystem, Gerichtbarkeit
8.5.1	FIDIC (Fédération Internationale des Ingénieurs-Conseils)	Internationale Vereinigung der Beratenden Ingenieure
	cross-border operations	grenzüberschreitende Tätigkeiten
	provision	Versorgung, Bereitstellung
	turnkey project	schlüsselfertiges Projekt
	national jurisdiction	nationales Recht
8.5.2	tender report	Ausschreibungsbericht, Vergabeempfehlung
	articles of agreement	Vertragsklauseln
	to add, delete, amend a clause	eine Klausel ergänzen, entfernen, modifizieren
8.5.3	contract termination	Vertragsbeendigung

8.6 Vocabulary

to cease	aufhören zu
agreement	Übereinkommen, Vereinbarung
frustration	Wegfall der Geschäftsgrundlage
breach	Vertragsbruch, -verletzung
contractual obligation	vertragliche Verpflichtung
innocent party	unschuldig Vertragspartei
to sue for damages	auf Schadensersatz klagen
notice period	Frist
claim for a loss of profit	Anspruch auf entgangenen Gewinn erheben
suspension	Aufschub, Verschiebung
default	Nichterfüllung, Versäumnis
8.5.4 remuneration	Bezahlung, Entlohnung

9 Pre-Construction Phase

9.1 Background to building operations

As explained at the beginning of the book, a building project may begin fairly simply, perhaps merely a conversation between a client and an architect. Over the ensuing months, the project team grows as other services and advisors, such as structural and mechanical consultants, are brought in and the cost commitment builds rapidly. The *run-up* to the construction phase is especially critical. It is a time when a number of new companies are contracted to offer advice, to supply specialist services, materials or components. Very often this number has to be further increased in order to ensure an appropriate level of competition. At the time of the contract award, a project of even modest proportions can involve dozens of people. For this reason it is absolutely necessary for team members to understand each other's *area of responsibility* and for *contractual obligations* to be clearly defined.

As soon as the contract is signed, the roles of those involved change. The contractors and the sub-contractors, who up until this stage have only given advice, become the constructors; the architect and the consultants, who have been responsible for the design, become *inspectors*. It has to be acknowledged that the creative part of an architect's work, except for detail planning and finishes, is virtually complete when the job starts on site.

According to German practice, the architect is the *client's representative*. In case of disputes regarding contractual obligations, the architect is obliged to represent the client's interests. In contrast, British guidelines, which have been adopted in the FIDIC books, see the architect not only as the client's representative but also as a *mediator* charged with balancing the interests of both parties.

9.1.1 Responsibilities

The client will have worked closely with the architect and consultants up until the contract stage. The contract documents define the client's requirements and expectations and the amount that will have to be paid. Once the contract is signed the client's functions are limited. Nevertheless, the client will be curious to see the project developing on site and, depending on the client's vicinity to the site and time available, will pay visits to the construction site to visualise what has so far only been on paper. If the client sees something not corresponding to plans or desire, he/she should under no circumstances instruct the contractor or any of the contractor's employees directly, but contact the architect. The architect is the agent and will act on behalf of the client.

The architect continues to co-ordinate the job as a whole and takes on the task of inspecting the building construction as the job proceeds on site. Architects have to recognise that the site and the work on it are generally the responsibility of the contractor, from the *date of possession* until the building is *handed over*. The architect's duties on site are to ensure that the contractor acts in accordance with the instructions given in the drawings, bills and other contract documents and that the *quality of workmanship* and materials comply with the standards specified. The architect has to *be kept up-to-date* by the contractor and receive all relevant documents and test reports. The architect in turn has to provide all drawings necessary for the contractor to complete work on time. A *release schedule* states the dates by which the architect should provide the drawings.

The contractor has been selected by the client to realise the architect's design. The contractor is obliged to plan, carry out and complete the work described in the contract. The contractor is also responsible for the site, which covers site access, site staff and their safety as well as all services up until completion.

In small or even one-person businesses, the contractor will be both, manager and constructor, at the same time bearing the sole responsibility for the whole operation. In larger firms, the contractor is represented by a *construction manager*. He/she is responsible for the management of the work and is the direct counterpart to the architect. The construction manager, who has effective control of the entire building operation from the day the contract is signed, works in the contractor's main office and visits the site frequently to co-ordinate work and ensure that the execution is in accordance with the agreed terms. Depending on the size of the firm, the construction manager may be responsible for controlling costs and organising plant, materials, labour, meetings, sub-contractors and *programming*.

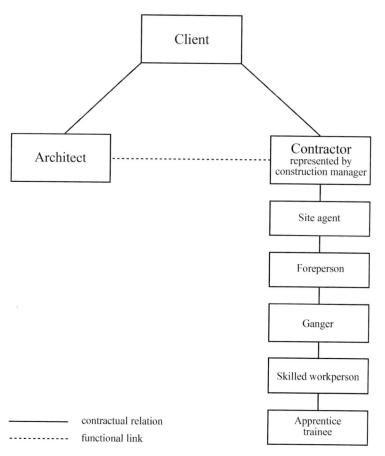

The site agent, who receives instructions from the construction manager, has direct control of all *site operations*. Trade forepeople, e.g. a bricklayer foreperson, a joiner foreperson, etc., receive their instructions from the site agent. Despite being responsible for the work as a whole, the site agent is primarily concerned with initiating each particular operation, co-ordinating it with other trades in order to ensure that it has a clear run and is supplied with the appropriate plant, labour and materials.

Each foreperson is responsible for his/her trade. On large projects a foreperson will manage several gangers, who are in charge of and work with a number of skilled and/or unskilled labourers and apprentices.

9.1.2 Grammar: Present Perfect

Within the lifetime of a construction project, the commencement of work on site is a very significant phase producing many changes. The people involved take on different roles and perform different activities. The tenses we use to describe activities which have been completed or those which continue differ.

The present perfect tense is used to describe activities which started in the past, continue up until today and will most probably continue into the future.

Example: The architect has been the client's agent.

It is used for activities which took place in the past but are mentioned without a time reference.

Example: The architect has prepared the contract documents.

As soon as a point in time is mentioned (except in combination with since), simple past is used.

Example: The client commissioned the architect in June.

Form: The present perfect is formed with have or has for the 3rd person singular plus the past participle. In regular verbs, the past participle is formed by adding -ed to the infinitive. In irregular verbs, the past participle varies considerably and the forms simply have to be learnt. Most dictionaries include a list of irregular verbs.

The inflection takes place in the helping verb "have". The negative is formed by inserting not between the helping verb and the full verb. The short forms "hasn't" and "haven't" are used in speech.

Signal words: recently, lately (either at the beginning or end of the sentence, or between the helping verb and full verb)

ever, never (between the helping verb and full verb)

yet (usually at the end of the sentence)

since + a point in time; for + period of time

9.1.3 Exercise: Present Perfect

Complete the text below by putting the verb in brackets into either the simple past or present perfect tense. Where "since or for" are offered, decide whether it is a point in time or a period of time.

The design team …………………. (work) on the Brown's house ………. (since/for) last April. They ……………… (be) very thorough. They ……………… (discuss) many options and ………………… (prepare) detailed contract documents. ………. (Since/For) the last weeks, they ………………… (work) on the procurement procedure. Last Thursday, the successful tendering company ……………. (sign) the contract. Work on site ……………….………… (not yet, commence). So far the client ……………..…………… (be involve, very). He ………………… (take part) in many meetings with consultants and ……………..… (make) lots of important decisions. He will now have to stand back and watch the work being realised on site.

9.2 Time management

Time management is a set of skills, tools and systems for planning and scheduling time. The aim of time management is to support an orderly accomplishment of tasks increasing the effectiveness and efficiency of not only work, but everyday life. Time is a resource, which cannot be stored and saved for later. Everyone gets exactly the same amount of time each and every day. The difference lies in the way in which it is used.

Time management strategies are fundamental to effective *scheduling*, the process by which you plan your time. Tools range from simple *to-do-lists* to sophisticated computer programmes. No matter which format is chosen, all help to set *deadlines* and priorities, highlight urgent, *high-priority activities* as well as leave margins such as *contingency times* for *unpredicted interruptions*.

Procrastination is a major hindrance to effective time management. Everyone likes to *defer* or avoid less attractive tasks. However, all aspects of accepted work need to be completed in the same way and with the same degree of *diligence* as for all jobs. Being punctual, delivering on time and meeting deadlines are characteristics that every professional should *strive* for.

A useful saying for everybody is: Don't put off until tomorrow what you can do today.

9.2.1 Time terms

Timing is very important throughout the *course* of every project. A good architect will often be recognised for his or her good time management. However, from time to time, even good *timekeepers* find that there are not enough hours in the day and are given a hard time.

9.2 Time management

As can be seen from the paragraph above, there are lots of useful expressions and idioms dealing with time. Take a look at the following overview for more.

Expression	Meaning/Idiomatic expression	Example
time	<ul><li>on time – according to schedule, punctual in time – before a time limit expires high time – the appropriate or urgent time in no time – almost instantly, immediately from time to time – once in a while</li><li>to waste time; to make up for lost time; to give sb a hard time; to take time; to have time on ones hands</li></ul>	The contractor took so much time preparing the site, now they are going to have to make up for lost time.
date	<ul><li>a time stated in terms of day, month, year</li><li>date can also mean appointment, but a social one and often with a romantic interest</li><li>to set/arrange/cancel/observe a date; to update sth</li></ul>	The date set for completion is 23 June 2008.
schedule	<ul><li>a plan for performing work with a specified order and an allotted time</li><li>to be ahead of/on/behind schedule</li></ul>	Work on site is absolutely on schedule.
duration	<ul><li>the time required for a certain task</li></ul>	The clerk of works will be on site for the duration of the construction.
durability	<ul><li>the period of *withstanding wear and tear* or *decay*</li></ul>	The architect has selected high-quality goods; their durability is excellent.
deadline	<ul><li>a time limit with a target date by which sth must be completed</li><li>to meet/exceed/postpone a deadline; to set/fix a deadline</li></ul>	The roofing company is not going to meet the deadline; we will have to postpone the starting date for subsequent trades.
period	<ul><li>an interval of time</li><li>to extend a period; the period has expired</li></ul>	The period assigned for tiling has expired.
appointment	<ul><li>an arrangement to do sth or meet sb at a particular time and place</li><li>to make/arrange/cancel an appointment with sb</li><li>the other meaning of appointment is the act of designating sb for a position/task</li></ul>	The architect has arranged an appointment with the client on site.

9.2.2 Exercise: Time terms

Enter the following words into the text below. Make sure to use the correct tense.

to postpone · period · to make up for lost time · just in time · deadline · to interrupt · delay · date period · on schedule · to meet deadlines · to waste time · behind schedule · to take time · to update

George Brown's project is more or less .... The procurement .... was quite tense as the tenders all only arrived .... Then the evaluation .... and a few items had to be negotiated with the lowest bidder. The pre-start meeting had to be .... by a week. Luckily the contractor .... by bringing the .... to take possession of the site forward. The .... set for completion is realistic. The contractor does not want ...., but make use of the .... before winter sets in. The contractor is optimistic and wants .... Hopefully nothing unpredictable will .... building operations, which would cause .... and put work .... The contractor is obliged to keep the client and the architect ....

9.3 Construction programme

Before work commences on site, a construction programme should be drawn up. A programme is a *forecast* of activities with a precise indication of the progress planned for each trade each week. It enables all participants in the building project, planners as well as constructors, to plan ahead, order materials in good time and reinforce or reduce the labour force according to demand. On large contracts, it is customary to include the dates of *information release* for imminent operations. No matter how small the project, the benefits of a well thought-through programme are immense in terms of achieving the timely commencement and completion of site operations.

The schedule should be placed in a prominent position in the architect's office as well as the site office where it will signal whether or not work is proceeding at a satisfactory rate. Both architect and contractor should *monitor* the programme and update it whenever necessary. The only really significant date in contract terms is the *completion date*. Even if the *sequence of construction* alters slightly during the progress of the project, the architect should, with the help of the programme, ensure that the end date is met.

The most common programme is the *Gantt or bar chart*. Bars are used to represent each trade of the contract; the length of a bar indicates the *anticipated duration* of each particular element. The bars might be continuous or *suspended* to allow other operations to proceed before work is *resumed* again. A *network diagram*, which is a logical schematic picture of a project, has the advantage that it not only shows the expected duration of operations but also the relationships between the individual activities.

9.3 Construction programme

9.3.1 Gantt chart

The figure below shows the programme Tim Smith has drawn up for the construction work on the Brown's family home. Because it is a fairly straightforward project, the architect has chosen a Gantt chart with bars for each trade. The weeks are indicated in the time line at the top of the table. The trades are listed on the left according to their date of appearance on site. *Milestones* are shown to highlight key dates.

Job No. 0712	Contract:	Brown single family home, Mill Road, Chesham	
Architect: Tim Smith	Consultants: Mechanical: Electrical:	White Engineers J. Peters	Main contractor: John White

No.	Trade	Executing company	anticip. dur / actual dur
1	Earthwork	John White	4+5
2	Sewer construction	John White	10
3	Carcass work	John White	35
4	Scaffolding	Stewart	2+2
5	Carpentry	Ford	5
6	Roofing	Ford	15
7	Joinery work	Williams	10+5
7	Electrical installation	T+P	15+5
8	Heating/Plumbing work	Frazer	15+5
9	Plastering/Rendering	S. Dennis	15
10	Floor screeding	S. Dennis	2
11	Painting work	unknown	5
12	Tiling/Flooring	unknown	10

9.3.2 Prepositions of time

When talking about periods, dates and deadlines, prepositions are indispensable. There are many different prepositions, which are used in different cases. What they all have in common, in the case of time factors, is that they are placed before nouns.

Preposition	Uses	Examples	Exceptions/Notes
at	+ clock time	at 4.30 p.m, at 9 o'clock	at midnight
on	+ day/date	on Monday, on 4 June	at the weekend, at Christmas
in	+ time of the day/ week/month	in the morning/afternoon, in week 23, in August, in 2007	at night, at noon
by	+ a deadline	by 4 p.m., by Friday, by May	
from …to/ until/till	+ time/date	from 8 to 4 o'clock; from Monday to Friday	

Preposition	Uses	Examples	Exceptions/Notes
since	+ point in time	since 10 a.m., since Monday, since this morning	Always used with a perfect tense, e.g. the foreman has been waiting for the delivery since this morning.
for	+ period of time	for 3 hours, for 2 weeks	Often used with a perfect tense, e.g. The foreman has been waiting for 4 hours.
-	+ this, next, last	next Monday, last month, this morning	No prepositions are used!

9.3.3 Exercise: Prepositions of time

 Look at the Gantt chart in 9.3.1 and complete the memo. If no preposition is required, leave the space blank.

The construction work for the Brown single family home is due to start ...... week 30. The main contractor, John White, will be on site ...... a total of 8 weeks. Their work has to be completed .... 14 September in order to allow enough time for the other trades. The joiner Williams is due to start work ...... 3 September. Once he has fitted the windows, he will be off site .... 17 September .... 29 October. The companies Frazer and T + P will also suspend their work .... 3 weeks while the plastering and screeding work is being carried out. It is absolutely essential that the screeder finishes .... 9 October allowing the screed to dry sufficiently before the parquet flooring is installed. The painters should be out .... the end of week 44. However, there is a buffer of 5 days for *overruns* and *remedial work*.

9.4 Site set-up

The site set-up has a major influence on the smooth running of a contract. The location of the main features, such as *access roads, material compounds, storage sheds, general plant,* offices, etc., is significant. Adequate water and electricity supplies are essential at any site from the very start of the work. Where there is no *electricity supply network*, generators will be necessary to provide *temporary power* for lighting and power. Similarly, if a *water supply main* is not available, a *temporary water supply* will have to be arranged, possibly the installation of a storage tank with regular *top-ups* assured. If the operation is not planned properly beforehand, time and money will be wasted needlessly. All of those involved in site organisation should get together to determine the best site set-up from efficiency and safety points of view.

9.4 Site set-up

9.4.1 Site layout

A *site layout plan* enables contractors to understand whether the important items are correctly placed in accordance with the general organisation of the site. In most contracts access roads constitute an important part of the site set-up. To avoid *obstructions* and delays, sufficient space should be allowed for *lorries* to load and unload. Access roads must be properly maintained, especially during wet weather.

All contracts usually include a *tower crane*, either a static one, requiring very little space, or one running *on rails*. It goes without saying that the radius of the *crane jib* as well as the *lifting capacity* at the *jib nose* have to be suited to the job. Sometimes *mobile cranes* are required to perform single operations, which exceed the capacities and accessibility of static plant.

Safety measures cover both, *security* and *protection*. *Perimeter fences* are primarily intended to guard the site against *trespass* and *theft*. Usually *fencing* is made of *steel mesh* fixed to concrete block fence bases. Sites directly adjoining *public footpaths* or roads must provide protection to the public. *Hoardings*, protected walkways and *guard rails* are installed for the duration of the site work. The contractor's insurance policy includes clauses relating to the provision of all necessary safety measures.

According to an EEC directive, a *safety and health coordinator* has to be appointed if the work on site exceeds a certain volume, for example more than 500 person-days. The task of the coordinator is to ensure that construction regulations are adhered to and health and safety measures conform to the rules set out. The work of a safety and health coordinator also includes drawing up a safety and health plan before work commences and a safety and health file on completion.

All equipment, plant and material belonging to the construction companies have to be positioned on the client's property. If additional space is required, temporarily or permanently, a permit must be obtained from the local government before work commences. The permit for a *road closure* usually involves a fee. Furthermore, all construction companies have to adhere to legal requirements regarding aspects such as working hours, noise and vibration, *waste management*, etc. *Emission standards*, for example, prescribe the volume of noise permitted at each hour of the day.

9.4.2 Construction site

Construction sites are busy and noisy places. For *passers-by*, a construction site often resembles a beehive – it appears to be chaotic, but nevertheless everybody seems to know what they should be doing. Take a look at the drawing below and find the following items.

tower crane · lifting crab · hardhat · reinforcement · architect · safety shoes · shovel
ready-mixed concrete · hook · concrete skip · plan · bucket

9.5 Vocabulary

9		pre-construction phase	Bauvorbereitungsphase
9.1		in the run-up to	im Vorfeld eines Ereignisses
		area of responsibility	Aufgabenbereich
		contractual obligation	vertragliche Verpflichtung
		inspector	Bauaufseher
		client's representative	Bauherrenvertreter
		mediator	Vermittler (in Streitfällen)
9.1.1		possession date	Übergabetermin für Baustelle
		to hand over	übergeben
		quality of workmanship	Ausführungsqualität
		to keep sb up-to-date	jmdn. auf dem laufenden halten
		release schedule	Zeitplan für Planfreigabe
		construction manager	Oberbauleiter (der ausführenden Firma)
		programming	Bauzeitenplan
		site agent	Bauleiter (der ausführenden Firma)
		foreperson, pl forepeople foreman, pl foremen forewoman, pl forewomen	Polier/in
		ganger	Vorarbeiter/in
		skilled workperson, pl workpeople skilled workman, pl workmen skilled workwoman, pl workwomen	Facharbeiter/in
		unskilled workperson, pl workpeople unskilled workman, pl workmen unskilled workwoman, pl workwomen	ungelernte/r Arbeiter/in, Hilfsarbeiter/in
		apprentice	Auszubildende/r
		site operations	Baustellentätigkeiten
9.2		time management	Zeitplanung
		scheduling	Terminplanung
		to-do-list	Aufgabenliste
		deadline	Endtermin, Schlusstermin, Termin
		high-priority activity	Tätigkeit mit hoher Dringlichkeit
		contingency time	Zeitreserve, Zeitpuffer
		unpredicted interruption	unvorhergesehene Unterbrechung
		procrastination	Aufschieben, Saumseligkeit
		to defer	aufschieben
		diligence	Fleiß, Eifer
		to strive for sth	anstreben
9.2.1		timing	zeitliche Abstimmung
		course	Ablauf

	timekeeper	Zeitnehmer/in
	date	Datum, Termin, Verabredung
	schedule	Zeitplan, Terminplan
	duration	Zeit, Zeitdauer
	durability	Dauerhaftigkeit, Beständigkeit
	to withstand wear and tear	Verschleiß, Abnutzung widerstehen
	decay	Verfall
	period	Frist, Zeitraum
	appointment	Termin; Beauftragung
9.3	construction programme	Bauzeitenplan
	forecast	Vorhersage
	information release	Informationsfreigabe
	to monitor	überwachen, kontrollieren
	completion date	Fertigstellungszeitpunkt
	sequence of construction	Bauabfolge
	Gantt chart, bar chart	Gantt-Diagramm, Balkendiagramm
	anticipated duration	erwartete Dauer
	to suspend	unterbrechen
	to resume	wiederaufnehmen
	network diagram	Netzplan
9.3.1	milestone	Meilenstein
	to erect	aufbauen
	to dismantle	abbauen
	pre-assembly	Rohmontage
	final assembly	Endmontage
	buffer	(Zeit-)Puffer
9.3.3	overrun	(Termin-)Überschreitung
	remedial work	Nachbesserungsarbeiten
9.4	site set-up	Baustelleneinrichtung
	access road	Zufahrtsstraße
	material compound	Baustofflager
	storage shed	Lagerschuppen, Magazin
	general plant	allgemeine Baustellengeräte
	electricity supply network, mains	Strom(versorgungs)netz
	temporary power	Baustrom
	water supply main	Wasserversorgungsleitung
	temporary water supply	Bauwasser
	top-up	Auffüllung
9.4.1	site layout plan	Baustelleneinrichtungsplan
	obstruction	Behinderung
	lorry, pl lorries BE; truck AE	Lastwagen, LKW

9.5 Vocabulary

	tower crane	Turmkran
	on rails	auf Schienen
	crane jib	Kranausleger
	lifting capacity	Krantragfähigkeit
	jib nose	Auslegerkopf
	mobile crane	Mobilkran
	safety measure	Sicherheitsmaßnahme, -vorkehrung
	security measure	Sicherheitsmaßnahme (gegen Einbruch, Diebstahl, unbefugtes Betreten)
	protective measure	Schutzmaßnahme
	perimeter fence	Sicherheitszaun, Bauzaun
	trespass	unbefugtes Betreten
	theft	Diebstahl
	fencing	Ein-/Umzäunung
	steel mesh	Stahldrahtgewebe, Stahlgitter
	public footpath	öffentlicher Fußweg
	hoarding	Bretterzaun
	guard rail	Schutz-/Sicherheitsgeländer
	safety and health coordinator	Sicherheits- und Gesundheitsschutz-koordinator (SIGE Koordinator)
	road closure	Straßensperrung
	waste management	Abfall-/Entsorgungswirtschaft
	emission standards	Emissionsgrenzwerte
9.4.2	passer-by, pl passers-by	Passant
	lifting crab	Laufkatze
	hardhat	Bauhelm
	safety shoes	Sicherheitsschuhe
	shovel	Schaufel
	ready-mixed concrete	Transportbeton
	hook	Haken
	concrete skip	Betonkübel
	bucket	Eimer

10 Construction

10.1 Work progress

Once all the background information has been clarified and the commencement date approaches, the contractor takes possession of the site. A once desolate site comes to life as numerous *tradespeople* move in and set to work. The type and the scale of work will determine the number of trades involved, the volume of noise to be expected and the duration of the project. For neighbours and surrounding plots, a very wearing period commences. A *construction site sign* informs neighbours and passers-by of the future development and all the companies involved.

The operations on site from the day of taking possession until the completion date require good organisation, time management and negotiation skills. Depending on the type of contract, the person responsible for the work on site and managing all operations varies. All companies, who were commissioned with work through tendering, need to be contacted in advance and commencement dates need to be agreed. The aim is to achieve a smooth run with as few interruptions and *obstructions* as possible.

10.1.1 Trades

This list of trades and building processes is far from complete. The intention is to give the reader a general understanding of the work on site. For further information on building practices please refer to the list of additional reading material on page 161.

Trade **Persons involved**		**Building process**
Excavation work Building contractor		The site is cleared, and the ground is prepared. *Profile boards* are pegged with the help of a level indicating the exact location of the building. *Excavators* dig the construction *pit*, which has to either be secured by planking or sloped to prevent collapse. Excavated material is either stored in *spoil heaps* or removed.
Concrete work Concrete worker		Ready-mixed concrete is poured into *formwork*, compacted by vibrators to ensure solidity and *cured* with sprinklers. Pre-cast concrete is cast and cured in factories and transported to the site. The components, aggregate, cement and water, define the strength, durability, density, *impermeability* and stability of the concrete.

Formwork Formworker	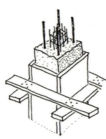 Before *in-situ concrete* can be poured, *formwork*, which is also known as shuttering, has to be prepared. It needs to be sufficiently tight to prevent leakage and smooth to impart a smooth finish to the concrete surface – this especially applies to *exposed concrete*. After an adequate *striking time*, the formwork is removed. For repetitive elements, *sliding formwork* is used. Occasionally, the formwork remains in the structure; this is then called *permanent formwork*.
Reinforcement Steelfixer	Steelfixers bend and fix reinforcement bars and cages and install them in formwork to strengthen concrete. *Barspacers* are used to guarantee a certain *concrete cover*. Bar intersections are securely tied with wire.
Structural steelwork Steel erector	Steel profiles are often used to form the structure of a building. Standard profiles with I-shaped, T-shaped, etc. cross sections are welded or bolted together to form stiffened frames.
Brickwork Mason	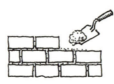 Bricks or larger blocks are layered with *mortar* to form walls, piers, chimneys etc. All combinations of *stretcher* and *header* bonds are termed *English bond*. *Face brickwork* is built to a fair face and *pointed*. *Cavity walls* consist of two skins joined together by wall ties.
Timberwork Carpenter	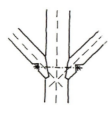 A carpenter's work includes the construction, erection and installation of timber structures. This may involve joining *purlins* and *rafters* to assemble a roof; it might involve posts and beams for a whole structure. A carpenter usually has a circular saw on site, other tools include milling and drilling machines, grinders and, not to be forgotten, the carpenter's hammer.
Roofing Roofer	 The roofer is responsible for covering the roof and making the structure *watertight*. Most roofs involve a combination of structure, *waterproofing*, heat insulation and *vapour barrier*. Whereas a gable roof is covered with roof tiles, a flat roof is sealed with bituminous materials.
Sheet metal work Tin smith or sheet metal worker	A tin smith is the person who makes and repairs things made of light metal, copper, stainless steel, aluminium, zinc, etc. Most buildings, especially regarding roofs, require *flashings* or *copings*. Fixing *gutters*, *downpipes* and *sills* is usually also the work of a tinsmith.

10.1 Work progress

Roof plumbing work
Roof plumber

It is essential for a building to be watertight. In the roof area, *roofing felt* is installed to prevent the *penetration of moisture*. A vertical *damp proof course* (DPC) is usually applied around the base of the building using a *bituminous paint coat*.

Thermal insulation work

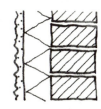

Insulation material is either fixed or installed in or on walls, ceilings and roofs to prevent heat loss. Vapour barriers are installed on the warm side of the insulation to prevent moisture developing.

Dry construction work
Dry construction builder

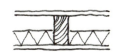

Dry construction builders fix *plasterboards* as internal linings. Their work includes preparatory measures such as erecting frames and *battens* to fix boards, installing insulation and vapour barriers, as well as decorative measures.

Floor screeding
Floor screeder

Screed is a layer of concrete or plaster is installed on top of the structural slab. Usually the mix is pumped into a specified area and levelled creating a smooth surface for floor coverings.

Plaster work
Plasterer

Generally gypsum-based plasters are applied to internal walls in order to create smooth and uniform surfaces.

Rendering
Renderer

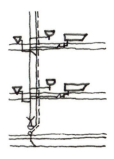

Render is applied to external walls. Usually cement-based materials are used to protect and smoothen brickwork.

Plumbing work
Plumber

Plumbing work involves all of the *pipework* within a building. This includes *water supply, discharge* and *drainage*, heating and gas. They also fit all *sanitary appliances* and radiators. Plumbing embraces a large area of work and most plumbers specialize in one specific field.

Electrical installations
Electrician

Electrical work includes the installation of electrical and electronic equipment for industrial, commercial and domestic purposes, such as *lighting, plugs, switches*, etc. Electricians are responsible for laying cables in buildings and connecting a *distribution board* to the main supply. Electricians have to work in stages, alternating their visits on site with plasterers, painters, etc.

Blacksmith's work
Blacksmith

A blacksmith creates objects from iron or steel by *forging* the metal, i.e. by using tools to hammer, bend, cut and shape metal. Blacksmiths create products such as *wrought iron* gates, grills, railings, etc.

Joinery work Joiner		Joinery work involves all tasks from fabricating to installing architectural woodwork. The building components can include doors, windows, stairs, wooden panelling, shop cabinets, kitchens, etc. The skills of a joiner are somewhere between a carpenter and a *cabinet maker*.
Tiling Tiler		A tiler sets tiles made of ceramic, stone or glass in mortar or uses a *tile adhesive* to arrange tiles on floors and walls. *Grout* is used to fill and seal the joints between the tiles.
Locksmith's work Locksmith		Locksmiths traditionally secure buildings with locking mechanisms. Today electronic lock services involve overall security systems of complex structures.
Glazing Glazier		The trade involves selecting, cutting, installing, replacing and removing glass. *Double-glazing* and *triple-glazing*, insulated glazing units with a hermetically sealed air spaces between the layers, have replaced *single glazing*. Glaziers work together with joiners in workshops, they also work on site installing *curtain walls*, glass floors, partitions, shelving, etc.
Painting and wall-papering work/ decorating Painter/decorator		Usually the decorating concludes all activities on site. The work includes painting, varnishing and wallpapering in order to protect and decorate interior and exterior surfaces.
Flooring Floor layer		Flooring is a general term for a permanent covering of a floor. It can refer to carpets, parquet, *raised flooring*, laminate and linoleum. The work of a floor layer also includes *levelling*, the installation of insulation and *skirting boards*.

10.1.2 Who does what?

According to the descriptions above, decide which tradesperson performs the work below.

1. They work with a *trowel* and are responsible for creating the shell of a building..............
2. They will be on site to fit *built-in wardrobes* in the bedrooms.   ……………………………..
3. When it comes to a roof conversion, they will erect dormers.   ……………………………..
4. They are responsible for wall and floor finishes in kitchens and bathrooms.   ………………
5. They use wet materials to prepare internal walls for painting.   ……………………………..
6. The owner commissions one to repair a *leak* in a flat roof.   ……………………..……..
7. They will produce and install a railing on a balcony.   ……………………………...
8. They work with *wire* and *pliers* to make the building *tension resistant*.   ………….....……..

10.2 Site meetings

The architect is responsible for arranging and *conducting* site meetings. Usually these take place at regular intervals, either on a weekly, *fortnightly* or monthly basis. It is an opportunity to bring all participants involved to the table in order to provide and exchange information, answer queries and *check actual against expected progress*. Site meetings are always *preceded* by site inspections. An inspection can, however, be carried out independent of site meetings.

Regular site meetings do not remove the need for telephone calls or correspondence, as most queries, which need answering immediately, arise between meetings. Meetings are known *to swallow up* a lot of expensive *manhours* and many people attending may only have an interest in a small part of the proceedings. Meetings should therefore be reserved for specific purposes and prepared carefully. It is useful to prepare an agenda and circulate it to participants before the meeting.

The *agenda* of a meeting will usually include the following:
- Record of all participants as well as *absentees*
- Acceptance of previous *minutes*
- Items arising from the previous *minutes*
- Progress related to programme
- Labour strength and materials required
- Drawings received or due
- *Financial review*
- Any other business
- Date of next meeting

Minutes should be taken at a meeting and copies should be sent to everyone concerned, the participants, absentees as well as the client. Minutes should be brief, recording decisions and not the, perhaps, endless discussions leading up to them. They should always include a column indicating the persons responsible for dealing with any action points.

One of the most important meetings during a project is the *pre-start meeting*. It should take place once the contract has been signed but before work commences. The aim of the meeting is to give everybody the opportunity to meet and hopefully form the beginning of a team. There will also be business matters to attend to, for example the *release of production information*, the construction programme and matters such as *insurance policies* and *bonds*.

10.2.1 Site inspection

The words inspection and *supervision* are often confused. An inspection, in this sense, is the work of an architect or a consultant. It involves visiting the site and checking that work completed and in progress is in accordance with the drawings and specifications. Progress against the construction programme will also be checked. Supervision is concerned with the monitoring of the workforce and includes giving instructions regarding the execution of work. Supervision is carried out by the contractor.

Once work has commenced, a site inspection usually precedes every site meeting. An inspection involves visual checks and taking notes, and possibly also carrying out tests. The architect should prepare for the site inspection, possibly by drawing up a list of items, which need to be inspected. These will be apparent from the construction programme, which also needs to be reviewed in terms of progress against timetable. It is wise for the architect to vary the times of inspections and inspect *at random* to avoid contractors covering up poor work.

Any defects identified or work, which does not meet the contract requirements, has to be pointed out and will need to be rectified. It is best to put any such matters in writing.

10.2.2 Dos and don'ts

Due to the architect's position and the importance of a good relationship between client and contractor, the behaviour of the architect as the client's representative should be *impeccable*. There are many aspects on site, which can be categorised as "dos and don'ts". Combine a beginning with an end of a sentence and decide whether the behaviour is appropriate or not.

				true	false
1.	The architect doesn't have to wear	a.	in order to give *devious* contractors time to cover up poor work.		
2.	Architects should look out for *infringements*	b.	a hard hat or any other protective clothing.		
3.	The architect should let the client	c.	of safety regulations.		
4.	It is wise to put all comments regarding defective work	d.	should be assessed in the office before answered.		
5.	Before leaving the site	e.	in writing.		
6.	Architects should always perform inspections at the same time	f.	the architect should make a few random inspections.		
7.	The architect should waste time	g.	with particular construction stages.		
8.	Complicated *queries* on site	h.	instruct builders directly.		
9.	Inspections don't have to *coincide*	i.	talking about the site agent's cold.		

10.3 Variations

A variation is an *alteration* or *modification* to the design, quantity or quality of the works compared to what is shown in the contract drawings and is described in the contract documents. A variation can result from a change in the client's requirements, revisions to the design by the architect or other design consultants, or can arise from construction activity on site. Variations can be both time-saving and more reasonable and *disruptive* and more expensive than the item in the *priced bill*. Architects will gladly accept cost and time-saving solutions so long as these do not reduce the quality of workmanship. Variations, which increase the construction period as well as the cost, need to be thought about very carefully before being authorised. Any variations requested by the client outside the tendered price have to be paid for by the client. The costs deriving from variations required due to a fault in the contractor's work are borne by the contractor.

10.3 Variations

Variations are generally subject to the architect's instructions or confirmation. A form, letter or even memo showing the date and basic details of the instruction signed by the architect is important to keep track of variations and their valuation. Depending on the degree of the variation, it might be covered by the contingency sum. Where an instruction involves something quite different, an estimate should be obtained from the contractor. Modified drawings clearly indicating the alteration need to be prepared and distributed to all persons affected by the change.

The bill rates form the key to the valuation of variations. Especially regarding the quantity, *omission* or addition, the rates and prices quoted in the priced bills apply. Fair prices, in line with those in the bills, should be quoted for all alterations. Variations, which cannot be valued by measurement, are usually valued as daywork. *Daywork sheets* have to be delivered for verification at regular intervals, usually on a weekly basis.

10.3.1 Alteration

For slightly more elaborate alterations, the normal procedure is for the architect to approach the contractor and ask for a quote. Once the price offered is approved by the client, a *variation order* drawn up by the architect on behalf of the client is submitted to the contractor.

Here, the client, George Smith, requests the architect to add a further window on the ground floor. The architect sends a fax with the request and a drawing to the site office where it can receive the immediate attention of the contractor. A follow-up phone call will ensure matters are sorted out promptly.

Tim Smith & Partners

Fax to John White

Hello John,

The client, George Smith, paid a visit to the site at the weekend and contacted me requesting an additional window in the dining room. I know that you have almost completed the exterior walls on the first floor and are getting ready to put in the roof slab, and I explained as much to our client. He is aware of the additional costs and understands that he will be giving up valuable wall space, but regards extra light as having greater value – he is very insistent regarding this change. Could you please take a look at the drawing attached and quote a price for the alteration. It is, of course, quite urgent, as the windows are due be fitted. As soon as the client has approved the additional costs, I will release an official variation order.

I would be grateful if you could see to this immediately. Thanks for your help.

Regards

Tim Smith

Encl: Extract from ground floor plan showing additional window in dining room.

10.3.2 Cause and effect

If you take another look at the letter, you will come across events which have a knock-on effect, for example the visit George Brown pays to the site followed by the request for an additional window, or the windows which are due to be fitted leading to the urgency expressed in the fax. The relationship between two aspects, dependent on or responsible for one another, is called cause and effect. Sentence connectors are used to express these relationships and to combine clauses.

There are many possibilities to express cause and effect. The intention of the following section is to point out the differences and the varieties, which help to make expressions and speech more appropriate and accurate.

Example: As a result of the client's visit to the site, a further window is to be added to the dining room.

The cause is the client's visit to the site; the effect is the additional window. The sentence connector chosen here is "as a result of". There are numerous sentence connectors, which can be used to express a cause/effect relationship.

- Verb and verb phrases:
  <u>The bad weather</u>   <u>is responsible</u>   <u>for the delay</u>.
     cause   verb link   effect
  Alternative verb links with a similar meaning:
  to account for, to result in, to bring about, *to give rise to*, to lead to, etc.

  It is also possible to reverse the elements of the sentence above:
  <u>The delay</u>   <u>stems from</u>   <u>the bad weather</u>.
    effect   verb link   cause
  Alternative verb links with a similar meaning:
  to arise from, to result from, *to be attributable to*, etc.

- Clauses of cause:
  <u>The contractor selected an alternative material</u>   <u>because</u>   <u>the tender item was not available</u>.
                          effect   conjunction   cause
  A subordinating conjunction links the effect and cause clauses.
  Alternative subordinating conjunctions are:
  as, since, etc.

- Phrases of cause:
  <u>Due to the delayed delivery of supplies,</u>   <u>operations on site are behind schedule</u>.
               cause   effect
  In this case, an adverb phrase introduces the cause.
  Alternative expressions with a similar meanings are:
  as a result of, because of, on account of, owing to, etc.

When an adverb clause begins the sentence, use a comma to separate the two clauses. When the adverb clause finishes the sentence, there is no need for a comma.

Example: The operations on site are behind schedule due to the delayed arrival of supplies.

10.3.3 Exercise: Cause and effect

Enter the following words into the text below. Make sure to use the correct verb form.

> as a result of · to lead to · to be attributable to · to bring about · owing to · due to
> not to give rise to · since

In addition to the extra window in the dining room, the client also requested a second washbasin in the family bathroom. A visit to a friends house ……...………. this idea. …….….……. the already spacious layout of the bathroom, this request was fairly easy to fulfil. ……..………. the variation, the architect had to draw a new plan showing the modification. ………..………. the sanitary appliances had not yet been ordered, the additional washbasin caused no delays. A mistake in the *door schedule* ……..………. a slight delay. The mistake …….…………. the architect, who noted a wrong number in the contract documents. …….………. the speedy reaction of the joiner on site, the correct door was delivered quickly and the mistake ………….….…… any delays.

10.4 Project diary

No matter how big or small the project, a project diary is a good way of keeping track of site activities. It is quite normal for building sites to receive frequent telephone calls, faxes, deliveries, etc. Even though some things may seem insignificant at the time, they may turn out to be relevant later on in the project. Our human memory is *fallible* and, if not *jotted down*, trivial matters, which may turn out to be critical at a later date, are simply forgotten. A few minutes is all that it takes to write down the main events of the day, while the memory is still fresh.

The project diary should include anything that could affect completion, cost and workmanship. The diary should include a list of all persons present on site and their accomplished work. A note should be made of deliveries, phone calls and not to be forgotten the weather. A *notice of obstruction* filed by a contractor can easily be evaluated if a project diary is kept.

Even though the diary is personal and not part of the contract documents, it may be a valuable source of information in the case of legal disputes. It is not the style of writing, but the facts contained in the writing that are important. It merely has to be legible. Nowadays software packages offer note pads to keep track of daily events.

10.5 Ceremonies

There are three ceremonies that are traditionally associated with new buildings and which most clients like to *perpetuate*. The first to take place is the laying of the *foundation stone*, the second is the *topping-out ceremony* and the third, marking the completion of the building, is the *opening ceremony*.

Foundation stone: The ceremony is conducted to mark the beginning of construction work and record the building's development for *posterity*. The foundation stone often has a cavity containing a time capsule holding objects appropriate to the occasion and the building, such as a newspaper of the day, a coin, etc. The stone normally carries an *inscription* of who laid the stone and when.

Nowadays the event takes place later than the foundation stage, once there is enough evidence of building work, which can function as a stage for the ceremony. The stone is then placed in a visible position in a course of stones or bricks above the actual foundations. The foundation stone laying effectively becomes a corner stone ceremony. It is a client's event and, depending on the importance of the building, a celebrity or a political figure may be invited to place the stone and tap it into place.

Topping out: Whereas foundation stones have been found in ancient buildings, the origins of the topping out ceremony seem to be lost in history. However, it is a ceremony performed all over the world and is associated with the fixing of the topmost stone or beam to a building. Usually a fir tree or some evergreen is hoisted to the topmost structural element and a toast is drunk by everyone on site to celebrate the completion of the building structure. In practical terms, it defines the point at which the client is able to thank and pay his/her respect to those who have actually been involved in the construction of the building.

Opening ceremony: If the client has an opening ceremony, it will usually be some time after occupation, when the building is looking clean, trim and in good working order. Generally the client has lived with the construction site since the commencement date and, despite defects, misunderstandings and *teething troubles*, most probably feels part of the achievement. The opening ceremony declares and confirms the client as the owner of the building. Depending on the size of the event, it may include a description of the design, the planning and construction process as well as the credits, a list recognising the contribution of everybody involved in the project.

10.6 Vocabulary

10.1	work progress	Baufortschritt
	tradesperson, pl tradespeople; also tradesman, pl tradesmen and tradeswoman, pl tradeswomen	Handwerker/in
	construction site sign	Bau(stellen)tafel
	obstruction	Behinderung
10.1.1	trade	Gewerk
	building process	Bauprozess
	excavation work	Aushubarbeiten
	profile boards	Schnurgerüst
	excavator	Bagger
	pit	Baugrube
	spoil heap	Aushublagerhaufen
	concrete work	Betonarbeiten
	formwork	Schalung, Schalarbeit

10.6 Vocabulary

to cure concrete	nachbehandeln (von Beton), abbinden
impermeability	Undurchlässigkeit, Dichtheit
in-situ concrete	Ortbeton
formwork	Schalung
exposed concrete	Sichtbeton
sliding formwork	Gleitschalung
permanent formwork	verlorene Schalung
striking time	Ausschalzeit
reinforcement	Bewehrung
steelfixer	Betonstahlverleger, Eisenflechter
barspacer	Abstandshalter für Betondeckung
concrete cover	Betonüberdeckung
structural steelwork	Stahlbauarbeiten
steel erector	Stahlbauer
brickwork	Mauerwerk
mason	Maurer
mortar	Mörtel
stretcher	Läufer
header	Binder
English bond	Blockverband
face brickwork	Verblendmauerwerk
to point	auskratzen und ausfugen (Mörtelfuge)
cavity wall	zweischaliges Mauerwerk
timberwork	Zimmerarbeit
carpenter	Zimmerer, Zimmermann
purlin	Pfette
rafter	Sparren
roofing	Dach(ein)deckung
roofer	Dachdecker
watertight	wasserdicht, -undurchlässig
waterproofing	Abdichtung
vapour barrier	Dampfbremse, Dampfsperre
sheet metal work	Metalldacharbeiten
tinsmith, sheet metal worker	(Bau-)Spengler
flashing	Spritzblech
coping	Mauerabdeckung
gutter	Rinne
downpipe	Fallrohr
sill	Fensterblech
roof plumbing work	Dachklempnerarbeit
roof plumber	Dachklempner

roofing felt	Dachpappe
penetration of moisture	Eindringung von Feuchtigkeit
damp proof course (DPC)	Feuchtigkeitssperre
bituminous paint coat	Bitumenanstrich
thermal insulation work	Dämmarbeiten
dry construction work	Trockenbauarbeiten
dry construction builder	Trockenbaumonteur
plasterboard	Gipskartonplatte
batten	Latte
floor screeding	Estricharbeiten
floor screeder	Estrichleger
plaster work	Putzarbeiten
plasterer	Putzer
rendering	Außenputzarbeit
render	Außenputz
plumbing work	Sanitärinstallation
plumber	Sanitärinstallateur, Klempner
pipework	Leitungs- u. Rohrverlegearbeit
water supply	Wasserversorgung
discharge	Schmutzwasser
drainage	Kanalisation
sanitary appliance	Sanitärobjekt
electrical installation	Elektroinstallation
electrician	Elektriker
lighting	Beleuchtung
plug	Steckdose
switch	Schalter
distribution board	Verteiler
blacksmith's work	Schmiedearbeit
blacksmith	Schmied
to forge	schmieden
wrought iron	Schmiedeeisen
joinery work	Bauschreinerarbeit
joiner	Bauschreiner
cabinet maker	Möbelschreiner
tiling	Fliesenlegearbeit
tiler	Fliesenleger
tile adhesive	Fliesenkleber
grout	Vergussmörtel
locksmith's work	(Bau-)Schlosserarbeit
locksmith	Bauschlosser

	glazing work	Glaserarbeit
	glazier	Glaser
	single, double, triple glazing	einfach, zweifach, dreifach Verglasung
	curtain wall	Vorhangfassade
	painting and wallpapering work, decorating	Maler- u. Tapezierarbeiten
	decorator	Maler
	to varnish	lackieren
	flooring	Bodenbelagsarbeit
	floor layer	Bodenleger
	raised flooring	aufgeständerter (Fuß-)Boden
	to level	ausgleichen, glätten
	skirting board	Sockelleiste
10.1.2	trowel	(Maurer-)Kelle
	built-in wardrobe	Einbauschrank für Kleidung
	leak	undichte Stelle, Leck
	wire	Draht
	pliers	Beißzange
	tension resistant	zugfest
10.2	site meeting	Baustellenbesprechung
	to conduct a meeting	eine Besprechung führen
	fortnightly	vierzehntägig, zweiwöchentlich
	to check actual against expected progress	Ist- u. Sollfortschritt gegenüberstellen
	to precede	vorangehen
	to swallow up	schlucken
	manhour	Arbeitsstunde
	agenda	Tagesordnung
	absentee	Abwesende/r
	minutes	Protokoll
	financial review	finanzielle Prüfung
	pre-start meeting	Vorbesprechung
	release of production information	Freigabe der Ausführungspläne
	insurance policy	Versicherungsschein
	bond	Bürgschaft
10.2.1	site inspection	Baustellenbesichtigung, -begehung
	supervision	Bauüberwachung
	at random	stichprobenartig
10.2.2	impeccable	makellos, tadellos
	infringement	Verletzung (der Vertragspflicht)
	query, pl queries	Anfrage
	to coincide	zeitlich zusammenfallen
	devious adj	verschlagen, hinterhältig

10.3		variation	Bauvertragsänderung
		alteration, modification	Änderung, Abwandlung
		disruptive adj	störend
		priced bill	ausgefülltes Leistungsverzeichnis
		omission	Auslassung, Wegfall
		daywork sheet	Stundenlohnzettel
10.3.1		variation order	Bauänderungsanweisung, Änderungsauftrag
10.3.2		cause and effect	Ursache und Folge
		to give rise to	führen zu, Anlass geben zu
		to be attributable to	jmdm. zuzuschreiben sein
10.3.3		door schedule	Türliste
10.4		project diary	Bautagebuch
		fallible adj	fehlbar
		to jot down sth	rasche Notizen machen
		notice of obstruction	Behinderungsanzeige
10.5		to perpetuate	aufrechterhalten
		foundation stone	Grundstein
		topping-out ceremony	Richtfest
		opening ceremony	Eröffnungsfeier
		posterity	Nachwelt
		inscription	Inschrift
		teething troubles fig	Anlaufschwierigkeiten

11 Completion

11.1 Completion stage

The completion stage is a significant phase in the course of a project. After months, sometimes even years, of construction work, the building, which was originally developed on paper, finally appears in its true dimensions. The client, who relied on the architect's competence to transform the contents of the brief, is now able to experience the completed building. The contractor, who took possession of the site to perform the work, hands it back to the client.

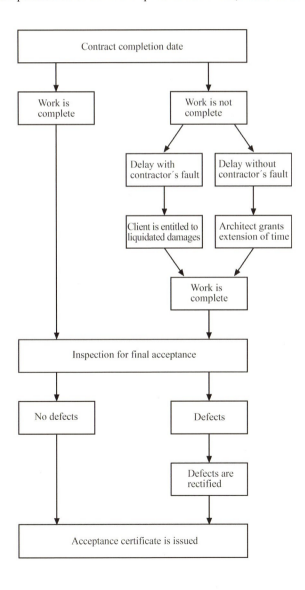

Despite the festive character of this phase, it is also one governed by *inspections*, *certificates* and *payments*. Furthermore, it is not always one which is completed in agreement, but one which may end up in disagreement and *legal disputes*. For this reason, it is absolutely necessary for all parties to *adhere* to their contractual obligations and to do their best to avoid expensive and time-consuming *lawsuits*.

The diagram above shows the various phases of completion. The process is similar throughout the world. The number of certificates, however, varies as does the length and the character of the *defects liability period*.

11.2 Delays

There are few businesses for which the saying "time is money" is more appropriate than the construction industry. Construction work is extremely time sensitive. Construction contracts specify the sum of money due for the work and the period in which the work must be undertaken. The contract agreements therefore show a commencement and completion date or an *anticipated construction period*. In both cases, a contract completion date is established. Failure to meet dates specified is a *breach of contract*. Whereas the client loses opportunities and profit in waiting for completion of delayed projects, the contractor carries the *financial burden* of running the site beyond the date anticipated at tendering stage.

In many cases and for numerous reasons, jobs *overrun* and finish on a later date than originally agreed. This later date is then the *actual contract completion date*. Most contracts provide a buffer and grant the architect the power to extend the original contract completion date. If the cause for the delay is not the contractor's fault, the architect will allow an extension of time. A new contract completion date is fixed, and the threat to the contractor of liquidated damages being implemented is lifted for the extended period.

If the contractor is responsible for the delay and an extension of time is not awarded, the contractor is in *culpable delay* and *liable for damages*. In this case the client is entitled to deduct *liquidated and ascertained damages* (LADs) from moneys otherwise payable to the contractor for every day the contractor fails to meet the completion date. The rate, which is stated in the contract, is the amount the contractor agreed to pay the client to cover *losses*, *expenses* and *damages* up until completion.

Events which would usually allow an extension of time:

- Variations
- *Deferment of possession*
- Inaccurate forecast of quantities
- *Suspension* of contractor's obligations
- *Impediment*, *prevention* or *default* on behalf of the client
- Delays resulting from other trades not completing on schedule
- Exceptional weather conditions
- Loss or damage caused by *perils*, such as fire
- Civil commotion
- Strikes
- *Force majeure*

11.2.2 Extension of time

During the construction of George Brown's single-family home, several events outside the contractor's control gave rise to delay. Read the e-mail from the contractor to the architect. Which of the following suggestions is the most appropriate subject line?

- Nearly finished
- Request for extension of time
- Too many changes have caused delays

Dear Tim,

As you are most probably aware, the building will not be in a satisfactory state and ready for handover on the completion date. Too many unforeseen events have prevented work from progressing according to schedule.

As a reminder these were:

- Torrential rainfall in week 12 preventing us from pouring concrete
- Misestimate of required insulation material
- Obstruction caused by tiling company

Despite having two extra men on site, we are still approximately four days behind schedule. For this reason, I would like to request an extension of time and postpone our site meeting for the inspection by one week. The extra time will allow us to complete all outstanding work and hand-over the building to the client in a tidy and finished state.

Please inform the client, and let us know whether our request has been granted. A detailed report is attached.

I look forward to hearing from you.

Best wishes

John White

11.2.3 Collocations

A collocation is an expression in which words are habitually combined. Some words sit together well and sound very natural in speech and script, whereas combinations using other words with similar meanings, can sound quite awkward and unnatural.

There are different patterns of collocations:

- verb + noun: e.g. to accept responsibility
- adverb + verb: e.g. to strongly suggest
- adverb + adjective: e.g. completely useless
- noun + noun: e.g. window frame
- verb + adjective + noun: e.g. to make steady progress

 Before continuing with this section, take another look at the e-mail in 11.2.2 and underline the collocations. Which patterns do they follow?

Identify the following verb + noun collocations which commonly appear in everyday business situations.

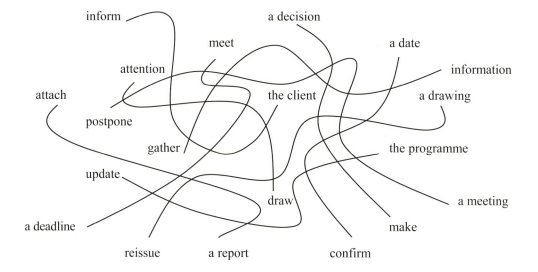

11.3 Acceptance

Acceptance is the task of inspecting and approving work performed on site. It is a process which takes place at various stages during the course of a project. As soon as an operation has been completed, the tradesperson who undertook the work requests formal acceptance in order to leave the site and receive payment. It would not be appropriate to have a company wait until the final completion date. Furthermore, some work needs to be accepted before it is covered up by other work. One example would be the acceptance of the reinforcing steel before the concrete is poured.

The inspection for *final acceptance* is, in a sense, the most important because it not only marks the completion of construction work, but also the *hand-over* to the client. For the final acceptance, the building should be in a state ready for *occupation* by the client without *inconvenience*. There are conflicting views regarding the meaning of completion. It certainly does not have to be certified simply because the client has occupied the building or the contractor is trying to meet the completion date stipulated in the contract without the liquidated damages clause being *invoked*.

A date for the final inspection is arranged once completion is imminent. The final inspection focuses on the correct operation of all equipment, completion and state of all *finishes* and the recording of defective or *omitted* items. The purpose is not one of catching up on points noted or missed at regular site inspections, although some of these may be open issues recorded at final inspection. All items, either incomplete or requiring *remedial work*, are then put on the so-called *snagging list*.

Depending on the extent or significance of remedial work, the client may have to decide whether he/she is prepared to receive the building in an incomplete state, or whether to fix a new date for a second acceptance. In both cases, the contractor is responsible for performing the remedial work, however, in the second case, the client may be entitled to liquidated and ascertained damages.

If the client wishes to take possession and move in before completion has been achieved, he/she may, in agreement with the contractor, be granted *partial possession*, which must be clearly documented. Some contracts incorporate provisions for *sectional completion*. In this case the client does not take over the entire building at one time, but in several phases. The same clauses regarding liquidated damages, liability periods, retention sums etc. apply to each section in the same way as they do for the full completion.

11.3.1 Acceptance certificate

The acceptance certificate, also referred to as taking-over certificate, is formal evidence of the architect's opinion regarding his/her satisfaction that the works are in accord with the contract with no obvious defects.

The acceptance certificate marks the end of the construction phase and the beginning of the defects liability period. It is the transfer from the contractor to the client and the date from which the client must undertake insurances.

The acceptance certificate marks an important stage and the contractor will be anxious to receive it for the following reasons:

- The contractor's liability for damage to the works ends.
- The contractor's *liability insurance* expires.
- The danger of liquidated damages being invoked no longer exists.
- Part of the *retention* is released.
- A *final invoice* can be drawn up.

It is general practice either during or after the inspection at completion to hand over the keys and all *maintenance manuals* to the client. The client should also receive a full set of the *as-built drawings* together with information regarding construction materials, *user instructions* for technical equipment, possible contact numbers, etc.

11.3.2 International differences

British building legislation, which has been adopted in the FIDIC conditions, provides for the acceptance of construction work being performed in two stages. Once work has been completed and an acceptance certificate issued, the *care for the works is transferred* to the client. The certificate marks the beginning of the *defects notification period*, the first half of the retention monies is released and the contractor prepares a *provisional final invoice*.

After a period of 6 months or 365 days and once all the defects have been remedied, a second certificate, the *performance certificate,* is issued. The second half of the retention monies is released, and the contractor prepares the final invoice. The performance certificate marks the *completion of the contract*, which, however, does not mean the *elimination of contractual obligations*. Any matters arising after issuing the performance certificate are covered by *statutory defects liability* clauses. In many countries, the date of the performance certificate is the commencement date for *decennial liability* under civil law. During what is usually a 10-year period, the contractor is liable for any hidden defects. This excludes damage resulting from *extraneous events* or *wear and tear*.

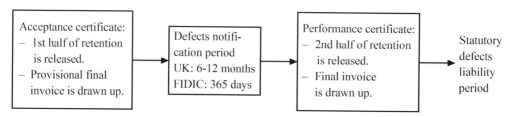

11.4 Remedial work

Remedial work includes all operations taking place on site after final acceptance and after the building has been handed over to the client. The contractor is obliged to perform all outstanding work, remedy the defects noted on the snagging list as well as see to all defects which appear after having left the site and cannot be categorised as maintenance caused by ordinary wear and tear.

It is the contractor's contractual obligation to perform the remedial work at his/her own cost within the determined period. If the contractor fails to perform the work within the specified timescale, the client is entitled to engage another contractor to make good the defects. All costs incurred are deducted from the *outstanding retention*.

Exercise: Remedial work

Having settled into the building, the client contacts the architect to talk about a number of items, which need to be taken care of. Decide which of these items are maintenance and which ones are defects requiring remedial work.

1. *Skirting board* has come away from the wall
2. Broken tile in the bathroom
3. No *logs* for open fireplace
4. Kitchen door scrapes floor
5. *Leak* in flat roof over garage
6. Red wine *stain* on *parquet flooring*
7. Dirty fingerprints on walls
8. *Tilt-turn window* only turns, doesn't tilt
9. *Flush plate* still missing in utility room

11.5 Payment procedures

All *payment conditions* are laid down in the contract. The terms and conditions determine whether payments are to be made at a set date or according to progress. In case of a *lump sum contract*, the dates for *instalments* are agreed in the contract. *Progress payments*, also called *interim payments*, refer to a completed activity or a particular stage or *percentage* of work. Progress payments are subject to adjustment depending on whether the contractor is ahead or behind schedule. A *payment schedule* clearly indicates when payments are due.

Independent of the payment conditions, all *invoices* prepared by contractors include a *measurement sheet*, assigning quantities to the completed work. *Unfixed materials* can be included. Unfixed materials are either items already delivered to site, but not yet fixed, or materials off-site, ready to be included in the works, e.g. pre-cast concrete elements, windows, etc. The contractor sends the invoice and all other necessary documents to the architect. The architect checks the invoice and defines the amount due in a *payment certificate*, which is then forwarded to the client.

It is the architect's task to certify the amounts due and keep track of the overall construction costs. The payment certificates include the value of work properly executed and the unfixed materials, less a percentage to be held back, which is known as the retention sum. If unsure about the valuation, the architect may request further information from the contractor or pay a visit to the site specifically to check items listed on the invoice. It is helpful if the architect and the contractor agree on the final figure. If this is not the case, the client has to be informed accordingly. All items paid for become part of the client's possession.

If the client fails to pay the requested amount within the period specified in the certificate, the contractor is entitled to *interest* on the amount *in default*.

11.5.1 Final statement

The final statement is an itemised list of construction work, which should take into account all variations agreed during the period of the contract. It sets the original provisional sums or prime cost assessments against the actual sums and includes all information provided by the contractor, which the architect, or, if commissioned, the quantity surveyor, carefully checks beforehand. It should present a complete picture of the financial situation for the project as a whole. The quantity surveyor, if appointed, is responsible for preparing the final statement according to the information received from the architect. However, since the architect is much more closely involved, the final statement should not be left entirely up to the quantity surveyor but checked carefully by the architect.

The final statement should not be a surprise to the client. It is the architect's responsibility to keep the client up-to-date throughout the contract. The client should be aware that most changes result in extra cost. As mentioned earlier, the architect is not entitled to instruct variations involving extra cost without prior agreement of the client.

11.5.2 Retention

Retention is a percentage of monies owed to the contractor for work performed. It serves as security for later work stages through until completion of a project. The retention monies are held until all defects are remedied and work is completed to the satisfaction of the client and the architect. In the event of the client's default or *bankruptcy*, the monies become available to pay off the contractor.

Every invoice shows the amount to be held back or retained. The sum, usually ranging from 5% to a maximum of 10% of the building costs, is released in two stages. The first half of the retention is released as soon as the acceptance certificate has been issued. In Germany, the second half is released after the defects liability period has elapsed. Contracts incorporating the VOB guidelines allow for a period of 4 years; the *Civil Code (BGB)* grants a period of 5 years. In the UK, the second half of the retention monies is released once the performance certificate has been issued i.e. 6 or 12 months after the acceptance certificate was issued.

The retention monies have to be set-aside in a separate account in the joint names of the client and the contractor. The contractor can achieve the release of retention monies by providing a *surety bond* as security.

If the contractor fails to fulfil his/her contractual obligations and make good the defects identified during the defects liability period within a reasonable time, the client may engage others to do the work and charge the full cost to the original contractor. The costs for the remedial work would then be deducted from the retention fund.

11.5.3 Fee calculation

The fees are the costs for professional services provided during the course of a project. Since fees are usually a percentage of the *actual construction costs* (see section 3.3), the architect and other consultants cannot perform their fee calculations until the costs have been determined in the final statement. The fee statement should describe all stages through which the contract has passed, list all *interim accounts* and include all *outstanding expenses*. The final account for fees represents the completion of the services to the client.

Any information of interest to the client, such as maintenance information, as-built drawings or photographs, should be handed over to the client at this point. It may also be necessary to inform the client about copyright in connection with the building's *artistic merit* and any drawings. Copyright remains with the originator for his or her lifetime and for 50 years thereafter.

11.5.4 Lexis: Payments

Match the terms on the left with the correct definition on the right.

1.	unfixed materials	a.	a certificate usually issued by a bank as a guarantee for the client in case the contractor fails to fulfil the contractual obligations
2.	measurement sheet	b.	an amount of money due to the architect and other consultants for their professional services
3.	retention	c.	items manufactured and/or supplied, but not yet installed
4.	instalment	d.	a document listing the prices charged for providing a service
5.	surety bond	e.	to subtract or take away an amount
6.	invoice	f.	a payment for a stage or percentage of work completed

7.	final statement	g.	money spent in connection with the supply of services, e.g. travel
8.	to deduct	h.	a document or diagram showing the quantities of completed works
9.	fee	i.	a list of the actual building costs drawn up after the acceptance certificate is issued
10.	expenses	j.	a percentage of a payment withheld as a security

11.6 Vocabulary

11	completion	Fertigstellung
11.1	delay	Verzögerung, Verzug
	with/without fault	mit/ohne Verschulden
	to be entitled to liquidated damages	Anspruch haben auf vertraglich festgesetzte Schadenssumme
	extension of time	Bauzeitverlängerung
	inspection for final completion	Besichtigung zur Endabnahme
	defect	Mangel
	acceptance certificate	Abnahmebescheinigung
	inspection	Kontrolle, Überwachung
	certificate	Bescheinigung
	payment	Zahlung
	legal dispute	Rechtsstreitigkeit
	to adhere to sth	befolgen
	lawsuit	Prozess, Klage
	defects liability period	Gewährleistungsfrist, Mängelhaftungszeitraum
11.2	anticipated construction period	vorgesehene Bauzeit
	breach of contract	Vertragsverletzung, -bruch
	financial burden	finanzielle Last
	to overrun	überschreiten
	actual contract completion date	tatsächlicher Fertigstellungszeitpunkt
	culpable delay	schuldhafter Verzug
	to be liable for damages	schadensersatzpflichtig
	liquidated and ascertained damages	Verzögerungsschadensersatz
	losses	Verlust
	expenses	Kostenaufwand, Auslagen
	damages	Entschädigung

	deferment of possession	Verzögerung der Übergabe an den Auftragnehmer
	suspension	Aufschub
	impediment	Behinderung
	prevention	Verhinderung
	default	Versäumnis
	peril	Gefahr
	force majeure	Höhere Gewalt
11.2.2	misestimate	Fehlkalkulation
	obstruction	Behinderung
11.3	acceptance	Abnahme
	final acceptance	Endabnahme
	hand-over	Übergabe
	occupation	Besitznahme
	inconvenience	Unannehmlichkeit
	to invoke	anrufen
	finishes	Oberflächengestaltung, -ausführung
	to omit	auslassen, weglassen
	remedial work	Nachbesserungsarbeiten
	snagging list	Mängelliste
	partial possession	teilweise Inbesitznahme
	sectional completion	Fertigstellung in Bauabschnitten
11.3.1	liability insurance	Haftpflichtversicherung
	retention	einbehaltener Betrag, Einbehalt
	final invoice	Schlussrechnung
	maintenance manual	Wartungshandbuch
	as-built drawings	Bestandspläne
	user instructions	Gebrauchsanleitung
11.3.2	to transfer the care for the works	Gefahrenübergang
	defects notification period	Mängelanzeigefrist
	provisional final invoice	vorläufige Schlussrechnung
	performance certificate	Erfüllungsbescheinigung
	completion of the contract	Vertragserfüllung
	elimination of contractual obligations	Erlöschung der Vertragspflicht
	statutory defects liability	gesetzliche Gewährleistung
	decennial liability	zehnjährige Haftung
	extraneous events	Fremdeinwirkung
	wear and tear	Verschleiß, Abnutzung
11.4	outstanding retention	ausstehender Einbehalt
11.4.1	skirting board	Sockelleiste
	logs	Brennholz

11.6 Vocabulary

	English	German
	leak	undichte stelle, Leck
	stain	Fleck, Verfärbung
	parquet flooring	Parkettboden
	tilt-turn window	Drehkippfenster
	flush plate	(Schalter-)Abdeckplatte
11.5	payment conditions	Zahlungsbedingungen
	lump sum contract	Pauschalvertrag
	instalment	Rate, Zwischenzahlung
	progress payment, interim payment	Abschlagszahlung, Zahlung nach Leistungsabschnitten
	payment schedule	Zahlungsplan
	percentage	prozentualer Anteil
	invoice	Rechnung
	measurement sheet	Aufmassblatt
	unfixed material	noch nicht eingebaute Materialien
	payment certificate	Zahlungsbescheinigung
	interest	Zinsen
	to be in default	in Verzug sein
11.5.1	final statement	Schlussrechnung
11.5.2	bankruptcy	Konkurs
	Civil Code	BGB, Bürgerliches Gesetzbuch
	surety bond	Bürgschaft
11.5.3	fee calculation	Honorarberechnung
	actual building construction costs	tatsächlichen Baukosten
	interim accounts	Zwischenabrechnung
	outstanding expenses	ausstehende Ausgaben
	artistic merit	künstlerischer Verdienst

12 Education, registration and more

12.1 Education

The word architect is derived from the Greek word "arch" meaning chief and the word "teckton" meaning carpenter or builder. As the roots imply the architect is a master builder, or one might refer to him/her as being the leader of a construction team. Architects are not only responsible for designing a building but also for managing its realisation. It follows that architects require theoretical as well as practical knowledge, which is acquired through a combination of academic education and professional training.

Qualification as an architect requires *enrolment* in an academic programme and *practice-based training*. Universities and Universities of Applied Sciences offer a variety of programmes with differing emphases, durations and requirements. In order *to enrol* in architectural courses, the applicant has to have completed *secondary education* to the requisite standard.

The Bologna Agreement, signed in June 1999, introduced the European Higher Education Area (EHEA) aimed at *increasing competitiveness* between European universities and adopting a system with comparable *degrees*. The system comprises three cycles, Bachelor, Masters and Doctorate. Depending on the emphasis of the course, either a Master of Arts (MA or M.A.), Master of Science (MSc or M.Sc.) or a Master of Engineering (MEng or M.Eng.) is awarded on completion. The same titles and abbreviations apply to Bachelor degrees.

A system of academic credits was introduced to make achievements at European universities comparable and to make it easier to transfer between universities, including those abroad. The European Credit Transfer System (ECTS) awards *credit points* to students who successfully complete modules, seminars, workshops, examinations, etc. A full-time student can receive a maximum of 60 credits per year. The credits reflect the quantity of work required to achieve the objective. Most university homepages and brochures list modules with the number of credits they are worth. The performance of students is documented by *grades*. Grades range from A (very good) to F, which is a fail.

The website of the European Commission www.ec.europa.eu offers information regarding education and programmes.

12.1.1 Studying architecture in Germany

In Germany applicants need either Abitur or Fachabitur to enrol at a university. They must apply directly to the university and their admission is subject to *passing an aptitude test*, which is aimed at evaluating their talent and enthusiasm for the profession. Courses in Germany are numerous and differ greatly with regard to the number of semesters. There is, however, a clear leaning towards the internationally recognised Bachelor/Master courses.

The possibilities currently offered in Germany are:

- *Degree courses* at Universities of Applied Science incorporating 8 semesters, usually with an integrated practical semester, lead to the German title of Diplomingenieur (certified engineer). These courses are gradually being replaced by the internationally recognised Bachelor and Masters programmes.

- *Traditional* University courses, which are usually less practical than the courses at Universities of Applied Sciences, can be completed in 10 to 12 semesters and generally consist of a basic and an advanced course. Work experience in a construction-related profession is required before and/or during the course. A *thesis* has to be completed in the last semester. The title awarded on completion is still Diplomingenieur (certified engineer). Universities are also in the process of reforming their courses and introducing Bachelor and Masters programmes in line with the Bologna Agreement. A Doctorate can be obtained by spending further semesters at a University and compiling an additional, more extensive, doctoral thesis.

- Bachelor courses incorporate at least 6 semesters. The degree enables graduates to start work in the construction industry at a younger age and, if they wish, to continue on a Masters *degree* course after the compulsory 1-year work experience.
  The difference between a Bachelor course at a University and a Bachelor course at a University of Applied Science is the focus. Whereas the teaching and research focus at a University of Applied Science is on, as the name applies, the practical application of science, a University focuses on scientific studies.

- Masters courses require a good Bachelor degree and at least 1 year of practical experience. They *incorporate* 4 semesters at the end of which the students compile a thesis. Most Masters courses are offered as part-time programmes, which enable students to continue their professional careers.
  There are many different Masters courses to choose from. Some are oriented towards management, while others lean towards construction. The compulsory period of work experience – one year or more – is usually sufficient to give postgraduates a clear idea of their strengths and interests and provide guidance as to the most suitable course to follow.

12.1.2 Studying architecture in the UK

In the UK there are two routes to become a qualified architect:
- A full-time *education* and training programme
- A practice-based *education* and training

The full-time education is comparable with the Bachelor and Masters courses now offered in Germany. Universities offer sandwich courses, which include a 3-year Bachelor course followed by a year of practical training. For those pursuing the Masters course, studies continue with a two-year *postgraduate course*, which is then followed by a further year of practical training. The Masters course concludes with a final examination.

Practice-based education is a combination of practical training in an office and short academic programmes. This method suits those who cannot engage in full-time education and those looking for a more practical approach. The time factor attached to this route can be a disadvantage. On the other hand, the income from the employment compensates for the extended training period. Students selecting this route still have to go through the three phases applicable to full-time students. Job advertisements often indicate whether a company is looking for a registered or senior architect, a Part 1, Part 2 or Part 3 architect, which means that the stage reached in one's studies is very relevant for those seeking new positions.

12.1.3 Exchange programmes

There is more to studying today than just visiting *lectures* and participating in workshops at the local university. International mobility is recognised as an important attribute for a successful career and anything that helps to build international experience can be of enormous value. The facility to interrupt a course for a semester or more can provide an excellent opportunity to travel abroad to gain work experience or to participate in a language course. Both can pay dividends in the later career.

The changes across Europe brought about by the Bologna Agreement, which is aimed at making European higher education programmes more comparable, enable students to interrupt a course and enrol at another University without losing time. The European credit point system (ECTS) allows students to accumulate credits independent of their location.

Exchange programmes encourage the mobility of students worldwide. Programmes such as Erasmus, which stands for European Action Scheme for the Mobility of University Students, was introduced in 1987 to enable students to continue their studies while spending time abroad. For more information see www.erasmus.ac.uk or www.daad.de.

12.2 Registration

Successful completion of studies does not automatically grant the right to practise as an architect and use the title. Architect is a *registered profession* and the title is protected. Although in theory, the role of an architect can be carried out by anyone, use of the title is restricted to those registered according to the applicable regulations. Any person who publicly uses the title and is not qualified to do so can be sanctioned or *prosecuted* by the responsible body.

In Germany, applications for registration are made to the Federal Chamber of Architects in the land where the applicant is resident. Applicants must have passed the final examination at a school of architecture and provide proof of two years' experience working as an architect.

In the United Kingdom persons wishing to use the title architect have to apply to the Architects Registration Board (ARB). The website of the Architects Registration Board (ARB) www.arb.org.uk offers information concerning registration. There is also the possibility to contact them directly with any questions.

12.2.1 Practising architecture in the UK

Most German graduates have a very good command of English, which is of course helpful when looking for work in an English-speaking country. So long as there is a demand for architects, which seems to be the case at the time of writing, architectural practices are very willing to employ students and graduates from abroad.

In order to actually set up a company and obtain planning permission for construction work, registration is required. As long as the person wishing to work in the UK satisfies the requirements of the European Commission Architects' Directive 85/384/EEC, architects may register with the ARB and practise without any further restrictions.

The website www.bdonline.co.uk has an international section with some success stories of foreign architects working in the UK. There is also a website offering general advice and support for those wishing to seek work in the UK: www.arbeiten-in-england.de.

12.3 Practicing architecture

Years ago, the opportunities for the employment of architects were more limited than they are today. Architects tended to be employed either in a private practice or in local government. A relatively small number of architects worked in other areas. For a variety of reasons this is now changing. In part, this is supported by a much broader education, in terms of the range of subjects offered, which opens up new career possibilities. In some occupations the architect will make use of all skills, in others only one facet of the architectural services will be applied.

Apart from the obvious employment positions in local governments, which still employ approximately 10% of all architects, architectural departments in large companies, contractors and manufacturers of building components also employ architects. If the job-seeker has an interest in teaching, there are positions available in the architectural faculties at universities. There are also good opportunities for architects in IT, especially regarding the development and application of architectural software, in *property transaction*, survey work and many other fields.

Nevertheless, working in a private practice is still the preferred career route for the majority. The opportunities to be creative, to work in a particular field of construction and take on responsibility are greater here than in the public sector. Small to medium-sized practices offer work to more than 50% of all architects, and undoubtedly, working locally in a small unit, usually in friendly and familiar surroundings, is a major attraction.

Types of practice

Architects practices range from small one-person businesses to large practices with several partners and many employees. Approximately 50% of all practices are run by a *sole principal*, who either works entirely alone or employs staff. For some this is an ambition, for others factors such as the economic situation may have influenced scale and structure. For whatever reason, it can be difficult and demanding bearing the sole responsibility each and every day. However, many will see substantial benefits in terms of job satisfaction and having greater control over one's own destiny.

In a partnership, the ups and downs of everyday business life are shared and the same applies to the *profits and the losses*. Partners are *jointly liable* for the actions of the partnership. Indeed, the partners are responsible to the full extent of their *personal wealth* unless the business is run as a *limited liability company*. Partnerships make up approximately 40% of all practices. It is often argued that a larger team brings benefits in terms of flexibility and creativity, and is therefore able to attract more work than those who work alone. Even though partners share similar views regarding the general philosophy of the partnership, a written agreement can be helpful in the case of disputes.

A group practice shares features of both, a one-person business and a partnership. The concept is that independent architects associate themselves to *mutual benefit*. They do not share the profits, but access the same staff and office resources. Each partner bears the responsibility for his or her own clients. Nevertheless the partners can support one another by helping to even out the *peaks and troughs* of too many and too few *assignments*.

12.4 Finding work

Depending on the economic situation, it may be fairly easy to get a job, but not necessarily the right one. A good presentation of talent, experience and personality is advantageous, because the art of finding employment is very much about the art of *self-presentation*. *Job-seekers* need to market themselves effectively. A first step is to carry out a *self-assessment*, which should include qualifications and experience. The job-seeker needs to be aware of his/her talents and objectives.

It is not easy to plan a career, and few people do, but it pays to think carefully about the type of work and the role one aspires to. The *remuneration package* is also very important and there may be a balance to strike between short term and longer term interests, e.g. a position offering great career development opportunities may not offer the best starting salary.

There is also of course the possibility to make a speculative approach to particular architects or firms. The choice may be influenced by a number of factors such as reputation, knowledge of the type of work undertaken and matches with one's own area of expertise. *Word of mouth* recommendations through contacts in the industry are always useful and one should not ignore *recruitment consultants* or approaches from *head-hunters*, who may introduce opportunities which otherwise would not have been considered.

12.4.1 Opportunities

If you do not receive unexpected phone calls offering just the job you are looking for, there are many other ways of going about locating job vacancies. Construction journals, professional press, national and regional newspapers advertise *job vacancies*. These should be answered according to the request either by sending for an *application form*, sending a *CV* or phoning for further detail. The aim here is to get through to the interview stage, which provides applicants with the opportunity to meet the employer and demonstrate suitability for the job in person.

The Internet is also a fruitful source of jobs. There are thousands of sites for job-seekers, and the difficulty lies in finding the right one. The following British websites are examples of online career and recruitment services committed to connecting organisations with individuals.

Sites with an architectural background:
www.ribaappointments.com
www.architecturejobs.co.uk

General job-matching websites:
www.monster.co.uk, www.guardian.co.uk;
www.fish4jobs.co.uk

12.4.2 Job advertisement

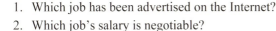

Take a look at the two following job advertisements and answer the following questions:

1. Which job has been advertised on the Internet?
2. Which job's salary is negotiable?
3. Which advertisement is looking for a graduate architecture?
4. Which job requires a very dynamic, energetic applicant?

A

Job Title:	Architect (pt3)
Contract:	Permanent
Salary:	£38k
Location:	London
Closing Date:	06 September 2007
Ref. No:	LR-Arch
Date Posted:	14 August 2007

IDSA
Construction

We are currently seeking a part 3 qualified architect to enhance our team.

The individuals must have qualifications recognised by RIBA. Knowledge of UK building regulations is preferred as is the ability to "*hit the ground running*".

In return we offer excellent salary for the right candidate.

If you feel you have the skills and experience *to be an asset to* our progressive company and help push the business forward, look no further.

Send CV and selection of A4 illustrations to:

IDSA Construction, 28 Edward Street, London SW5 8GK

B

We require talented and enthusiastic Part I, II and III Architects in our busy office to work on a variety of commercial, educational and residential schemes.

Please apply in writing with your CV and A4 examples of your work to:

David Owen
Duncan Architects
25 Burton Way
Leeds LS8 9YJ

Duncan Architects

12.4.3 Self-appraisal

Even if an architect is in employment, he/she should perform a self-appraisal from time to time. Job satisfaction and reward are extremely important and, all too often, an excess of work prevents employees, as well as employers, from reflecting on the current work situation. It is sensible, every now and then, to take time out to ask oneself a few questions. The answers may help to get one's career and performance into perspective and perhaps highlight a need for change.

A self-appraisal could include the following questions:

- Have your responsibilities changed since the last appraisal?
- Are there any changes you would like to make to increase your effectiveness?
- How well do you assess relationships with your colleagues, your boss, your clients and your contractors?
- Are your skills being used to the full?
- Were your recent assignments interesting and did they provide you with a sense of achievement?
- How well do you meet your targets?
- Are you entitled to a pay rise or a bonus?

Changes from every day office life refresh the mind and generate ideas. Employees should therefore be encouraged to take part in professional activities and *continuing professional development (CPD)*.

12.5 Curriculum Vitae

CV stands for curriculum vitae, which is Latin and means the story of life. Most companies are not actually interested in your life story, but your career history. When companies request a CV, they are usually only interested in facts relevant to the application. Although a CV is, in many ways, a formal document it conveys the first impression of the applicant to the potential employer. This first impression can be critical. The CV should therefore be written with care and tailored to suit the needs of the post for which one is applying.

There is a great range of books and websites giving advice on how to write the perfect CV and many offers to perform the task for a small fee. A useful website with a clear layout and good examples is www.tcd.ie/careers. Offering all the advice here would go beyond the scope of this book, however, some aspects need to be mentioned.

There is a significant difference between the style of the more traditional *chronological CV* and a *skills-based CV*. A chronological CV lists education and practical experience according to their occurrence, usually starting with the most recent first and working backwards; the reverse order is also acceptable. A chronological CV underlines the continuity of a career and is suitable if the history is consistent without interruptions. A skills-based CV eliminates the listing of repetitive work details and emphasises skills and abilities, such as accomplishments, organisational skills and strengths. It is a style, which is becoming more common in the UK. Despite being more difficult to write, it is a targeted CV and can be written specifically to answer the demands of an advertisement. It goes without saying that a combination of the two styles is also possible.

Features of a CV

- A CV should be clear and concise, ideally no longer than 2 A4 pages, especially for job applications in the UK.
- It should be easy to read with an attractive layout. Imagine an employer reading several hundred CVs and separating them into two piles – possible candidate and bin.
- Always send the CV with a cover letter addressed in the formal manner using Dear Mr/Ms for the salutation and Yours sincerely for the close.
- The cover letter provides the opportunity to include some comments not appropriate for the CV, such as why motivated to apply, but keep it short and to the point.
- Use the spell-check facility on your computer – there should be no spelling mistakes.
- Use a format and style which best reflects your experience and your skills.
- If you are e-mailing your CV make sure your e-mail address is business-like. Use a suitable name to save the CV.

12.6 Job application and interview

As mentioned above, the offer of an interview is the first hurdle every job-seeker strives to overcome. The interview is concerned with matching the applicant's skills and experience with the employer's demands. It may not seem so for graduates, but interviews are two-way affairs and not only the interviewer must decide whether the applicant is suitable, but the interviewee must decide whether he/she wants the post. Both parties should be well-prepared and, even if it is not specifically requested, the job-seeking architect or architectural student should take along visual material to demonstrate his/her skills.

12.6.1 Interview questions

 Every interview contains awkward questions. The ability to deal with them depends on experience and competence. Decide which of the answers are more appropriate for these typical interviewer's question.

1. Why are you leaving your present post?
   a. I would like to move on and see this post as an opportunity to meet new challenges.
   b. I *was made redundant*.

2. Who is your favourite architect?
   a. I'm a great admirer of Frank Lloyd Wright, who created functional architecture conform to the setting.
   b. I haven't really thought about that question before.

3. What has been your greatest disappointment?
   a. I failed to solve the escape route situation in Building X.
   b. The award-winning design was not realised due to financial difficulties.

4. Where do you see yourself in 10-years time?
   a. I'd like to take early retirement. So I might be on a beach somewhere.
   b. If the opportunities allow it, I'd like to concentrate on creating master plans and supervise a small group of architects.

5. Do you think you are too young for this post?
   a. I may be young, but I'm motivated and willing to learn.
   b. Has age got anything to do with experience?

6. How would you motivate others?
   a. I'd look for special talents and skills and praise them for these capabilities.
   b. I'd bribe them and take them out for drinks.

7. What salary are you looking for?
   a. I'll take what is going.
   b. I'm looking for something between £20,000 and £22,000.

12.6.2 Outcome

Depending on how many candidates are being interviewed, the outcome of the interview may be announced the same day but seldom longer than a week after the meeting. The result of an interview is hopefully a job offer or at least confidence and experience earned, from sometimes yet another interview. If the outcome is a job, a written *contract of employment*, setting out the terms and conditions of employment, should be drawn up and signed by both employer and employee. Every employee will be eager to find the following points in writing:

- The job title
- Remuneration (salary, bonuses and fringe benefits, such as pensions)
- Hours of work and the regulations concerning overtime
- Holiday entitlement
- The period of notice required to terminate the contract.
- The statutory minimum of 4 weeks before month end applies in Germany; the period increases according to the length of employment. In the UK the notice period is also dependant on the length of employment. For an employment lasting between 2 and 5 years, the minimum notice period is two weeks, but an architect would expect longer, probably at least one month.

12.7 Vocabulary

12.1	enrolment	Immatrikulation, Einschreibung
	practice-based training	praxisbezogene Ausbildung
	to enrol in sth	sich immatrikulieren, einschreiben
	secondary education	weiterführende Schule (z.B. Gymnasium)
	to increase competitiveness	Wettbewerbsfähigkeit erhöhen
	degree	akademischer Grad
	credit point	Leistungspunkt
	grade	Note
12.1.1	to pass sth	bestehen
	aptitude test	Eignungstest
	degree course	Diplomstudiengang
	thesis	Dissertation
12.1.2	postgraduate course	weiterführendes/postgraduales Studium, Aufbaustudium
12.1.3	exchange programme	Austauschprogramm
	lecture	Vorlesung
12.2	registration	Eintragung (hier in die Architektenliste)
	registered profession	eingetragener Beruf
	to prosecute sb	jmdn. strafrechtlich verfolgen
12.3	property transaction	Immobiliengeschäfte
12.3.1	sole principal	alleiniger Geschäftsführer

	English	German
	profit and loss	Gewinn und Verlust
	to be jointly liable for sth	gemeinsam haftbar sein
	personal wealth	Privatvermögen
	limited liability company	Gesellschaft mit beschränkter Haftung
	mutual benefit	beiderseitiger Vorteil
	to even out the peaks and troughs	die Höhen und Tiefen ausgleichen
	assignment	Aufgabe, Arbeit
12.4	self-presentation	Selbstdarstellung
	job-seeker	Arbeitssuchende/r
	self-assessment	Selbsteinschätzung
	remuneration package	Gehalt
	by word of mouth	durch mündliche Mitteilung
	recruitment consultancy	Personalagentur
	head-hunter	Personalbeschaffer, -vermittler
12.4.1	job vacancy	unbesetzte Stelle
	application form	Anmeldeformular
12.4.2	CV, Curriculum Vitae	Lebenslauf
	£38k = £38,000.00	38.000,00 engl. Pfund im Jahr
	to hit the ground running	sofort voll einsatzfähig sein, unermüdlich
	to be an asset to sth	eine wichtige Stütze sein
12.4.3	self-appraisal	Selbsteinschätzung
	continuing professional development (CPD)	berufliche Weiterbildung
12.5	chronological CV	chronologischer Lebenslauf
	skills-based CV	stärkenbetonter Lebenslauf
12.5.1	cover letter	Anschreiben zum Lebenslauf
12.6.1	to be made redundant	entlassen werden
12.6.2	contract of employment	Arbeitsvertrag
	notice period	Kündigungsfrist

Answer Key

Unit 1

1.2.8 Who is who?
1. Structural engineers
2. Client
3. Quantity surveyors
4. Structural engineers
5. Clerk of works
6. Subcontractors
7. Client
8. Quantity surveyors

1.3.2 Design and build contract

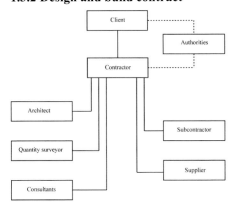

1.4.2 Lexis: Architect's appointment
1h   2a   3f   4e   5i   6b   7d   8c   9g

1.5.2 Exercise: Simple present versus simple past
designed, managed, sat, invented, appeared, did not become, sit, give, still use

1.5.3 Office equipment

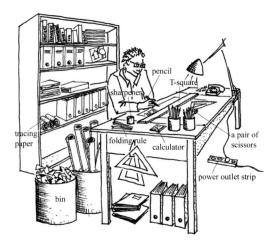

Unit 2

2.1.4 Exercise: Questions and answers
1b 2g 3f 4a 5c 6e 7d

2.2.1 Comprehension
1. true
2. false
3. false
4. true
5. true
6. false
7. false
8. true

2.3.2 Situations

on a slope
spacious, rural
small buildings
narrow roads
in the countryside
friendly
distant neighbours

in town
constricted
commercial, busy
wide roads
narrow plots
close neighbours
urban, dense,
large buildings

2.5.1 E-mail
site location plan, boundaries, properties, planning permission, restrictions, constraints, water level, soils report, ground consultant, services, site, measurements, photographs

2.5.2 Register
to inform   = to let you know
to receive = was able to get
to present = it clearly shows

to contact = to give him a ring
to return   = have been back to
to arise   = questions have cropped up

Unit 3

3.1.2 Needs and worries

Client's needs	Architect's worries
We'd like an office integrated in the main living area.	Does the office need a separate entrance?
We'd like a cellar for technical equipment and storage facilities.	A cellar makes the building very expensive. Is the site big enough to offer the necessary space on the ground floor?
We'll need four bedrooms on the first floor.	Should all bedrooms have an *en-suite bathroom*?
There has to be a terrace for dining in the summer.	Does the kitchen have to be linked to the terrace?
We'll be needing a guest bedroom.	Would it be possible to locate the guest bedroom on the ground floor?
I'd like *loft* space for storage.	A loft assumes a *gable roof*. Could storage space be located somewhere else? Could the roof also have a different shape?

Answer Key

3.2.3 Exercise: Telephoning

George Brown:	George Brown.
Tim Smith:	Hello, George. It's Tim.
George Brown:	Hello, Tim. Nice to hear from you. What can I do for you?
Tim Smith:	I'm just phoning to let you know that I've spoken to Jo White and he'd be interested to do the structural planning for your house.
George Brown:	Oh, that's good news. Should I arrange a meeting with him?
Tim Smith:	Yes, definitely, but there's no rush at the moment. I'd like you to take a look at some sketches first and confirm the brief. And once I have got some preliminary drawings prepared, we could all sit down together.
George Brown:	That sounds good. So how about our meeting then? How does Thursday late afternoon suit you?
Tim Smith:	Thursday would be fine. Shall we say 5 o'clock? Would you like to come round to the office?
George Brown:	Yes that suits me fine. I'll be round at 5.
Tim Smith:	Excellent, I look forward to seeing you. Goodbye George.
George Brown:	Goodbye.

3.3.4 Lexis: Building costs

1b 2f 3h 4c 5g 6d 7a 8e

Unit 4

4.1.1 Presentation form

1c 2f 3e 4a 5g 6b 7d

4.2.2 Modifiers

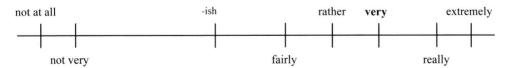

4.3.2 Exercise: Comparisons

the tallest, the most recent, higher, taller, the highest, lower, the most ancient, as tall as, older

4.4.1 Standard shapes

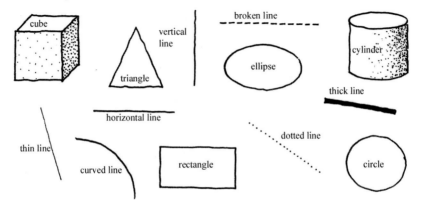

4.5.1 Roof shapes

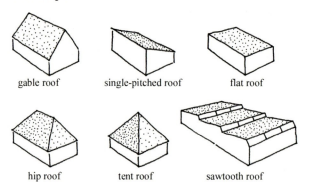

gable roof   single-pitched roof   flat roof

hip roof   tent roof   sawtooth roof

4.6.2 Exercise: Building materials

From left to right (from outside to inside)

Brickwork: 100 mm fair-faced concrete blocks fixed to load-bearing wall with stainless-steel cavity ties, 40 mm cavity, 60 mm insulation, 200 mm concrete blockwork, 13 mm gypsum plaster

Metal façade: 18mm boarding, waterproof membrane, mineral-wool insulation, steel tube shore, vapour barrier, 8 mm plywood, 12 mm plasterboard

aluminium clamping strip holds the double glazing in place

Unit 5

5.1.2 Informing the design team

An appropriate subject line could be: Brown, alteration

5.1.3 Exercise: Register

1. to inform you
2. to postpone
3. as soon as possible
4. to confirm
5. to enclose
6. to be on a tight schedule
7. the alterations
8. to be taken with an idea

5.2.3 Exercise: Connectors

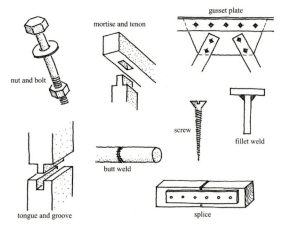

nut and bolt   mortise and tenon   gusset plate   screw   fillet weld   tongue and groove   butt weld   splice

Answer Key   155

5.3.3 Lexis: Structural engineering

A	B	C
in	equilibrium	the active external forces are balanced with the internal forces
live	load	load imparted by the external environment and intended occupancy or use
dead	load	load generated by the weight of the structural member being considered
stresses	and strains	related terms defining the intensity of internal reactive forces caused by external forces
bending	moment	the result of internal forces in a member caused by external loads
shearing	force	a force acting parallel to a plane
uniformly	distributed load	A load imposed evenly on a load-bearing member
bearing	capacity	the load-bearing properties of the ground
column	buckling	bending of a vertical member due to a compressive load
reinforced	concrete	concrete with steel mesh or bars embedded in order to increase the tensile strength

5.4.1 Plan

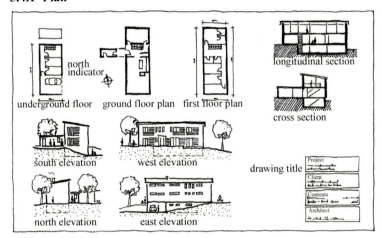

5.4.2 Presentation language

1. a simple and clear structure
2. a smart and professional appearance
3. a good sense of humour
4. good eye contact
5. an enthusiastic attitude
6. a strong voice
7. expressive body language
8. careful preparation

5.4.4 Presentation

1. Good morning everybody,

2. It's nice to be here with you again today. I think we're nearly there, and if there are no major alterations to be made, we'll be able to submit the planning application next week.
   But before we start talking about business matters, let me talk you through the design. First of all I'm going to take you through the various floors, beginning on the ground floor, and then we'll look at the sections and the elevations.

3. Let's begin at the main entrance. You enter the building here and step into a large hall. Here you can see that the hall functions as both a *distributor* and as a separator. On the ground floor it separates

the kitchen, dining and living area from the office, and on the first floor it separates the adult area from the children's area.

Now let's take a look at the stairs. This set takes you up to the first floor. The stairs to the cellar are behind this door.

Finally, the bedrooms on the first floor. The master bedroom with an en-suite bathroom and a walk-in wardrobe is situated above the office. The children's bedrooms are arranged in a row above the living and dining area.

4. If you take a look at the cross section, you'll see that the single pitched roof rises towards the garden, which emphasizes the open character of the façade. The *overhang* of the roof is approximately 1m offering some structural shading to the sunny side of the house. As you can see here, the overhang is less on the north façade allowing as much light as possible to penetrate through the small windows.

5. We'll now move onto the elevations. All bedrooms and living areas face southwest. Large windows with *movable shutters* look out onto the garden. All other facades, especially the north and east facing, are closed except for a few small windows.

6. So, I've completed the little tour of the house. I think you can see that it is a very clear design. I know you envisioned a private adult area on a separate storey, however the extra height would be very difficult to manage on this site. Nevertheless, I think we have succeeded in offering clearly separated parent and children zones by adding the spacious hall on the first floor.

7. Well, I hope the proposal meets your expectations. Have you got any questions regarding any aspects of the house?

5.4.6 Exercise: Conditional sentences

1f   2g   3h   4c   5a   6b   7e   8d

Unit 6

6.2.2 Exercise: Permitted development?

1. UK: The porch exceeds the permissible total area of 3 m² and is closer than the requested 2 m distance to the road.
   Germany: Habitable extensions may not be built without planning permission.
2. UK: No problem, as long as it is at least 1 m away from the boundary.
   Germany: No problem.
3. UK: No problem as the added volume will be less than 10 per cent of the total floor area.
   Germany: Planning application is necessary.
4. Different regulations apply to all extensions in conservation areas.
5. Walls up to 2 m do not require planning permission.
6. UK: If garages are positioned more than 5 m away from the main building, they are considered to be a shed. Sheds must be positioned at least 1 m away from the site boundary.
   Germany: Garages may be built anywhere so long as they do not exceed an average height of 3 m and a total length on the boundary of 9 m.
7. No problem
8. UK: Extensions may not be any higher than 4 m. This extension will also exceed the 15 per cent rule regarding the volume of the extension in relation to the original building.
   Germany: Habitable extensions may not be built without planning permission.

Answer Key

6.3.1 Exercise: Planning application and planning permission

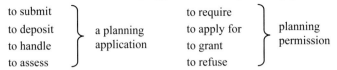

assess, submits, will grant, refuse, apply for, handles, assess, require

6.4.4 Lexis: Fire safety
1b   2g   3h   4f   5c   6a   7d   8e

Unit 7

7.2.3 Exercise: Dimensions
2.51 m   2.88^5 m   7.24 m²   1.01 m   1.26 m   4.26 m   3.25 m   14.95 m²   88^5
63^5 240   80

7.3.3 Lexis: Procurement
1f   2j   3h   4g   5b   6i   7c   8e   9a   10d

7.4.2 Exercise: Active versus passive
are made up, is made, is plastered, is not rendered, is placed, enclose, consists, are required, are embedded, are left open

7.5.3 Exercise: Business letter

Tim Smith & Partners
6 Willow Road
Chorleywood
Herts WD4 3RS

Pepper Road
Great Missenden
Bucks HP6 2BP

5th April 2007

~~Hi~~Dear Tim~~!~~,

~~I received your letter with~~Thank you for your very informative letter and the list of contractors. Your selection looks fine to me/I generally approve of your selection. Some of the names ring a bell/are familiar, but most companies are unknown to me.

A friend of mine has used Company X on your list and had great difficulties with the quality of workmanship and meeting deadlines; therefore I would like to take them off/remove them from the list. I have added two further companies: Company Y, for whom my brother-in-law works and Company Z, who built our current neighbour's house.

If you have no objections to these changes, I suggest you ~~go ahead and we get this tendering business sorted out~~proceed and complete the tendering phase as soon as possible. Please don't ~~ask any more questions~~hesitate to contact me if you have any questions.

~~Cheers,~~ Best regards

George

Encl.: Altered ~~L~~list of contractors

Unit 8

8.3.2 Exercise: Comparison of tendered prices

the most favourable; the lowest; the highest; higher; lower; as high as; more labour-intensive; more expensive; the most reasonable

8.4.3 Comprehension

1.	false	3.	true	5.	false	7.	true
2.	false	4.	false	6.	true	8.	true

Answer Key

8.5.4 Lexis: Contracts

A	B	C
contract	award	decision on which company will be performing the work
risk	distribution	responsibility for dangers is shared between contract partners
terms and	conditions	all agreements making up the contents of a contract
breach	of contract	contract termination due to failure of performing contractual obligations
tender	report	a document put together by the architect enabling the client to award a company with a contract
contract	parties	companies or individuals signing an agreement
payment	method	agreement concerning the details of remuneration
turnkey	project	a service including everything, from the design to the pictures on the wall
comparative	analysis	overview of prices offered by tenderers as a basis for comparison

Unit 9

9.1.3 Exercise: Present Perfect

has worked, since, have been, have discussed, (have) prepared, For, have worked, signed, has not yet commenced, has been very involved, took part, made

9.2.2 Exercise: Time terms

on schedule, period, just in time, took time, postponed, made up for lost time, date, deadline, to waste time, period, to meet deadlines, interrupt, delay, behind schedule, updated

9.3.3 Exercise: Prepositions of time

in, for, by, on, from, to, for, by/on, by

9.4.2 Construction site

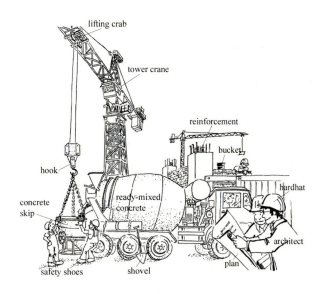

Unit 10

10.1.2 Who does what?
1. mason
2. joiner
3. carpenter
4. tiler
5. plasterer
6. roof plumber
7. blacksmith
8. steelfixer

10.2.2 Dos and don'ts
True: 2c   4e   5f   8d
False: 1b   3h   6a   7i   9g

10.3.3 Exercise: Cause and effect
brought about, Due to, As a result of, Since, led to, is attributable to, Owing to, did not give rise to

Unit 11

11.2.2 Extension of time
Most appropriate subject line: Request for extension of time

11.4.1 Exercise: Remedial work
Maintenance: 3, 6, 7
Remedial work: 1, 4, 5, 8
Remedial work or maintenance, depending on the cause: 2
Outstanding work: 9

11.5.4 Lexis: Payments
1c   2h   3j   4f   5a   6d   7i   8e   9b   10g

Unit 12

12.4.2 Job advertisement
1. A   2. B   3. A   4. A

12.6.1 Interview questions
1a   2a   3b   4b   5a   6a   7b

Bibliography

Green, Ronald, **The Architect's Guide To Running A Job**, 6th edition, Architectural Press

Baden-Powell, Charlotte, **Architect's Pocket Book**, 2nd edition, Architectural Press

Lange, Klaus, **Wörterbuch Auslandsprojekte Deutsch-Englisch**, Dictionary of Projects Abroad German-English, 2nd edition, Vieweg Verlag

Lange, Klaus, **Dictionary of Projects Abroad English-German**, Wörterbuch Auslandsprojekte Englisch-Deutsch, 2nd edition, Vieweg Verlag

HOAI Textausgabe/Text Edition, 3rd edition, Vieweg Verlag

Wallnig, Günter und Evered, Harry, **Englisch für Baufachleute 1, 2 und 3**, Bauverlag

Killer, W.K., **Bautechnisches Englisch im Bild**, Illustrated Technical German for Builders, Bauverlag

Chappell, David and Willis, Andrew, **The Architect in Practice**, 9th edition, Blackwell Publishing

FIDIC Red Book, VBI

Lange und Rogers, **Musterbriefe in Englisch für den Auslandsbau**, Bauverlag

English for Emails, Cornelsen

Brieger, Nick and Pohl, Alison, **Technical English** Vocabulary and Grammar, Summertown Publishing

Müller, Jochen, **Planen und Bauen in Großbritannien**, Hauptseminarbeit WS 1999/2000, Grin

Vocabulary English–German

absentee Abwesende/r 119
accept *v* abnehmen 55
acceptability Genehmigungsfähigkeit 15
acceptance Abnahme 132
acceptance certificate Abnahmebescheinigung 129
access Zufahrt, Zugang 15
access road Zufahrtsstraße 108
accessible *adj* zugänglich 27
act, to act on sth auf etwas wirken, einwirken .. 53
actual building construction costs tatsächliche Baukosten 136
actual contract completion date tatsächlicher Fertigstellungszeitpunkt 130
actual costs tatsächliche Kosten 31
add v ergänzen 95
additional (planning) service besondere Leistung 31
adequate support ausreichende Stützung 53
adhere to sth *v* befolgen 130
adjacent property Nachbarbebauung 19
adjoining *adj* angrenzend 19
adjudication system Rechtssystem, Gerichtbarkeit 94
advice Beratung 4
affordability Erschwinglichkeit 31
after practical completion nach Fertigstellung 3
agenda Tagesordnung 119
agreement Übereinkommen, Vereinbarung 95
alignment Ausrichtung 51
allocate a sum of money to sth eine Geldsumme für etw. zur Verfügung stellen 33
allowance Spielraum, Toleranz 76
alteration Änderung, Abwandlung 3, 50, 120
alternate specification item Alternativposition 78
amendment Berichtigung, Nachtrag 66, 74
amenities nützliche Anlagen 78
amplify sth *v* etw. ergänzen, ausführlicher erläutern 74
angle Blickwinkel 56
anticipated construction period vorgesehene Bauzeit 130
anticipated duration erwartete Dauer 106
appeal Berufung, Einspruch 63

applicant Antragsteller 64
application form Antrag, Anmeldeformular 63, 145
appoint sb *v* beauftragen 6
appointment Termin; Beauftragung 8, 105
appraisal Bewertung, Evaluierung 3
apprentice Auszubildende/r 102
approval Genehmigung, Zustimmung 64
approximately ungefähr 42
aptitude test Eignungstest 141
architect's fee Architektenhonorar 3
area Fläche 27
area load Flächenlast 53
area of responsibility Aufgabenbereich 101
arrangement of rooms Raumanordnung 28
arrangement of the interior Anordnung im Innenbereich 37
articles of agreement Vertragsklauseln 95
artistic merit künstlerischer Verdienst 136
asap, as soon as possible so bald wie möglich 50
as-built drawings Bestandspläne 133
ashlar stone facing Natursteinverkleidung 45
asset, to be an a. to sb/sth eine wichtige Stütze sein 146
assignment Aufgabe, Arbeit 144
associated works Nebenleistungen 88
at random stichprobenartig 120
attitude Haltung, Einstellung 56
attributable, to be a. to sb jmdm. zuzuschreiben sein 122
authorise a variation *v* eine Änderung genehmigen, billigen 89
award a contract einen Auftrag vergeben 78

back-up services Hilfsbetriebe 89
bankruptcy Konkurs 136
bar system Stabbauweise 51
bargain for an advantage over sb sich einen Vorteil über jmdn. erschaffen 91
barspacer Abstandshalter für Betondeckung 116
based on trust auf Vertrauen basieren 4
batten Latte 117
beam Balken 52
bearing capacity Tragfähigkeit 55
bending moment Biegemoment 54

benefit, to b. from sth von etw. profitieren 91
best alternative to a negotiated agreement (BATNA) Nichteinigungsalternative 91
bid, to b. for sth ein Angebot machen 87
bill of quantities Leistungsverzeichnis 5, 73
bin (rubbish bin) BE, trashcan AE Mülleimer, -kübel 11
binding agreement verbindliche Vereinbarung .8
bird's eye view Vogelperspektive 42
bituminous materials bituminöse Materialien .43
bituminous paint coat Bitumenanstrich 117
blacksmith Schmied 117
blacksmith's work Schmiedearbeit 117
blanket insurance allgemeine Versicherung 89
blend, to b. in sich harmonisch einfügen 44, 63
bolting Verschrauben 52
bond Bürgschaft, Verbund 52, 119
borehole, to sink a b. Bohrloch ausheben 21
borrow, to b. sth sich etwas leihen 32
boundary wall Grenzmauer 65
breach Vertragsbruch, -verletzung 95
breach of contract Vertragsbruch 130
breakdown, to b. sth etw. aufschlüsseln, -gliedern 88
breakthrough Durchbruch 92
brickwork Mauerwerk 116
brief Übermittlung der Planungsgrundlagen an den Planer durch den Bauherrn 3, 27
brief, to b. sb jmdn. unterrichten, informieren ...27
briefing Vorbesprechung, Bedarfsermittlung 27
bring sth into line with sth in Einklang bringen 31
broken line gestrichelte Linie 41
bucket Eimer 110
buckle v knicken 54
budget Haushalt 31
budgetary approval Kostengenehmigung 78
buffer (Zeit-)Puffer 107
building authority Baubehörde 63
building contract Bauvertrag 4, 94
building costs Baukosten 31
building line Baulinie 15
building process Bauprozess 115
building regulation Baubestimmung, -vorschrift 64
building services engineer Haustechnik-Ingenieur 4
building society Bausparkasse 32

built-in wardrobe Einbauschrank für Kleidung 118
butt weld Stumpfnaht 52
by word of mouth durch mündliche Mitteilung 145

cabinet maker Möbelschreiner 118
cable clutter Kabelsalat 9
cable connection Kabelanschluss 31
cadastral office Katasteramt 19
cantilever Auskragung 52
carcass Rohbau 76
carcass work Rohbauarbeiten 80
carpenter Zimmerer, Zimmermann 116
carpentry connection Zimmermannsverbindung 52
cause and effect Ursache und Folge 122
cavity Hohlraum 45, 80
cavity wall zweischaliges Mauerwerk 116
cease v aufhören zu 95
certificate Bescheinigung 130
certification mark Zertifizierungszeichen 68
check actual against expected progress Ist- u. Sollfortschritt gegenüberstellen 119
chronological CV chronologischer Lebenslauf 147
claim for a loss of profit Anspruch auf entgangenen Gewinn erheben 96
clamping strip Klemmprofil 45
class of inflammability Brandschutzklasse 68
clerk of works Bauaufseher (meist des Auftraggebers) 5
client Auftraggeber, Bauherr 3
client's means Bauherrenmittel 31
client's representative Bauherrenvertreter 4, 101
coincide v zeitlich zusammenfallen 120
collaboration with in Zusammenarbeit mit 49
combustibility Verbrennbarkeit 66
command, to have a good c. of sth gute Beherrschung von etw. haben 56
commencement Baubeginn 94
commission Beauftragung 3
commitments Verpflichtungen 17
comparative analysis of tender items Preisspiegel 88
compartmentalisation Einteilung in Brandabschnitte 67
compass Zirkel 11
competition, to be in c. with sb mit jmdm. konkurrieren/im Wettbewerb stehen 88

competitive tender Ausschreibung 5, 73, 74
compilation of sth Zusammenstellung von etw. 37
compile sth *v* etw. zusammenstellen 74
complaints handling Beschwerdebearbeitung ... 8
completion Fertigstellung 94, 129
completion date Fertigstellungszeitpunkt 106
completion of the contract Vertragserfüllung 134
comply, to c. with sth erfüllen, nachkommen .. 63
compressive force Druckkraft 54
concentrated load Einzellast, Punktlast 53
concise report kurzer und prägnanter Bericht ... 38
concrete cover Betonüberdeckung 116
concrete skip Betonkübel 110
concrete work Betonarbeiten 115
conduct Verhalten, Betragen 8
conduct a meeting eine Besprechung führen . 119
conduct a negotiation eine Verhandlung führen 91
confidentiality Vertraulichkeit 88
confirm, to c. sth bestätigen 27
conservation area Denkmalerhaltungsgebiet 15, 64
conservation of resources Ressourcenerhaltung, -schonung 66
conservatory Wintergarten 64
constraints Beschränkung 23
construction costs Baukosten 31
construction manager Oberbauleiter (der ausführenden Firma) 102
construction programme Bauzeitenplan 106
construction site sign Bau(stellen)tafel 115
construction to practical completion Bauausführung bis zur Fertigstellung 3
consult sb/sth *v* jmdn./etw. zu Rate ziehen 64
consultant Fachplaner, Fachingenieur 4, 28
contingency item Eventualposition 78
contingency sum Summe für Unvorhergesehenes 31
contingency time Zeitreserve, Zeitpuffer 104
continuing professional development (CPD) berufliche Weiterbildung 147
contract award Auftragsvergabe, - erteilung 87
contract of employment Arbeitsvertrag 149
contract termination Vertragsbeendigung 95
contractual disputes Vertragsstreitigkeiten 5
contractual link Vertragsverhältnis 29
contractual obligation vertragliche Verpflichtung 95, 101

contractual relation Vertragsverhältnis 6
convenience of the public Wohl der Öffentlichkeit 66
coordination Abstimmung, Koordination 49
coping Mauerabdeckung 116
core insulation Kerndämmung 45
corrugated roof panel Welldachplatte 43
cost calculation Kostenberechnung 50
cost categories Kostengruppen 31
cost determination Kostenermittlung 50
cost estimate Kostenanschlag, Kostenschätzung 6, 31, 50
cost finding Kostenfeststellung 50
cost plan Kostenaufstellung 33
council Gemeinderat, Stadtrat 64
counter proposal Gegenvorschlag 91
counterbalance *v* ausgleichen 53
counterparty (Verhandlungs-) Gegner 91
course Ablauf 104
cover letter Anschreiben (zum Lebenslauf) 147
covered area überbaute Fläche 38
crane jib Kranausleger 109
credit point Leistungspunkt 141
cross section Querschnitt 56
cross-border operations grenzüberschreitende Tätigkeiten 94
cross-reference *v* querverweisen 55
cubage Kubatur, umbauter Raum 38
culpable delay schuldhafter Verzug 130
cure concrete nachbehandeln (von Beton), abbinden 115
current workload momentane, aktuelle Arbeitsbelastung 88
curtain wall Vorhangfassade 45, 118
curtilage Hausgrundstück 19, 65
curved line gebogene Linie 41
CV, Curriculum Vitae Lebenslauf 145

damages Entschädigung 130
damp proof course (DPC) Feuchtigkeitssperre 75, 117
date Datum, Termin, Verabredung 105
daywork sheet Stundenlohnzettel 121
dead load unveränderliche Last, Eigenlast 53
dead-end corridor Sackflur 68
deadline Endtermin, Schlusstermin, Termin 104
decay Verfall 105
decennial liability zehnjährige Haftung 134
decorator Maler 118

default Nichterfüllung, Versäumnis 96, 130
default, to be in d. in Verzug sein 135
defect Mangel 129
defects liability period Gewährleistungsfrist, Mängelhaftungszeitraum 130
defects notification period Mängelanzeigefrist 133
defer *v* aufschieben 104
deferment of possession Verzögerung der Übergabe an den Auftragnehmer 130
deflection Verformung infolge von Biegung 51
deformation Verformung 51
degree akademischer Grad 141
degree course Diplomstudiengang 141
delay Verzögerung, Verzug 129
demolition Abbruch, Abriss 64
demountable *adj* demontierbar, abnehmbar 79
dense *adj* dicht besiedelt ....
depth *n*; **deep** *adj* Tiefe, tief 38
determination of cost Kostenermittlung 31, 55
development Bebauung 3
development charges Erschließungskosten 31
development plan Bebauungsplan 15, 63
devious *adj* verschlagen, hinterhältig 120
diaphragm action Scheibenwirkung 51
diligence Fleiß, Eifer 104
dimension line Maßkette 75
dimension Abmessung, Dimension 38
disabled people Körperbehinderte 66
disagreement Meinungsverschiedenheit, Uneinigkeit 91
discharge Schmutzwasser 117
disciplinary proceedings Disziplinärverfahren . 8
discount for early payment Skonto 93
discrepancy Unstimmigkeit 74
dismantle *v* abbauen 107
disruption Störung, Unterbrechung 55
disruptive *adj* störend 120
distribution board Verteiler 117
distribution of risk Risikoverteilung 94
distributor Verteiler 58
door schedule Türliste 123
dormer Gaube 44
dotted line gepunktete Linie 41
downgrade *v* niedriger einstufen, niederstufen .89
downpipe Fallrohr 116
draft *v* Zeichnen, entwerfen 37
drainage Kanalisation 117

draughtsperson Bauzeichner 11
drawing board Reißbrett, Zeichenbrett 9
drawing ink Tusche 9
drawing title Plankopf 56
drawing, to draw Zeichnung, zeichnen 37
dry construction builder Trockenbaumonteur 117
dry construction work Trockenbauarbeiten . 117
durability Dauerhaftigkeit, Beständigkeit 105
duration Zeit, Zeitdauer 105
dyeline (copy) Lichtpause 9

eaves Traufe 44
effectiveness Wirksamkeit 51
egg-shaped eierförmig 41
electrical engineer Elektroingenieur 28
electrical installation Elektroinstallation 117
electrician Elektriker 117
electricity supply network, mains Strom(versorgungs)netz 108
elemental drawing Teilzeichnung 74
elevation Ansicht 56
elimination of contractual obligations Erlöschung der Vertragspflicht 134
embed, to e. sth in eingliedern 44
emission standards Emissionsgrenzwerte 109
emphasise *v* betonen 39
employer Auftraggeber 4
encasing Ummantelung 67
end-terrace house Reiheneckhaus 19
enforcement notice Vollstreckungsankündigung 64
English bond Blockverband 116
enrol, to e. in sth sich immatrikulieren, einschreiben 141
enrolment Immatrikulation, Einschreibung 141
en-suite bathroom an ein Schlafzimmer direkt anschließendes Badezimmer 28
entitled to liquidated damages Anspruch haben auf vertraglich festgesetzte Schadenssumme 129
entrance area (hall) Eingangsbereich 27
equilibrium Gleichgewicht 53
erect *v* aufbauen 107
escape and rescue plan Flucht- u. Rettungsplan 68
escape route Fluchtweg 67
estimated final cost geschätzte Endkosten, Kostenanschlag 32
estimating Preisermittlung, (Baukosten-) Kalkulation 88

estimation Schätzung 73
estimator Kalkulator, Baukalkulator 77
excavation work Aushubarbeiten 115
excavator Bagger 115
exchange programme Austauschprogramm . 143
exempt, to be e. (genehmigungs-) frei sein 65
expense budget Kostenplan 31
expenses Aufwendungen, Kostenaufwand .. 31, 130
exposed concrete Sichtbeton 116
extended price Gesamtpreis einer Position 88
extension of time Bauzeitverlängerung 129
exteriors Außenanlagen 31
external appearance äußere Erscheinung 37
external wall Außenwand 38
extraneous events Fremdeinwirkung 134

face/fair-faced brickwork Verblendmauerwerk, Sichtmauerwerk 45, 80, 116
fall-back position Kompromiss 91
fallible *adj* fehlbar 123
feasibility Durchführbarkeit, Machbarkeit 15, 31
feasibility study Durchführbarkeitsstudie 15
fee Gebühr 63
fee calculation Honorarberechnung 136
fencing Ein-/Umzäunung 109
FFL finished floor level FFB Fertigfußboden .. 75
FIDIC (Fédération Internationale des Ingénieurs-Conseils) Internationale Vereinigung der Beratenden Ingenieure 94
filing cabinet Aktenschrank 9
fillet weld Kehlnaht 52
final acceptance Endabnahme 132
final account Schlussrechnung, Endabrechnung . 5
final assembly Endmontage 107
final design Entwurfsplanung 49
final invoice Schlussrechnung 133
final proposal Entwurf 3
final statement Schluss(ab)rechnung 31, 135
finance costs Finanzierungskosten 32
financial burden finanzielle Last 130
financial review finanzielle Prüfung 119
finishes Ausbau 27, 76, 133
fire endurance test Feuerwiderstandsprüfung . 68
fire extinguisher Feuerlöscher 67
fire hose Feuerlöschschlauch 68
fire precaution vorbeugender Brandschutz 67
fire protection authority Brandschutzbehörde 67

fire protection components Bandschutzmaßnahmen 67
fire protection plan Brandschutzkonzept 67
fire protection requirement Brandschutzanforderung 66
fire regulations Brandschutzrichtlinien 67
fire resistance Feuerwiderstand 66, 67
fire resistance rating Feuerwiderstandsklasse .68
fire safety Feuersicherheit 67
fire section Brandabschnitt 67
fire service Feuerwehr 67
fire-alarm and fire-detecting device Feuermeldeeinrichtung 67
fire-extinguishing system Feuerlöschsystem ..67
firewall Brandwand 67
firing system Feuerungsanlage 66
flashing Spritzblech 116
flashover Brandüberschlag 67
flat Etagenwohnung 18
float *v* schweben 44
floor layer Bodenleger 118
floor screeder Estrichleger 117
floor screeding Estricharbeiten 117
flooring Bodenbelagsarbeit 118
flow of information Informationsfluss 50
flush plate (Schalter-)Abdeckplatte 134
folding rule Zollstock 11
foolproof absolut sicher, narrensicher 82
force majeure höhere Gewalt 130
forces Kräfte 53
forecast Vorhersage 106
foreperson Polier 77, 102
forewarn, to f. sb jmdn. vorwarnen 29
forge *v* schmieden 117
form of tender Angebotsformular 77
formwork Schalung 79, 115
fortnightly vierzehntägig, zweiwöchentlich 119
foundation stone Grundstein 4
foundations Fundamente 123
frustration Wegfall der Geschäftsgrundlage 95
functional link funktionale Bindung 6

gable Giebel 44
gable roof Satteldach 20
gain space Platz gewinnen 58
ganger Vorarbeiter/in 102
Gantt chart, bar chart Gantt-Diagramm, Balkendiagramm 106

gap Baulücke 20
gas supply mains Gasanschluss 31
general contractor Generalübernehmer 74
general plant allgemeine Baustellengeräte 108
geological conditions geologische Bedingungen
.... 15
girder Träger 52
girth Abwicklung, Umfang 75
give rise to führen zu, Anlass geben zu 122
glazier Glaser 118
glazing work Glaserarbeit 118
global tender Gesamtvergabe 74
glued connection Klebeverbindung 52
grade Note 141
grant *v* bewilligen, gewähren 63
greenhouse Treibhaus, Gewächshaus 65
gross floor area Bruttogeschossfläche 38
ground consultant Bodengutachter 21
grout Vergussmörtel 118
guarantee bond Bürgschaft 80
guard rail Schutz-/Sicherheitsgeländer 109
gusset plate Knotenblech 52
gutter Rinne 116
gypsum plaster Gipsputz 45

habitable room Aufenthaltsraum (gemäß Bauordnung) 65
hand over *n, v* Übergabe, übergeben 101
hand-over 132
hardhat Bauhelm 110
hazard Gefahr 67
hazardous material Gefahrenstoff 67
header Binder 116
head-hunter Personalbeschaffer, -vermittler ... 145
health and safety matters Gesundheits- und Sicherheitsangelegenheiten 66
heat loss Wärmeverlust 43
height *n*; **high** *adj* Höhe, hoch 38
high-priority activity Tätigkeit mit hoher Dringlichkeit 104
hip roof Walmdach 43
hoarding Bretterzaun 109
hook Haken 110
horseshoe Hufeisen 42
hourly rate Stundensatz 32

impeccable makellos, tadellos 120
impediment Behinderung 130

impermeability Undurchlässigkeit, Dichtheit . 115
imposed load veränderliche Last, Nutzlast 53
incidental building costs Baunebenkosten 32
incombustible nicht brennbar 67
inconvenience Unannehmlichkeit 132
incorporate *v* aufnehmen, einbeziehen 50
increase competitiveness Wettbewerbsfähigkeit erhöhen ....
information release Informationsfreigabe 141
infringement Verletzung (der Vertragspflicht) 106
inherit, to i. sth erben 17
initial offer erstes Angebot 120
innocent party unschuldig Vertragspartei 91
inscription Inschriftv 95
in-situ concrete Ortbeton 124
inspection Kontrolle, Überwachung 116
inspection for final completion Besichtigung zur Endabnahme 130
inspector Bauaufseher 129
instalment Abschlagszahlung, Rate, Zwischenzahlung 32, 135, 101
insurance Versicherungen 32
insurance policy Versicherungsschein 119
interest Zins(en) 33, 135
interim account Zwischenabrechnung 136
interim payment Zahlung nach Leistungsabschnitten 135
interior construction work Ausbau 80
interior designer Innenarchitekt 28
internal dimension lichtes Maß 75
intersection Überschneidung, Durchdringung ... 44
invitation to tender Angebotsaufforderung 88
invoice *n, v* Rechnung, in Rechnung stellen
.... 31, 135
invoke *v* anrufen 132
iron out beseitigen, aus dem Weg räumen 50

jib nose Auslegerkopf 109
job vacancy unbesetzte Stelle 145
job-seeker Arbeitssuchende/r 145
joiner Bauschreiner 118
joinery shop Tischlerwerkstatt 89
joinery work Bauschreinerarbeit 118
joint configuration Gelenkausbildung 51
jointly liable, to be j. l. for sth gemeinsam haftbar sein 144
joist Stahlbalken 52
jot, to j. down sth rasche Notizen machen 123

keep sb up-to-date jmdn. auf dem laufenden halten 101

labour Arbeitskraft, -kräfte 87
land acquisition Grundstückserwerbskosten 31
landscape architect Landschaftsarchitekt, -planer 4, 28
larder Speisekammer 27
lawsuit Prozess, Klage 130
lead consultant leitender Fachplaner 29
leaf, *pl* **leaves** Mauerwerksschale (einer zweischaligen Wand) 80
leak undichte Stelle, Leck 118, 134
lecture Vorlesung 143
legal charges gesetzliche Gebühren 32
legal dispute Rechtsstreitigkeit 130
legislation Gesetzgebung 64
lender Kreditgeber 32
length *n*; **long** *adj* Länge, lang 42
let *v* vermieten 38
letter of acknowledgement Empfangsbestätigung 88
level *v* ausgleichen, glätten 118
levelling Höhenmessung, Nivellieren 21
levelling instrument Nivelliergerät 22
liability Haftung 29
liability insurance Haftpflichtversicherung ... 133
liability to flooding Überschwemmungsgefahr 15
liable for damages, to be l. schadensersatzpflichtig 130
liable *adj* haftbar 5
life safety Lebensrettung 67
lifting capacity Krantragfähigkeit 109
lifting crab Laufkatze 110
light *adj* leicht 44
lighting Beleuchtung 117
limited liability company Gesellschaft mit beschränkter Haftung 144
lintel Sturz 51
liquidated and ascertained damages Verzögerungsschadensersatz 130
listed building denkmalgeschütztes Gebäude 15, 64
live load Verkehrslast 53
load-bearing capacity Tragfähigkeit 67
loading arrangement Lastbild 54
loan Kredit, Darlehen 33
local planning authority kommunale Projektierungsbehörde 15, 64

location drawing Übersichtsplan 74
locksmith Bauschlosser 118
locksmith's work (Bau-)Schlosserarbeit 118
loft Dachboden 28
loft conversion Dachausbau 64
logs Brennholz 134
longitudinal section Längsschnitt 56
lorry, *pl* **lorries BE; truck AE** Lastwagen, LKW 109
loss Verlust 130
low-pitched roof Dach mit leichtem Gefälle 43
lump sum Pauschale 32
lump sum contract Pauschalvertrag 135
lump sum price Pauschalbetrag 88

maintenance manual Wartungshandbuch 133
mandatory obligatorisch, verbindlich 68
manhour Arbeitsstunde 119
margin Spanne 88
margin of error Abweichung 33
margin of negotiation Verhandlungsspielraum 92
mason Maurer 116
massing Massenverteilung, Ausmaße 37
master bedroom Elternschlafzimmer 27
master-builder Baumeister 11
material compound Baustofflager 108
material sample Bemusterung 38
measurement Aufmaß 21
measurement sheet Aufmassblatt 135
mechanical services engineer Haustechniker 28
mediator Vermittler 4, 101
mediator Vermittler (in Streitfällen) ....
milestone Meilenstein 107
minutes Protokoll 79, 119
misestimate Fehlkalkulation 131
misuse Missbrauch 66
mobile crane Mobilkran 109
mobilisation Mobilisierung, Bauvorbereitung 3
monitor *v* überwachen, kontrollieren 106
mono-pitched roof (single-pitched roof) Pultdach 42
mortar Mörtel 116
mortgage Hypothek 32
mortise and tenon Zapfen und Zapfenloch 52
movable shutter Schiebeladen 58
multi-family dwelling Mehrfamilienhaus 19
mutual benefit beiderseitiger Vorteil 144

national jurisdiction nationales Recht 94
nature of the subsoil Bodenbeschaffenheit 15
negotiate *v* verhandeln 89
negotiated tender freihändige Vergabe 73
negotiator Verhandlungsführer/in 91
net floor area Nettogeschossfläche 38
network analysis Netzplan 106
nominated subcontractor benannter Subunternehmer 78
nominated supplier benannter Lieferant 78
non-habitable room Raum ohne Aufenthalt 64
non-residential building Nichtwohnbau 18
north indicator Nordpfeil 56
notice of obstruction Behinderungsanzeige ...123
notice period Frist, Kündigungsfrist 96, 149
number of storeys Geschosszahl 15
nut and bolt Schraube und Mutter 52

obstruction Behinderung 109, 115, 131
occupation Besitznahme 132
occupier Bewohner 4
official scale of fees Honorarordnung 32
omission Auslassung, Wegfall 121
omit *v* auslassen, weglassen 133
open tender öffentliche Ausschreibung 73, 74
opening ceremony Eröffnungsfeier 123
opening of tenders Angebotseröffnung 87
oral contract mündlicher Vertrag 8
Ordnance Survey engl. Landvermessungsagentur 19
organigram Organisationsdiagramm 6
orientation Ausrichtung, Himmelsrichtung .19, 27
outline application Bauvoranfrage 15
outline proposal Vorentwurf 3
outstanding *adj* ausstehend, ungelöst 50
outstanding expenses ausstehende Ausgaben 136
outstanding retention ausstehender Einbehalt 134
overall dimension Außenmaß 75
overhang Ausladung, Überhang 43
overheads Gemeinkosten, indirekte Kosten 89
overlooking *adj* einsehend, mit Blick auf 19
overrun *n, v* (Termin-)Überschreitung, überschreiten 108, 130
owner Eigentümer, Besitzer 4

painting and wallpapering work, decorating Maler- u. Tapezierarbeiten 118

painting, to paint Gemälde, malen, zeichnen ... 37
panel system Plattenbauweise 51
panic bolt Notausgangsverriegelung 68
paperless office papierloses Büro 9
parapet wall Brüstung 51
parking provisions Stellplatzrichtlinien 15
parquet flooring Parkettboden 134
partial or additional services Teilleistungen oder bes. Leistungen 32
partial possession teilweise Inbesitznahme 133
partial tender Einzelvergabe 74
pass, to p. sth bestehen 141
passer-by, *pl* **passers-by** Passant 110
payment Zahlung 130
payment certificate Zahlungsbescheinigung . 135
payment conditions Zahlungsbedingungen ... 135
payment schedule Zahlungsplan 135
penetration of moisture Eindringung von Feuchtigkeit 117
percentage prozentualer Anteil 135
performance certificate Erfüllungsbescheinigung 134
peril Gefahr 130
perimeter fence Sicherheitszaun, Bauzaun 109
period Frist, Zeitraum 105
periodic valuation fortlaufende Kostenkontrolle 77
permanent formwork verlorene Schalung 116
permitted development nicht genehmigungspflichtiges Bauvorhaben 64
perpend Stoßfuge 80
perpetuate *v* aufrechterhalten 123
personal wealth Privatvermögen 144
pillar Pfeiler 52
pipework Leitungs- u. Rohrverlegearbeit 117
pit Baugrube 115
pitch (Dach-)Neigung 44
pitch sth on the low side unterschätzen 31
pitched roof geneigtes Dach 43
planning application Bauantrag, Baugesuch 15, 55
planning committee Planungsausschuss 63
planning permission Baugenehmigung 16, 63, 64
planning permission application Antrag auf Baugenehmigung 32
plant maschinelle Einrichtung, technische Ausstattung 87
plaster *v* Innenwände verputzen 80
plaster work Putzarbeiten (innen) 117

plasterboard Gipskartonplatte 45, 117
plasterer Putzer 117
plastering Putzarbeiten, innen 75
pliers Beißzange 118
plinth Sockel 51
plot Parzelle, Flurstück, Baugrundstück .. 19
plot of land Baugrundstück, Parzelle, Flurstück .. 3
plot ratio Grundflächenzahl 38
plug Steckdose 117
plumber Sanitärinstallateur, Klempner .. 117
plumbing work Sanitärinstallation 117
plywood Sperrholz 45
point *v* auskratzen und ausfugen (Mörtelfuge) 116
porch überdachter Eingangsbereich, Vorbau 65
possession date Übergabetermin für Baustelle 101
post (Stahl-)Pfosten 52
postgraduate course weiterführendes/postgraduales Studium, Aufbaustudium 142
postpone *v* verschieben 50
posts and mullions Pfosten und Riegel 45
power connection Stromanschluss 31
power outlet strip Mehrfachsteckdose 11
practice-based training praxisbezogene Ausbildung 141
pre-assembly Rohmontage 107
precede *v* vorangehen 119
pre-construction phase Bauvorbereitungsphase 101
preliminaries Vorbemerkungen 88
preliminary enquiries Voruntersuchungen 15
preservation order Denkmalschutzauflage 15
pre-start meeting Vorbesprechung 119
prevail *v* überwiegen, vorherrschen 42
prevent *v* verhindern 53
prevention Verhinderung 130
priced bill ausgefülltes Leistungsverzeichnis 77, 120
prime cost sum Selbstkostenbetrag 78
probable cost of a building voraussichtliche Baukosten 33
procurement procedure Vergabeverfahren 5, 73
product certification Produktzertifizierung 68
production information Ausführungsplanung 3, 74
professional association Berufsverband 8
professional fees Honorare für Freiberufler 32
profile boards Schnurgerüst 115
profit and loss Gewinn und Verlust 144
profit margin Gewinnspanne 89

programme of cost Kostenrahmen 17
programme of work Arbeitsaufwand 17
programming Bauzeitplan 102
progress payment, interim payment Abschlagszahlung, Zahlung nach Leistungsabschnitten 135
project diary Bautagebuch 123
project scope Leistungsbedarf 31
proofread *v* Korrektur lesen 82
property Immobilie 3, 19
property transaction Immobiliengeschäft 144
proportions Verhältnisse 38
proposal Vorschlag 15, 55, 91
prosecute, to p. sb jmdn. strafrechtlich verfolgen 143
protective measure Schutzmaßnahme 109
protrude *v* herausragen, vorstehen 42
provided/providing that angenommen dass .. 59
provision Vorkehrung, Vorsorge 32, 94
provisional final invoice vorläufige Schlussrechnung 133
provisional sum vorläufiger Betrag 78
proximity to sth Nähe zu etwas 23
public footpath öffentlicher Fußweg 109
public sector construction contract öffentlicher Bauvertrag 80
public sewer connection Kanalisationsanschluss 31
purchase *v* erwerben 18
purlin Pfette 116

quality of workmanship Ausführungsqualität 101
quantity surveyor or cost manager Kosten- u. Abrechnungsingenieur 5, 28
query, *pl* **queries** Anfrage 120
quotation Kostenanschlag 50
quote a price anbieten, einen Preis angeben 78
quote, to q. sth anbieten 32

rafter Sparren 116
rail, on rails Schiene, auf Schienen 109
raised flooring aufgeständerter (Fuß-)Boden .. 118
ready-mixed concrete Transportbeton 110
recommend, to r. sb/sth to sb empfehlen 17
recommendation Empfehlung 64
recruitment consultancy Personalagentur ... 145
redundant, to be made r. entlassen werden .. 148
refuge, to seek r. Schutz suchen 67

refuse *v* ablehnen, verweigern 63
registered profession eingetragener Beruf 143
registration Eintragung (hier in die Architektenliste) 143
registration conditions Eintragungsbedingungen 8
reinforcement Bewehrung 116
reinforcing steel Bewehrungsstahl 54
reissue *v* neu herausbringen, -geben 74
reject an offer ein Angebot ablehnen 91
relation Verhältnis 38
release of production information Freigabe der Ausführungspläne 119
release schedule Zeitplan für Planfreigabe 102
rely, to r. on sb sich auf jmdn. verlassen 93
remedial work Nachbesserungsarbeit 108, 133
remote possibility geringe Wahrscheinlichkeit 59
removal costs Umzugskosten 32
remuneration Bezahlung, Entlohnung 96
remuneration package Gehalt 145
render *n, v* Außenputz, Außenwände verputzen 45, 80, 117
rendering Außenputzarbeit 117
repellent *adj* abstoßend 44
resemble *v* ähneln, gleichen 42
residential and community needs Bedürfnisse der Anwohner u. Gemeinde 15
residential building Wohnungsbau 18
resist *v* sich widersetzen 53
responsibility Verantwortung 4
restricted tender beschränkte Vergabe 73, 74
resume *v* wiederaufnehmen 106
retention einbehaltener Betrag 133
retrospective approval rückwirkende Genehmigung 64
RIBA, Royal Institute of British Architects königlicher Britischer Architektenverband 3
ridge First 44
right angle rechter Winkel 42
rigid *adj* biegesteif 52
rive Niete 52
road closure Straßensperrung 109
roof area Dachfläche 43
roof covering Dacheindeckung 43
roof overhang Dachüberstand 58
roof parapet Attika 51
roof plumber Dachklempner 117
roof plumbing work Dachklempnerarbeit 117
roof sealing Dachabdichtung 43

roofer Dachdecker 116
roofing Dachdeckung 43, 116
roofing felt Dachpappe 117
roofing tile Dachziegel 43
room within a room gefangener Raum 68
rough sketch grobe Skizze 38
run-up to im Vorfeld eines Ereignisses 101
rural *adj* ländlich 3

safety and health coordinator Sicherheits- und Gesundheitsschutzkoordinator (SIGE Koordinator) 109
safety measure Sicherheitsmaßnahme, -vorkehrung 109
safety shoes Sicherheitsschuhe 110
sandlime Kalksandstein 93
sanitary appliance Sanitärobjekt 117
sawtooth roof Sheddach 43
scaffolding Gerüst 88
scale Größenordnung, Maßstab 15, 18
schedule Zeitplan, Terminplan 105
scheduling Terminplanung 104
scheme Plan, Projekt 15
scope of work Leistungsumfang 29
secondary education weiterführende Schule (z. B. Gymnasium) 141
sectional completion Fertigstellung in Bauabschnitten 133
security measure Sicherheitsmaßnahme (gegen Einbruch, Diebstahl, unbefugtes Betreten) 109
self-appraisal/-assessment Selbsteinschätzung 145, 146
self- Selbsteinschätzung 145
self-explanatory *adj* selbsterklärend 37
self-presentation Selbstdarstellung 145
semi, semi-detached house Doppelhaushälfte 17
sequence of construction Bauabfolge 106
services Leistungen 3
services Hausanschlüsse, Versorgungsleitungen 15
set of plans Plansatz 3
settlement Setzung 55
sewer Abwasserleitung 19
shearing force Scherkraft 54
sheathing Holzverkleidung, -verschalung 90
shed Schuppen 64
sheet metal work Metalldacharbeiten 116
shell (Außen-)Hülle 44
shell of the building Gebäudehülle 75
shop Werkstatt 52

Vocabulary English–German

shovel Schaufel 110
sill Fensterblech 116
similarity/ies Ähnlichkeit/en 42
single/double/triple glazing Einfach-/Doppel-/Dreifachverglasung 45, 118
single-family home, detached house Einfamilienhaus 19
site agent Bauleiter 5, 77, 102
site boundary Grundstücksgrenze 19
site diary Baustellentagebuch 79
site inspection Baustellenbesichtigung, -begehung 119
site investigation Baugrunderkundung 21
site layout plan Baustelleneinrichtungsplan 109
site location plan Lageplan 19, 65
site meeting Baustellenbesprechung 119
site operations Baustellentätigkeiten 103
site set-up Baustelleneinrichtung 108
site visit Ortsbegehung 17
skill Fertigkeit 4
skilled workperson, *pl* **workpeople** Facharbeiter/in 102
skills-based CV stärkenbetonter Lebenslauf ... 147
skin Außenoberfläche 44
skirting board Sockelleiste 75, 118, 134
slab action Plattenwirkung 51
sliding formwork Gleitschalung 116
smoke exhausting equipment Rauchabzugsvorrichtung 67
snagging list Mängelliste 133
soil sample Bodenprobe untersuchen 21
soils report Bodengutachten 16
sole principal alleiniger Geschäftsführer 144
space-utilisation schedule Raumprogramm ... 27
spacious *adj* geräumig 27
span Spannweite, Stützweite 54
specifications technische Daten 4
specifications (of works) Baubeschreibung 73
splice plate Stoßblech 52
spoil heap Aushublagerhaufen 115
spread *v* ausbreiten ....
staff Messlatte 22
stain Fleck, Verfärbung 134
stainless-steel cavity tie Edelstahlanker 45
stanchion Stahlstütze 52
stand out *v* auffallen 44
standard method of measurement Aufmassnorm 77

static system statisches System 53
statutory defects liability gesetzliche Gewährleistung 134
steel erector Stahlbauer 116
steel mesh Stahldrahtgewebe, Stahlgitter 109
steel tube shore Stahlrohrstütze 45
steelfixer Betonstahlverleger, Eisenflechter 116
stencil Schriftschablone 9
stiffening effect aussteifende Wirkung 51
storage facility Abstellraum, Lagermöglichkeit 17
storage shed Lagerschuppen, Magazin 108
storage space Lagerfläche, Stauraum 27
storey/s (AE story/ies) Geschoss, Stockwerk, Etage 27
stretcher Läufer 116
striking time Ausschalzeit 116
strive, to s. for sth anstreben 104
structural analysis statische Berechnung 53
structural dimension Rohbaumaß 76
structural engineer Statiker, Tragwerksplaner 4, 28
structural framework Tragwerk 51
structural steelwork Stahlbauarbeiten 116
study Arbeitszimmer (im Wohnhaus) 27
subcontractor Subunternehmen 5
subject line Betreffzeile 22
subject to conditions unter bestimmten Bedingungen 65
sublet *v* untervergeben 88
submit *v* unterbreiten, vorlegen 56, 63
submit a tender ein Angebot abgeben 73
sue for damages auf Schadensersatz klagen 96
supervision Bauüberwachung 4, 119
supplier Lieferant 6
supported beam Balken auf zwei Stützen 54
surety bond Bürgschaft 136
survey Aufnahme, Untersuchung 15, 21
surveying Vermessungsarbeit 21
surveying authority Vermessungsbehörde 21
surveying vehicle Vermessungsfahrzeug 21
surveyor Vermessungsingenieur 21
suspend unterbrechen 106
suspended ceiling abgehängte Decke 79
suspended construction Hängekonstruktion ... 54
suspension Aufschub, Verschiebung 96, 130
switch Schalter 117

target costs Zielkosten 89
technical installations betriebstechnische Anlagen 28
tee-square Reißschiene 9
teething troubles, fig Anlaufschwierigkeiten .124
temporary power Baustrom 88, 108
temporary water Bauwasser 88, 108
tender action Angebotseinholung 3
tender documentation Ausschreibungsunterlagen 3, 73
tender for a trade individually gewerkeweise Vergabe 74
tender price or amount Angebotssumme 77
tender report Ausschreibungsbericht, Vergabeempfehlung 95
tender sum Angebotssumme 88
tenderer Anbieter, Bieter 73
tendering Angebotseinholung 87
tensile force Zugkraft 54
tension resistant zugfest 118
tent roof Zeltdach 43
terms and conditions Konditionen 8
terms of appointment Bedingungen der Beauftragung 17
terrace house Reihenhaus 19
thatching Strohbedachung 43
theft Diebstahl 109
thermal insulation Wärmedämmung 66
thermal insulation calculation Wärmeschutznachweis 4
thermal insulation work Dämmarbeiten 117
thesis Dissertation 142
thick line dicke Linie 41
thin line dünne Linie 41
tight schedule enger Terminplan 50
tile adhesive Fliesenkleber 118
tiler Fliesenleger 118
tiling Fliesenlegearbeit 118
tilt-turn window Drehkippfenster 134
timberwork Zimmerarbeit 116
time charge Vergütung auf Stundenbasis 32
time management Zeitplanung 104
time schedule Zeitplan, Terminplan 55
timekeeper Zeitnehmer/in 104
timing zeitliche Abstimmung 104
tinsmith, sheet metal worker (Bau-)Spengler 116
to-do-list Aufgabenliste 104
tongue and groove Nut und Feder 52

top-heavy *adj* kopflastig 89
topping-out ceremony Richtfest 123
top-up Auffüllung 108
to-scale illustration maßstabsgetreue Darstellung 37
tower crane Turmkran 109
tracing paper Transparentpapier 9
trade Baugewerbe, Gewerk 4, 115
tradesperson, *pl* tradespeople Handwerker 115
transfer the care for the works Gefahrenübergang 133
trespass unbefugtes Betreten 109
triangle Dreieck 41
trowel (Maurer-)Kelle 118
truss Binder 52
turnkey development schlüsselfertige Bebauung 7
turnkey project schlüsselfertiges Projekt 94
two-storey *adj* zweigeschossig 42

UFL unfinished floor level RFB Rohfußboden 76
undertake an obligation Verpflichtung übernehmen, sich verpflichten 94
undue consumption unangemessener Verbrauch 66
unfixed material noch nicht eingebaute Materialien 135
uniformly distributed load gleichmäßig verteilte Last, Gleichlast 54
unit rate Stückpreis 88
unpredicted interruption unvorhergesehene Unterbrechung 104
unskilled workperson, *pl* workpeople ungelernte Arbeiter, Hilfsarbeiter 103
up-to-dateness Aktualität 74
urban *adj* städtisch 20
user instructions Gebrauchsanleitung 133
user requirement programme Bedarfsanalyse 27
U-shaped U-förmig 42
utility room Wirtschaftsraum 27

valley Kehle 44
vapour barrier Dampfbremse, Dampfsperre 45, 116
variation Bauvertragsänderung 120
variation order Bauänderungsanweisung, Änderungsauftrag 121
varnish *v* lackieren 118

Vocabulary English–German

verge Ortgang 44
vertically perforated brick Hochlochziegel ......
.... 80, 93
visual link Sichtbezug 44
virtual walk, take a v. einen virtuellen Spaziergang machen 37
volume Rauminhalt, Kubatur 27
volume method of construction cost estimate Kostenschätzung nach umbauten Raum 38

walk-away position Verhandlungsabbruch 91
walk-in wardrobe begehbarer Kleiderschrank . 27
wall tie Maueranker 80
waste management Abfall-/Entsorgungswirtschaft 109
waste prevention Abfallvermeidung 66
water contamination Wasserverschmutzung .. 66
water mains Wasseranschluss 31
water supply Wasserversorgung 117
water supply main Wasserversorgungsleitung 108
water table Grundwasserspiegel 15
waterproof membrane Dichtungshaut, Abdichtungsfolie 45
waterproofing Abdichtung 116
watertight wasserdicht, -undurchlässig 116

wear and tear Verschleiß, Abnutzung 134
weathering Wetterschutzabdeckung 75
weight Gewicht 53
welding Verschweißen 52
welfare Wohlergehen 66
width *n*; **wide** *adj* Breite, breit 38
win-lose negotiation Gewinner-Verlierer Verhandlung 91
winner-takes-it-all approach Einzelsieger Strategie 91
win-win approach Doppelsieg Strategie 91
wire Draht 118
with/without fault mit/ohne Verschulden 129
withstand wear and tear Verschleiß, Abnutzung widerstehen 105
work progress Baufortschritt 115
work stages Leistungsphasen 3
working drawing Werkplan 74
workmanship Ausführungsqualität, Bearbeitungsgüte 5, 77
workshop Werkstatt 27
wrought iron Schmiedeeisen 117

zinc sheet Zinkblech 43

Vocabulary German–English

abbauen to dismantle 107
Abbruch, Abriss demolition 64
Abdeckplatte(Schalter-) flush plate 134
Abdichtung waterproofing 116
Abfall-/Entsorgungswirtschaft waste management 109
Abfallvermeidung waste prevention 66
Ablauf course 104
ablehnen, verweigern to refuse 63
Abmessung, Dimension dimension 38
Abnahme acceptance 132
Abnahmebescheinigung acceptance certificate 129
abnehmen to accept 55
Abschlagszahlung, Rate instalment 32, 101, 135
Abschlagszahlung, Zahlung nach Leistungsabschnitten progress payment, interim payment 135
Abstandshalter für Betondeckung barspacer 116
Abstellraum, Lagermöglichkeit storage facility 17
Abstimmung, Koordination coordination 49
Abstimmung, zeitliche timing 104
abstoßend repellent *adj* 44
Abwandlung modification 120
Abwasserleitung sewer 19
Abweichung margin of error 33
Abwesende/r absentee 119
Abwicklung, Umfang girth 75
ähneln, gleichen to resemble 42
Ähnlichkeit/en similarity/ies 42
akademischer Grad degree 141
Aktenschrank filing cabinet 9
Aktualität up-to-dateness 74
allgemeine Versicherung blanket insurance .. 89
Alternativposition alternate specification item 78
anbieten, einen Preis angeben to quote a price 32, 78
Anbieter, Bieter tenderer 73
Änderung alteration 3, 50
Änderung genehmigen, billigen to authorise a variation 89
Anfrage query, pl. queries 120

Angebot abgeben to submit a tender 73
Angebot ablehnen reject an offer 91
Angebot machen to bid for sth 87
Angebot, erstes initial offer 120
Angebotsaufforderung invitation to tender 88
Angebotseinholung tender action, tendering 3, 87
Angebotseröffnung opening of tenders 87
Angebotsformular form of tender 77
Angebotssumme tender price or amount 77
Angebotssumme tender sum 88
angenommen dass provided/providing that 59
angetan sein to be taken with sth 50
angrenzend adjoining *adj* 19
Anlagen, betriebstechnische technical installations 28
Anlagen, nützliche amenities 78
Anlaufschwierigkeiten teething troubles, *fig* 124
Anordnung im Innenbereich arrangement of the interior 37
anrufen to invoke 132
Anschreiben cover letter 147
Ansicht elevation 56
Anspruch auf entgangenen Gewinn erheben claim for a loss of profit 96
anstreben to strive for sth 104
Anteil, prozentualer percentage 135
Antrag, Anmeldeformular application form 63, 145
Antragsteller applicant 64
Arbeitsaufwand programme of work 17
Arbeitsbelastung, momentane, aktuelle current workload 88
Arbeitskraft, -kräfte labour 87
Arbeitsstunde manhour 119
Arbeitssuchende/r job-seeker 145
Arbeitsvertrag contract of employment 149
Arbeitszimmer (im Wohnhaus) study 27
Architektenhonorar architect's fee 3
Attika roof parapet 51
aufbauen to erect 107
Aufbaustudium, weiterführendes/postgraduales Studium postgraduate course 142
Aufenthaltsraum (gemäß Bauordnung) habitable room 65
auffallen to stand out 44

Auffüllung top-up 108
Aufgabe, Arbeit assignment 144
Aufgabenbereich area of responsibility 101
Aufgabenliste to-do-list 104
aufhören to cease 95
Aufmaß measurement 21
Aufmassblatt measurement sheet 135
Aufmaßnorm standard method of measurement 77
Aufnahme, Untersuchung survey 15, 21
aufnehmen, einbeziehen to incorporate 50
aufrechterhalten to perpetuate 123
aufschieben to defer 104
aufschlüsseln, etw. aufgliedern to breakdown sth 88
Aufschub, Verschiebung suspension 96, 130
Auftrag vergeben award a contract 78
Auftraggeber employer 4
Auftraggeber, Bauherr client 3
Auftragnehmer, Bauunternehmen building contractor 4
Auftragsvergabe, -erteilung contract award ..87
Aufwendungen, Kostenaufwand expenses 31, 130
Ausbau finishes, interior construction work 27, 76, 80, 133
Ausbau 80
Ausbildung, praxisbezogene practice-based training 141
ausbreiten to spread 67
Ausführungsplanung production information 3, 74
Ausführungsqualität 101
Ausführungsqualität, Bearbeitungsgüte workmanship, quality of w. 5, 77, 101
Ausgaben, ausstehende outstanding expenses 136
ausgleichen to counterbalance 53
ausgleichen, glätten to level 118
Aushubarbeiten excavation work 115
Aushublagerhaufen spoil heap 115
Auskragung cantilever 52
auskratzen und ausfugen (Mörtelfuge) to point 116
Ausladung, Überhang overhang 43
auslassen, weglassen to omit 133
Auslassung, Wegfall omission 121
Auslegerkopf jib nose 109
Ausrichtung alignment 51
Ausschalzeit striking time 116

Ausschreibung competitive tender 5, 73, 74
Ausschreibung, öffentliche open tender . 73, 74
Ausschreibungsbericht, Vergabeempfehlung tender report 95
Ausschreibungsunterlagen tender documentation 3, 73
Außenanlagen exteriors 31
Außenmaß overall dimension 75
Außenoberfläche skin 44
Außenputz render 117
Außenputzarbeit rendering 117
Außenwände ausgenommen excluding external walls 38
Außenwände verputzen to render 45, 80
ausstehend, ungelöst outstanding adj 50
Austauschprogramm exchange programme . 143
Auszubildende/r apprentice 102

Badezimmer, an ein Schlafzimmer direkt anschließendes en-suite bathroom 28
Bagger excavator 115
Balken beam 52
Balkendiagramm, Gantt-Diagramm, bar chart, Gantt chart 106
Balken auf zwei Stützen supported beam 54
Bandschutzmaßnahmen fire protection components 67
Bau(stellen)tafel construction site sign 115
Bauabfolge sequence of construction 106
Bauänderungsanweisung, Änderungsauftrag variation order 121
Bauantrag, Baugesuch planning application 15, 55
Bauaufseher inspector 129
Bauaufseher (meist des Auftraggebers) clerk of works 5
Bauausführung bis zur Fertigstellung construction to practical completion 3
Baubeginn commencement 94
Baubehörde building authority 63
Baubeschreibung specifications (of works) 73
Baubestimmungen, -vorschriften building regulations 64
Baufortschritt work progress 115
Baugenehmigung planning permission 16, 63, 64
Baugenehmigung, Antrag auf planning permission application 32
Baugewerbe, Gewerk trade 4, 115
Baugrube pit 115
Baugrunderkundung site investigation 21

Vocabulary German–English

Baugrundstück, Parzelle, Flurstück plot of land 3
Bauhelm hardhat 110
Bauherrenmittel client's means 31
Bauherrenvertreter client's representative **4, 101**
Baukosten building/construction costs 31
Baukosten, tatsächliche actual building construction costs 136
Baukosten, voraussichtliche probable cost of a building 33
Bauleiter site agent **5, 77, 102**
Baulinien building lines 15
Baulücke gap 20
Baumeister master-builder 11
Baunebenkosten incidental building costs 32
Bauprozess building process 115
Bauschlosser locksmith 118
Bauschreiner joiner 118
Bauschreinerarbeit joinery work 118
Bausparkasse building society 32
Baustellenbesichtigung, -begehung site inspection 119
Baustellenbesprechung site meeting 119
Baustelleneinrichtung site set-up 108
Baustelleneinrichtungsplan site layout plan 109
Baustellengeräte, allgemeine general plant 108
Baustellentagebuch site diary 79
Baustellentätigkeiten site operations 103
Baustofflager material compound 108
Baustrom temporary power **88, 108**
Bautagebuch project diary 123
Bauüberwachung supervision **4, 119**
Bauvertrag building contract **4, 94**
Bauvertrag, öffentlicher public sector construction contract 80
Bauvertragsänderung variation 120
Bauvoranfrage outline application 15
Bauvorbereitungsphase pre-construction phase 101
Bauvorhaben, nicht genehmigungspflichtiges permitted development 64
Bauwasser temporary water supply **88, 108**
Bauzeichner draughtsperson 11
Bauzeit, vorgesehene anticipated construction period 130
Bauzeitenplan construction programme 106
Bauzeitenplan programming 102
Bauzeitverlängerung extension of time 129
beauftragen to appoint sb 6

Beauftragung commission 3
Bebauung development 3
Bebauung, schlüsselfertige turnkey development 7
Bebauungsplan development plan **15, 63**
Bedarfsanalyse user requirement programme ...27
Bedingungen der Beauftragung terms of appointment 17
Bedingungen, geologische geological conditions 15
Bedingungen, unter bestimmten B. subject to conditions 65
Bedürfnisse der Anwohner u. Gemeinde residential and community needs 15
befolgen to adhere to sth 130
Beherrschung, gute B. von etw. haben to have a good command of sth 56
Behinderung impediment 130
Behinderung obstruction **109, 115, 131**
Behinderungsanzeige notice of obstruction ...123
Beißzange pliers 118
Beleuchtung lighting 117
Bemusterung material sample 38
Beratung advice 4
Berechnung, statische structural analysis 53
Bericht, kurz und prägnant concise report ...38
Berichtigung amendment 66
Beruf, eingetragener registered profession 143
berufliche Weiterbildung continuing professional development (CPD) 147
Berufsverband professional association 8
Berufung, Einspruch appeal 63
Bescheinigung certificate 130
Beschränkung constraints 23
Beschwerdebearbeitung complaints handling ..8
Besichtigung zur Endabnahme inspection for final completion 130
Besitznahme occupation 132
besondere Leistung additional (planning) service 31
Besprechung führen conduct a meeting 119
Bestandsplan as-built drawing 133
bestätigen to confirm sth 27
bestehen to pass sth 141
Betonarbeiten concrete work 115
betonen to emphasize 39
Betonkübel concrete skip 110
Betonstahlverleger, Eisenflechter steel-fixer 116
Betonüberdeckung concrete cover 116

Betrag, einbehaltener retention 133
Betrag, vorläufiger provisional sum 78
Betreffzeile subject line 22
Bewehrung reinforcement 116
Bewehrungsstahl reinforcing steel 54
Bewertung, Evaluierung appraisal 3
bewilligen, gewähren to grant 63
Bewohner occupier 4
Bezahlung, Entlohnung remuneration 96
Biegemoment bending moment 54
biegesteif rigid *adj* 52
Binder header 116
Binder truss 52
Bitumenanstrich bituminous paint coat 117
bituminöse Materialien bituminous materials 43
Blickwinkel angle 56
Blockverband English bond 116
Boden (Fußboden), aufgeständerter raised flooring 118
Bodenbelagsarbeit flooring 118
Bodenbeschaffenheit nature of the subsoil 15
Bodengutachten soils report 16
Bodengutachter ground consultant 21
Bodenleger floor layer 118
Bodenprobe untersuchen to examine a soil sample 21
Bohrloch ausheben to sink a borehole 21
Brandabschnitt fire section 67
Brandabschnitt, Einteilung in compartmentalisation 67
Brandschutz, vorbeugender fire precaution .. 67
Brandschutzanforderung fire protection requirement 66
Brandschutzbehörde fire protection authority 67
Brandschutzklasse class of inflammability 68
Brandschutzkonzept fire protection plan 67
Brandschutzrichtlinien fire regulations 67
Brandüberschlag flashover 67
Brandwand firewall 67
Breite, breit width *n*; wide *adj* 38
brennbar combustible 67
Bretterzaun hoarding 109
Brüstung parapet wall 51
Bruttogeschossfläche gross floor area 38
Bürgschaft guarantee/surety bond 80, 119, 136

Dach, geneigtes pitched roof 43
Dach mit leichtem Gefälle low-pitched roof .. 43

Dachabdichtung roof sealing 43
Dachausbau loft conversion 64
Dachboden loft 28
Dachdecker roofer 116
Dachdeckung roofing 43, 116
Dacheindeckung roof covering 43
Dachfläche roof area 43
Dachklempner roof plumber 117
Dachklempnerarbeit roof plumbing work 117
Dachpappe roofing felt 117
Dachüberstand roof overhang 58
Dachziegel roofing tile 43
Dämmarbeiten thermal insulation work 117
Dampfbremse, Dampfsperre vapour barrier 45, 116
Darstellung, maßstabsgetreue to-scale illustration 37
Datum, Termin, Verabredung date 105
Dauer, erwartete anticipated duration 106
Dauerhaftigkeit, Beständigkeit durability .. 105
Decke, abgehängte suspended ceiling 79
demontierbar, abnehmbar demountable *adj* 79
Denkmalerhaltungsgebiet conservation area 15, 64
Denkmalschutzauflage preservation order 15
Dichtungshaut, Abdichtungsfolie waterproof membrane 45
Diebstahl theft 109
Diplomstudiengang degree course 141
Dissertation thesis 142
Disziplinärverfahren disciplinary proceedings . 8
Doppelhaushälfte semi, semi-detached house . 17
Doppelsieg Strategie win-win approach 91
Draht wire 118
Drehkippfenster tilt-turn window 134
Dreieck triangle 41
Druckkraft compressive force 54
Durchbruch breakthrough 92
Durchführbarkeit, Machbarkeit feasibility 15, 31
Durchführbarkeitsstudie feasibility study 15

Edelstahlanker stainless-steel cavity tie 45
eierförmig egg-shaped 41
Eigenlast, unveränderliche Last dead load .. 53
Eigentümer, Besitzer owner 4
Eignungstest aptitude test 141
Eimer bucket 110

Vocabulary German–English

einfügen, harmonisch to blend in 44, 63
Ein-/Umzäunung fencing 109
Einbauschrank für Kleidung built-in wardrobe 118
Einbehalt, ausstehender outstanding retention 134
Eindringung von Feuchtigkeit penetration of moisture 117
Einfach-/Doppel-/Dreifachverglasung single/double/triple glazing 45, 118
Einfamilienhaus single-family home, detached house 19
Eingangsbereich entrance area (hall) 27
Eingangsbereich, überdachter; Vorbau porch 65
eingliedern to embed sth in 44
Einklang, etw. in E. bringen to bring sth into line with sth 31
einsehend, mit Blick auf overlooking *adj* 19
Eintragung (hier in die Architektenliste) registration 143
Eintragungsbedingungen registration conditions 8
einwirken, auf etwas wirken to act on sth 53
Einzellast, Punktlast concentrated load 53
Einzelsieger Strategie winner-takes-it-all approach 91
Einzelvergabe partial tender 74
Elektriker electrician 117
Elektroingenieur electrical engineer 28
Elektroinstallation electrical installation 117
Elternschlafzimmer master bedroom 27
Emissionsgrenzwerte emission standards 109
Empfangsbestätigung letter of acknowledgement 88
empfehlen to recommend sb/sth to sb 17
Empfehlung recommendation 64
Endabnahme final acceptance 132
Endmontage final assembly 107
Endtermin, Schlusstermin, Termin deadline 104
entlassen werden to be made redundant 148
Entschädigung damages 130
entwerfen, zeichnen to draft 37
Entwurf final proposal 3
Entwurfsplanung final design 49
erben to inherit sth 17
erfüllen, nachkommen to comply with sth 63
Erfüllungsbescheinigung performance certificate 134

ergänzen, etw. ausführlicher erläutern to amplify sth 74
Erlöschung der Vertragspflicht elimination of contractual obligations 134
Eröffnungsfeier opening ceremony 123
Erscheinung, äußere external appearance 37
Erschließungskosten development charges 31
Erschwinglichkeit affordability 31
erwerben to purchase 18
Estricharbeiten floor screeding 117
Estrichleger floor screeder 117
Etagenwohnung flat 18
Eventualposition contingency item 78

Facharbeiter skilled workperson, *pl* work-people 102
Fachplaner, Fachingenieur consultant 4, 28
Fallrohr downpipe 116
fehlbar fallible *adj* 123
Fehlkalkulation misestimate 131
Fensterblech sill 116
Fertigkeit skill 4
Fertigstellung completion 94, 129
Fertigstellung, nach F. after practical completion 3
Fertigstellung in Bauabschnitten sectional completion 133
Fertigstellungszeitpunkt completion date 106
Fertigstellungszeitpunkt, tatsächlicher actual contract completion date 130
Feuchtigkeitssperre damp proof course (DPC) 75, 117
Feuerlöscher fire extinguisher 67
Feuerlöschschlauch fire hose 68
Feuerlöschsystem fire-extinguishing system 67
Feuermeldeeinrichtung fire-alarm and fire-detecting device 67
Feuersicherheit fire safety 67
Feuerungsanlage firing system 66
Feuerwehr fire service 67
Feuerwiderstand fire resistance 66, 67
Feuerwiderstandsklasse fire resistance rating 68
Feuerwiderstandsprüfung fire endurance test 68
FFB Fertigfußboden FFL finished floor level .75
Finanzierungskosten finance costs 32
First ridge 44
Fläche area 27
Fläche, überbaute covered area 38
Flächenlast area load 53

Fleiß, Eifer diligence 104
Fliesenkleber tile adhesive 118
Fliesenlegearbeit tiling 118
Fliesenleger tiler 118
Flucht- u. Rettungsplan escape and rescue plan 68
Fluchtweg escape route 67
Freigabe der Ausführungspläne release of production information 119
Fremdeinwirkung extraneous events 134
Frist, Kündigungsfrist notice period 96, 149
Frist, Zeitraum period 105
führen zu, Anlass geben zu to give rise to ... 122
Fundamente foundations 123
funktionale Bindung functional link 6
Fußweg, öffentlicher public footpath 109

Gasanschluss gas supply mains 31
Gaube dormer 44
Gebäude, denkmalgeschütztes listed building 15, 64
Gebäudehülle shell of the building 75
Gebrauchsanleitung user instructions 133
Gebühr fee 63
Gebühren, gesetzliche legal charges 32
Gefahr hazard, peril 67, 130
Gefahrenstoff hazardous material 67
Gefahrenübergang transfer the care for the works 133
Gegenvorschlag counter proposal 91
Gehalt remuneration package 145
Geldsumme für etw. zur Verfügung stellen to allocate a sum of money to sth 33
Gelenkausbildung joint configuration 51
Gemälde, malen painting, to paint 37
Gemeinderat, Stadtrat council 64
Gemeinkosten, indirekte Kosten overheads .89
Genehmigung, rückwirkende retrospective approval 64
Genehmigung, Zustimmung approval 64
Genehmigungsfähigkeit acceptability 15
genehmigungsfrei sein to be exempt 65
Generalübernehmer general contractor 74
geräumig spacious *adj* 27
Gerüst scaffolding 88
Gesamtpreis einer Position extended price 88
Gesamtvergabe global tender 74
Geschäftsführer, alleiniger sole principal 144
Geschäftsgrundlage, Wegfall der frustration 95

Geschoss, Stockwerk, Etage storey/s (AE story/ies) 27
Geschosszahl number of storeys 15
Gesellschaft mit beschränkter Haftung limited liability company 144
Gesetzgebung legislation 64
gesetzliche Gewährleistung statutory defects liability 134
Gesundheits- und Sicherheitsangelegenheiten health and safety matters 66
Gewährleistungsfrist, Mängelhaftungszeitraum defects liability period 130
Gewicht weight 53
Gewinn und Verlust profit and loss 144
Gewinner-Verlierer Verhandlung win-lose negotiation 91
Gewinnspanne profit margin 89
Giebel gable 44
Gipskartonplatte plasterboard 45, 117
Gipsputz gypsum plaster 45
Glaser glazier 118
Glaserarbeit glazing work 118
Gleichgewicht equilibrium 53
Gleitschalung sliding formwork 116
Grenzmauer boundary wall 65
grenzüberschreitende Tätigkeiten cross-border operations 94
Größenordnung scale 15
Grundflächenzahl plot ratio 38
Grundstein foundation stone 4
Grundstückserwerbskosten land acquisition 31
Grundstücksgrenzen site boundary 19
Grundwasserspiegel water table 15

haftbar liable *adj* 5
haftbar, gemeinsam h. sein to be jointly liable for sth 144
Haftpflichtversicherung liability insurance . 133
Haftung liability 29
Haftung, zehnjährige decennial liability 134
Haken hook 110
Haltung, Einstellung attitude 56
Handwerker tradesperson, *pl* tradespeople 115
Hängekonstruktion suspended construction ... 54
Hausanschlüsse, Versorgungsleitungen services 15
Hausgrundstück curtilage 19, 65
Haushalt budget 31
Haustechniker mechanical services engineer ... 28

Vocabulary German–English

Haustechnik-Ingenieur building services engineer 4
herausragen, vorstehen to protrude 42
Hilfsarbeiter, ungelernter Arbeiter unskilled workperson, *pl* workpeople 103
Hilfsbetrieb back-up services 89
Himmelsrichtung, Ausrichtung orientation 19, 27
Hochlochziegel vertically perforated brick .. 80, 93
Höhe, hoch height n; high *adj* 38
Höhere Gewalt force majeure 130
Hohlraum cavity 45, 80
Holzverkleidung, -verschalung sheathing 90
Honorarberechnung fee calculation 136
Honorare für Freiberufler professional fees . 32
Honorarordnung official scale of fees 32
Hülle, Außenhülle shell 44
Hufeisen horseshoe 42
Hypothek mortgage 32

Immatrikulation, Einschreibung enrolment 141
immatrikulieren, sich i., einschreiben to enrol in sth 141
Immobilie property 3, 19
Immobiliengeschäfte property transaction 144
Inbesitznahme, teilweise partial possession 133
Informationsfluss flow of information 50
Informationsfreigabe information release 141
Innenarchitekt interior designer 28
Innenwände verputzen to plaster 80
Inschrift inscription 95
Internationale Vereinigung der Beratenden Ingenieure FIDIC (Fédération Internationale des Ingénieurs-Conseils) 94
Ist- u. Sollfortschritt gegenüberstellen to check actual against expected progress 119

Kabelanschluss cable connection 31
Kabelsalat cable clutter 9
Kalksandstein sandlime 93
Kalkulator, Baukalkulator estimator 77
Kanalisation drainage 117
Kanalisationsanschluss public sewer connection 31
Katasteramt cadastral office 19
Kehle valley 44
Kehlnaht fillet weld 52
Kerndämmung core insulation 45

Klausel ergänzen, entfernen, modifizieren to add, delete, amend a clause 95
Klebeverbindung glued connection 52
Kleiderschrank, begehbarer walk-in wardrobe 27
Klemmprofil clamping strip 45
knicken to buckle 54
Knotenblech gusset plate 52
kommunale Projektierungsbehörde local planning authority 15, 64
Kompromiss fall-back position 91
Konditionen terms and conditions 8
Königlicher Britischer Architektenverband RIBA, Royal Institute of British Architects 3
Konkurs bankruptcy 136
Kontrolle, Überwachung inspection 116
kopflastig top-heavy *adj* 89
Körperbehinderte disabled people 66
Korrektur lesen to proofread 82
Kosten- u. Abrechnungsingenieur quantity surveyor or cost manager 5, 28
Kosten, tatsächliche actual costs 31
Kostenanschlag quotation 50
Kostenanschlag, geschätzte Endkosten estimated final cost 32
Kostenanschlag, Kostenschätzung cost estimate 6, 31, 50
Kostenaufstellung cost plan 33
Kostenberechnung cost calculation 50
Kostenermittlung cost determination ...31, 50, 55
Kostenfeststellung cost finding 50
Kostengenehmigung budgetary approval 78
Kostengruppe cost category 31
Kostenkontrolle, fortlaufende periodic valuation 77
Kostenplan expense budget 31
Kostenrahmen programme of cost 17
Kostenschätzung nach umbauten Raum volume method of construction cost estimate 38
Kräfte forces 53
Kranausleger crane jib 109
Krantragfähigkeit lifting capacity 109
Kredit, Darlehen loan 33
Kreditgeber lender 32
Kubatur, umbauter Raum cubage 38
künstlerischer Verdienst artistic merit 136

lackieren to varnish 118
Lageplan site location plan 19, 65

Lagerfläche, Stauraum storage space 27
Lagerschuppen, Magazin storage shed 108
ländlich rural *adj* 3
Landschaftsarchitekt, -planer landscape architect 4, 28
Landvermessungsagentur (englische) Ordnance Survey 19
Länge, lang length *n*; long *adj* ....
Längsschnitt longitudinal section 56
Last, finanzielle financial burden 130
Last, gleichmäßig verteilte; Gleichlast uniformly distributed load 54
Last, veränderliche; Nutzlast imposed load . 53
Lastbild loading arrangement 54
Lastwagen, LKW lorry, *pl* lorries BE; truck AE 109
Latte batten 117
Läufer stretcher 116
Laufkatze lifting crab 110
Lebenslauf CV, Curriculum Vitae 145
Lebenslauf, chronologischer chronological CV 147
Lebenslauf, stärkenbetonter skills-based CV 147
Lebensrettung life safety 67
Leck, undichte Stelle leak 118, 134
leicht light *adj* 44
Leistungen services 3
Leistungsbedarf project scope 31
Leistungsphasen work stages 3
Leistungspunkt credit point 141
Leistungsumfang scope of work 29
Leistungsverzeichnis bill of quantities 5, 73
Leistungsverzeichnis, ausgefülltes priced bill 77, 120
leitender Fachplaner lead consultant 29
Leitungs- u. Rohrverlegearbeit pipework .. 117
lichtes Maß internal dimension 75
Lichtpause dyeline (copy) 9
Lieferant supplier 6
Lieferant, benannter nominated supplier 78
Linie, dicke thick line 41
Linie, dünne thin line 41
Linie, gebogene curved line 41
Linie, gepunktete dotted line 41
Linie, gestrichelte broken line 41

makellos, tadellos impeccable 120
Maler decorator 118

Maler- u. Tapezierarbeiten painting and wallpapering work, decorating 118
Mangel defect 129
Mängelanzeigefrist defects notification period 133
Mängelliste snagging list 133
maschinelle Einrichtung, technische Ausstattung plant 87
Massenverteilung, Ausmaße massing 37
Maßkette dimension line 75
Maßstab scale 18
Materialien, noch nicht eingebaute unfixed material 135
Mauerabdeckung coping 116
Maueranker wall tie 80
Mauerwerk brickwork 116
Mauerwerk, zweischaliges cavity wall 116
Mauerwerksschale (einer zweischaligen Wand) leaf, *pl* leaves 80
Maurer mason 116
Maurerkelle trowel 118
Mehrfachsteckdose power outlet strip 11
Mehrfamilienhaus multi-family dwelling 19
Meilenstein milestone 107
Meinungsverschiedenheit, Uneinigkeit disagreement 91
Messlatte staff 22
Metalldacharbeiten sheet metal work 116
Missbrauch misuse 66
Mitteilung, mündliche by word of mouth 145
Möbelschreiner cabinet maker 118
Mobilisierung, Bauvorbereitung mobilisation 3
Mobilkran mobile crane 109
Mörtel mortar 116
Mülleimer, -kübel (rubbish) bin BE, trashcan AE 11

Nachbarbebauung adjacent property 19
nachbehandeln (von Beton), abbinden cure concrete 115
Nachbesserungsarbeiten remedial work 108, 133
Nachtrag amendment 74
Nähe zu etwas proximity to sth 23
nationales Recht national jurisdiction 94
Natursteinverkleidung ashlar stone facing 45
Nebenleistungen associated works 88
Neigung, Dachneigung pitch 44
Nettogeschossfläche net floor area 38

Netzplan network analysis 106
neu herausbringen, -geben to reissue 74
nicht brennbar incombustible 67
Nichteinigungsalternative best alternative to a negotiated agreement (BATNA) 91
Nichterfüllung, Versäumnis default 96, 130
Nichtwohnbau non-residential building 18
niedriger einstufen, niederstufen to downgrade 89
Nieten riveting 52
Nivelliergerät levelling instrument 22
Nivellierung, Höhenmessung levelling 21
Nordpfeil north indicator 56
Notausgangsverriegelung panic bolt 68
Note grade 141
Notizen machen (rasch) to jot down sth 123
Nut und Feder tongue and groove 52

Oberbauleiter (der ausführenden Firma) construction manager 102
obligatorisch, verbindlich mandatory 68
Organisationsdiagramm organigram 6
Ortbeton in-situ concrete 124
Ortgang verge 44
Ortsbegehung site visit 17

Parkettboden parquet flooring 134
Parzelle, Flurstück, Baugrundstück plot 19
Passant passer-by, pl passers-by 110
Pauschalbetrag lump sum price 88
Pauschale lump sum 32
Pauschalvertrag lump sum contract 135
Personalagentur recruitment consultancy 145
Personalbeschaffer, -vermittler headhunter 145
Pfeiler pillar 52
Pfette purlin 116
Pfosten, Stahlpfosten post 52
Pfosten und Riegel posts and mullions 45
Plan, Projekt scheme 15
Plankopf drawing title 56
Plansatz set of plans 3
Planungsausschuss planning committee 63
Plattenbauweise panel system 51
Plattenwirkung slab action 51
Platz gewinnen gain space 58
Polier foreperson, pl forepeople 77, 122

Preisermittlung, (Baukosten-)Kalkulation estimating 88
Preisspiegel comparative analysis of tender items 88
Privatvermögen personal wealth 144
Produktzertifizierung product certification 68
profitieren von etwas to benefit from sth 91
Projekt, schlüsselfertiges turnkey project 94
Protokoll minutes 79, 119
Prozess, Klage lawsuit 130
Prüfung, finanzielle financial review 119
Puffer, Zeitpuffer buffer 107
Pultdach mono-pitched roof (single-pitched roof) 42
Putzarbeit, innen plaster work, plastering 75, 117
Putzer plasterer 117

Querschnitt cross section 56
querverweisen to cross-reference 55

Rat, jmdn./etw. zu Rate ziehen to consult sb/sth 64
Rauchabzugsvorrichtung smoke exhausting equipment 67
Raum, gefangener room within a room 68
Raum ohne Aufenthalt non-habitable room ... 64
Raumanordnung arrangement of rooms 28
Rauminhalt, Kubatur volume 27
Raumprogramm space-utilisation schedule 27
Rechnung invoice 135
Rechnung, in R. stellen to invoice 31
rechter Winkel right angle 42
Rechtsstreitigkeit legal dispute 130
Rechtssystem, Gerichtbarkeit adjudication system 94
Reiheneckhaus end-terrace house ....
Reihenhaus terrace house 19
Reißbrett, Zeichenbrett drawing board 9
Reißschiene tee-square 9
Ressourcenerhaltung, -schonung conservation of resources 66
RFB Rohfußboden UFL unfinished floor level 76
Richtfest topping-out ceremony 123
Rinne gutter 116
Risikoverteilung distribution of risk 94
Rohbau carcass 76
Rohbauarbeiten carcass work 80
Rohbaumaß structural dimension 76
Rohmontage pre-assembly 107

Sackflur dead-end corridor 68
Sanitärinstallateur, Klempner plumber 117
Sanitärinstallation plumbing work 117
Sanitärobjekt sanitary appliance 117
Satteldach gable roof 20
Schadensersatz, auf S. klagen sue for damages
.... 96
schadensersatzpflichtig to be liable for
damages 130
Schadenssumme, Anspruch haben auf vertraglich festgesetzte entitled to liquidated
damages 129
Schalter switch 117
Schalung formwork 79, 115, 116
Schätzung estimation 73
Schaufel shovel 110
Scheibenwirkung diaphragm action 51
Scherkraft shearing force 54
Schiebeladen movable shutter 58
Schiene, auf Schienen on rails 109
Schlosserarbeit locksmith's work 118
Schluss(ab)rechnung final statement 31, 135
Schlussrechnung final invoice 133
Schlussrechnung, Endabrechnung final
account 5
Schmied blacksmith 117
Schmiedearbeit blacksmith's work 117
Schmiedeeisen wrought iron 117
schmieden to forge 117
Schmutzwasser discharge 117
Schnurgerüst profile boards 115
Schraube und Mutter nut and bolt 52
Schriftschablone stencil 9
Schule, weiterführende (z.B. Gymnasium)
secondary education 141
Schuppen shed 64
Schutz suchen to seek refuge 67
Schutz-/Sicherheitsgeländer guard rail 109
Schutzmaßnahme protective measure 109
schweben to float 44
Selbstdarstellung self-presentation 145
Selbsteinschätzung self-appraisal/-assessment
.... 145, 146
selbsterklärend self-explanatory adj 37
Selbstkostenbetrag prime cost sum 78
Setzung settlement 55
Sheddach sawtooth roof 43

Sicherheits- und Gesundheitsschutzkoordinator (SIGE Koordinator) safety
and health coordinator 109
Sicherheitsmaßnahme (gegen Einbruch,
Diebstahl, unbefugtes Betreten) security
measure 109
Sicherheitsmaßnahme, -vorkehrung safety measure 109
Sicherheitsschuhe safety shoes 110
Sicherheitszaun, Bauzaun perimeter fence . 109
Sichtbeton exposed concrete 116
Sichtbezug visual link 44
Sichtmauerwerk fair-faced brickwork 45, 80
Skizze, grobe rough sketch 38
Skonto discount for early payment 93
Sockel plinth 51
Sockelleiste skirting, skirting board 75, 118, 134
Spanne margin 88
Spannweite, Stützweite span 54
Sparren rafter 116
Speisekammer larder 27
Spengler tinsmith, sheet metal worker 116
Sperrholz plywood 45
Spielraum, Toleranz allowance 76
Spritzblech flashing 116
Stabbauweise bar system 51
städtisch urban adj 20
Stahlbalken joist 52
Stahlbauarbeiten structural steelwork 116
Stahlbauer steel erector 116
Stahldrahtgewebe, Stahlgitter steel mesh .. 109
Stahlrohrstütze steel tube shore 45
Stahlstütze stanchion 52
Statiker, Tragwerksplaner structural engineer 4, 28
Steckdose plug 117
Stelle, unbesetzte job vacancy 145
Stellplatzrichtlinien parking provisions 15
stichprobenartig at random 120
störend disruptive adj 120
Störung, Unterbrechung disruption 55
Stoßblech splice plate 52
Stoßfuge perpend 80
strafrechtlich verfolgen to prosecute sb 143
Straßensperrung road closure 109
Strohbedachung thatching 43
Strom(versorgungs)netz electricity supply
network, mains 108
Stromanschluss power connection 31

Vocabulary German–English

Stückpreis unit rate 88
Stumpfnaht butt weld 52
Stundenlohnzettel daywork sheet 121
Stundensatz hourly rate 32
Sturz lintel 51
Stützung, ausreichende adequate support 53
Subunternehmen subcontractor 5
Subunternehmer, benannter nominated subcontractor 78
Summe für Unvorhergesehenes contingency sum 31
System, statisches static system 53

Tagesordnung agenda 119
Tätigkeit mit hoher Dringlichkeit high-priority activity 104
technische Daten specifications 4
Teilleistungen oder bes. Leistungen partial or additional services 32
Teilzeichnung elemental drawing 74
Termin; Beauftragung appointment 8, 105
Terminplan, enger tight schedule 50
Terminplanung scheduling 104
Tiefe, tief depth *n*; deep *adj* 38
Tischlerwerkstatt joinery shop 89
Träger girder 52
Tragfähigkeit bearing capacity, load-b. 55, 67
Tragwerk structural framework 51
Transparentpapier tracing paper 9
Transportbeton ready-mixed concrete 110
Traufe eaves 44
Treibhaus, Gewächshaus greenhouse 65
Trockenbauarbeiten dry construction work .. 117
Trockenbaumonteur dry construction builder 117
Türliste door schedule 123
Turmkran tower crane 109

Übereinkommen, Vereinbarung agreement 95
Übergabe, übergeben hand-over 101, 132
Übergabetermin für Baustelle possession date 101
Übermittlung brief 3, 27
Überschneidung, Durchdringung intersection 44
Überschreitung, überschreiten overrun 108, 130
Überschwemmungsgefahr liability to flooding 15

Übersichtsplan location drawing 74
überwachen, kontrollieren to monitor 106
überwiegen, vorherrschen to prevail 42
U-förmig U-shaped 42
Ummantelung encasing 67
Umzugskosten removal costs 32
Unannehmlichkeit inconvenience 132
unbefugtes Betreten trespass 109
Undurchlässigkeit, Dichtheit impermeability 115
ungefähr approximately 42
Unstimmigkeit discrepancy 74
unterbrechen to suspend 106
Unterbrechung, unvorhergesehene unpredicted interruption 104
unterbreiten, vorlegen to submit 56, 63
unterrichten, informieren to brief sb 27
unterschätzen pitch sth on the low side 31
untervergeben to sublet 88
Ursache und Folge cause and effect 122

Verantwortung responsibility 4
verbindliche Vereinbarung binding agreement 8
Verblendmauerwerk face brickwork 116
Verbrauch, unangemessener undue consumption 66
Verbrennbarkeit combustibility 66
Verbund bond 52
Verfall decay 105
Verformung deformation 51
Verformung infolge von Biegung deflection 51
Vergabe, beschränkte restricted tender ... 73, 74
Vergabe, freihändige negotiated tender 73
Vergabe, gewerkeweise tender for a trade individually 74
Vergabeverfahren procurement procedure .. 5, 73
Vergussmörtel grout 118
Vergütung auf Stundenbasis time charge 32
Verhalten, Betragen conduct 8
Verhältnis relation 38
Verhältnisse proportions 38
verhandeln to negotiate 89
Verhandlung führen conduct a negotiation 91
Verhandlungsabbruch walk-away position ... 91
Verhandlungsführer/in negotiator 91
Verhandlungsgegner counterparty 91
Verhandlungsspielraum margin of negotiation 92

Verhinderung; verhindern prevention, to prevent 53, 130
Verkehrslast live load 53
verlassen, sich auf jmdn. V. to rely on sb 93
Verletzung (der Vertragspflicht) infringement 106
verlorene Schalung permanent formwork 116
Verlust loss 130
Vermessungsarbeit surveying 21
Vermessungsbehörde surveying authority 21
Vermessungsfahrzeug surveying vehicle 21
Vermessungsingenieur surveyor 21
vermieten to let 38
Vermittler mediator 4, 101
Verpflichtung übernehmen, sich verpflichten to undertake an obligation 94
Verpflichtung commitment 17
verschieben to postpone 50
Verschleiß, Abnutzung widerstehen to withstand wear and tear 105, 134
Verschrauben bolting 52
Verschulden, mit/ohne V. with/without fault 129
Verschweißen welding 52
Versicherung insurance 32
Versicherungsschein insurance policy 119
Versorgung, Bereitstellung provision ....
Verteiler distribution board 117
Verteiler distributor 58
Vertrag, mündlicher oral contract 8
vertragliche Verpflichtung contractual obligation 95, 101
Vertragsbeendigung contract termination 95
Vertragsbruch, -verletzung breach (of contract) 95, 130
Vertragserfüllung completion of the contract 134
Vertragsklausel article of agreement 95
Vertragspartei, unschuldige innocent party .. 91
Vertragsstreitigkeit contractual dispute 5
Vertragsverhältnis contractual link/relation 6, 29
Vertrauen, auf V. basieren based on trust 4
Vertraulichkeit confidentiality 88
Verzögerung der Übergabe an den Auftragnehmer deferment of possession 130
Verzögerung, Verzug delay 129
Verzögerungsschadensersatz liquidated and ascertained damages 130
Verzug, in V. sein to be in default 135
Verzug, schuldhafter culpable delay 130
vierzehntägig, zweiwöchentlich fortnightly 119

Vogelperspektive bird's eye view 42
Vollstreckungsankündigung enforcement notice 64
vorangehen to precede 119
Vorarbeiter/in ganger 102
Vorbemerkungen preliminaries 88
Vorbesprechung (der Bauarbeiten) pre-start meeting 119
Vorbesprechung, Bedarfsermittlung briefing 27
Vorentwurf outline proposal 3
Vorfeld, im V. eines Ereignisses in the run-up to 101
Vorhangfassade curtain wall 45, 118
Vorhersage forecast 106
Vorkehrung, Vorsorge provision 32, 94
vorläufige Schlussrechnung provisional final invoice 133
Vorlesung lecture 143
Vorschlag proposal 15, 55, 91
Vorteil, beiderseitiger mutual benefit 144
Voruntersuchungen preliminary enquiries 15
vorwarnen to forewarn sb 29

Wahrscheinlichkeit, geringe remote possibility 59
Walmdach hip roof 43
Wärmedämmung thermal insulation 66
Wärmeschutznachweis thermal insulation calculation 4
Wärmeverlust heat loss 43
Wartungshandbuch maintenance manual 133
Wasseranschluss water mains 31
wasserdicht, -undurchlässig watertight 116
Wasserverschmutzung water contamination .. 66
Wasserversorgung water supply 117
Wasserversorgungsleitung water supply main 108
Welldachplatte corrugated roof panel 43
Werkplan working drawing 74
Werkstatt workshop 27
Werkstatt, in der in shop 52
Wettbewerb, mit jmdm. konkurrieren/im W. stehen to be in competition with sb 88
Wetterschutzabdeckung weathering 75
widersetzen, sich w. to resist 53
wiederaufnehmen to resume 106
Wintergarten conservatory 64
Wirksamkeit effectiveness 51

Wirkung, aussteifende stiffening effect 51
Wirtschaftsraum utility room 27
Wohnungsbau residential building 18

Zahlung payment 130
Zahlung nach Leistungsabschnitten interim payment 135
Zahlungsbedingungen payment conditions .. 135
Zahlungsbescheinigung payment certificate 135
Zahlungsplan payment schedule 135
Zapfen und Zapfenloch mortise and tenon 52
Zeichnung, zeichnen drawing, to draw 37
Zeit, Zeitdauer duration 105
zeitlich zusammenfallen to coincide 120
Zeitnehmer/in timekeeper 104
Zeitplan für Planfreigabe release schedule . 102
Zeitplan, Terminplan (time) schedule 55, 105
Zeitplanung time management 104
Zeitreserve, Zeitpuffer contingency time 104
Zeltdach tent roof 43
Zertifizierungszeichen certification mark 68
Zielkosten target costs 89

Zimmerarbeit timberwork 116
Zimmerer, Zimmermann carpenter 116
Zimmermannsverbindung carpentry connection 52
Zinkblech zinc sheet 43
Zins(en) interest 33, 135
Zirkel compass 11
Zollstock folding rule 11
Zufahrt, Zugang access 15
Zufahrtsstraße access road 108
zugänglich accessible *adj* 27
zugfest tension resistant 118
Zugkraft tensile force 54
Zusammenarbeit, in Z. mit in collaboration with 49
zusammenstellen to compile sth 74
Zusammenstellung von etw. compilation of sth 37
zuzuschreiben, jmdm. z. sein to be attributable to 122
zweigeschossig two-storey *adj* 42
Zwischenabrechnung interim account 136

Das Bauwörterbuch für Auslandsprojekte und Baurecht

Mit 26.000 Begriffen und NEC

(deutsch – englisch)
Wörterbuch Auslandsprojekte
Dictionary of Projects Abroad
Vertrag, Planung und Ausführung
Contracting, Planning, Design and Execution
2., erw. und akt. Aufl. 2004, 660 S.
Vieweg Verlag 88,00 EUR
ISBN 978-3-528-01757-6

(englisch – deutsch)
Dictionary of Projects Abroad
Wörterbuch Auslandsprojekte
Contracting, Planning, Design and Execution
Vertrag, Planung und Ausführung
2., erw. und akt. Aufl. 2004, 777 S.
Vieweg Verlag 88,00 EUR
ISBN 978-3-528-11677-4

von Klaus Lange

Die beiden Bände wenden sich an alle, die mit Auslandsprojekten beschäftigt sind. Neben dem Hauptwortschatz des Bauwesens und Anlagenbaus finden sich Ausdrücke aus zahlreichen Fachgebieten des Auslandsbaus, was dem Nutzer in vielen Fällen das Nachschlagen in mehreren Spezialwörterbüchern erspart. Eine Besonderheit bildet die Aufnahme von Ausdrücken der folgenden Vertragsbedingungen: Internationale FIDIC Vertragsbedingungen, New Engineering Contract (NEC), Honorarordnung für Architekten und Ingenieure (HOAI). Ergänzt wird das Werk durch ein umfangreiches Abkürzungsverzeichnis in englischer Sprache und einen Abschnitt „Zahlen im Englischen".

Inhalt

Architektur – Hochbau – Haustechnik – Ingenieurbau mit Brückenbau – Wasserbau – Hydrologie – Siedlungswasserwirtschaft – Bewässerung – Grundbau – Bodenmechanik – Tunnelbau – Bergbau – Bohrtechnik – Sanitärtechnik mit Deponiebau – Verkehrswesen (Straßen– und Eisenbahnbau) – Stadt- und Landesplanung – Baustoffe – Baugeräte – Baustelleneinrichtung – Werkzeuge – Feuerschutz – Arbeitssicherheit – Maschinen– und Apparatebau – Elektrotechnik (Energieanlagen) – Natur– und Umweltschutz – Technische Zusammenarbeit – Immobilienmanagement – Transport– und Versicherungswesen – FIDIC–Vertragsbedingungen (Fédération Internationale des Ingénieurs Conseils, International Federation of Consulting Engineers) – New Engineering Contract – HOAI – Kalkulation – Angebotsbearbeitung – Vertragsgestaltung – Nachforderungen – Wirtschaftlichkeitsberechnungen – technische und finanzielle Abwicklung – Personalwesen – Lebensbedingungen im Ausland – Zahlen im Englischen – Abkürzungsverzeichnis.